Citizens in Arms

Studies on
Armed Forces and Society
Published in association with the Inter-University
Seminar on Armed Forces and Society

SERIES EDITOR
Sam C. Sarkesian, Professor of Political Science,
Loyola University

Lawrence Delbert Cress

Citizens in Arms

The Army and the Militia

in American Society to

the War of 1812

The University of North Carolina Press Chapel Hill

© 1982 The University of North Carolina Press
All rights reserved

Library of Congress Cataloging in Publication Data
Cress, Lawrence Delbert.
   Citizens in arms.
   (Studies on armed forces and society)
   Bibliography: p.
   Includes index.
   1. United States—History, Military—To 1900.
2. Civil supremacy over the military—United
States. 3. United States. Army—History—18th
century. 4. United States. Army—History—19th
century. 5. United States—Militia—History—18th
century. 6. United States—Militia—History—19th
century. I. Title. II. Series.
E181.C83   973   81-15945
ISBN 9780807896419 (pbk.)   AACR2

FOR LINDA
and in memory of Ruby John Cress

Contents

Acknowledgments ix

Introduction xi

PART ONE — Ideas and Institutions on the Eve of the American Revolution 1

Chapter 1 — The Military in American Colonial Society 3

Chapter 2 — Citizens and Soldiers in English Political Theory 15

Chapter 3 — The British Army in Prerevolutionary American Political Theory 34

PART TWO — Society, Arms, and the Republican Constitution 51

Chapter 4 — The Wartime Army 53

Chapter 5 — Liberty and Security in the Postwar Period 75

Chapter 6 — The Military and the Federal Constitution 94

PART THREE — Creating a Peace Establishment 111

Chapter 7 — Policy and Ideology in the Washington Administration 115

Chapter 8 — The Crisis of Ninety-Eight 135

Chapter 9 — Jeffersonian Victory and Defeat 150

Chapter 10 — Coda: A Call for Military Professionalism 172

Notes 179

Bibliography 217

Index 233

Acknowledgments

Merrill D. Peterson directed this study from its inception, giving many hours of his time, countless insights into the problems of the early national period, and an example of professional excellence toward which to aspire. William W. Abbot read the manuscript in its earliest form and offered advice, direction, and encouragement as it progressed. Richard Kohn provided extensive and penetrating criticism at a critical juncture. His own work in the military history of the early republic and his eagerness to assist me in my work proved invaluable. Russell Weigley read an early draft of the manuscript and offered counsel and commentary that strengthened its final form. Brent Tarter, George Billias, and Theodore Crackel offered advice, criticism, and encouragement, as did Donald Jackson. Charles Royster read the final draft and suggested some important revisions.

The Alderman Library and the McGregor Collection at the University of Virginia proved invaluable for much of my research. Folger Shakespeare Library, the Humanities Research Center at the University of Texas, the Historical Society of Pennsylvania, the American Antiquarian Society, and the Maryland Hall of Records also provided willing assistance and service. An American Council of Learned Societies Fellowship provided me with eight months of uninterrupted time for researching and writing. Summer grants from the National Endowment for the Humanities and the College of Liberal Arts at Texas A&M University also allowed me to complete important segments of the research. The Society of the Cincinnati in the State of Virginia provided financial support during an early stage of the research. The History Department at Texas A&M University provided secretarial assistance. Carol Knapp and Mary Watson, under the supervision of Rosa Richardson, typed the manuscript.

My parents, Delbert H. and Faye E. Cress, helped in ways they probably do not realize. James Halseth, Peter Ristuben, and Arthur Martinson, all members of the history faculty at Pacific Lutheran University during my undergraduate days, have been an important source of moral support over the past fifteen years. Joseph and Marjory Hanson provided a home away from home on many a research trip to Washington, D.C. A long time ago, James Forsyth encouraged me. Donald J. Pisani did not read the manuscript, but he made writing it a more pleasant task. Linda helped most.

Introduction

This is a book about America's early military history. It is not, however, concerned with the tactical, strategic, or administrative development of American military institutions. Rather, this is a study of ideology and policy. It examines the relationship between eighteenth-century perceptions of the military needs of a free society and the development of political policy intended to secure and preserve traditional English liberties in America. No one in the eighteenth century believed that a society could long endure without the means to preserve domestic order and guarantee external security. There was, however, considerable disagreement about how best to accomplish those ends. By their nature, military institutions held the power to destroy as well as to preserve; hence the character and composition of the military was an issue of major importance. For Americans, the issue evoked fundamental questions about the nature and viability of republican society.

First a word about ideology. Ideology can best be defined by its purpose or function.[1] It serves to "make facts amendable to ideas, and ideas to facts, in order to create a world image" convincing enough to support meaningful explanations for social and political circumstances. An ideology integrates the assertions, theories, and aims necessary for linking "particular actions and mundane practices with a wider set of meanings," providing a more explicit moral basis for an action or an attitude. This integration process may be consciously or unconsciously performed, but it is usually founded on real sociopolitical experience and is not the product of passive reflection.

Ideology is distinct from truth. An ideology is a coherent system of "distorted ideas" which purports to be factual and carries with it a more or less explicit evaluation of the "facts." Ideology mobilizes public opinion by articulating and fusing "into effective formulations opinions and attitudes that are otherwise too scattered and vague to be acted upon." It simplifies complex situations, allowing diverse groups and individuals to cooperate toward the same political and social goals. Distortions and simplification of fact, however, must ultimately be in tune with moral parameters which are linked to sources of social solidarity and political authority within a particular culture. Ideological constructs are not created; nor do they operate in a vacuum. The purpose or function of an ideological system is to provide a meaningful explanation for new or developing social or political circumstances. Its influence in a given political situation depends upon the ideology's ability to "formulate, reshape, and direct forward moods, attitudes, ideals, and aspirations that in some form, however crude or incomplete, already exist" within a society. Ideologies provide formulas for reacting to social or political strain by defining alternatives and providing justification for a particular course of action or attitude. In short, the role of ideology is to define a particular program as legitimate and worthy of support.

Partly because of its tendency to simplify complicated situations, ideology can suggest something of the internal unity and intellectual foundations of a given social system. Expressed in literary and legislative forms, ideology can provide the historian with ideas about the character of a particular society, as well as insights into events taking place within it. Care, however, must be taken to separate ideological axioms from policy alternatives and other political behavior produced by the defining function of ideology. The failure properly to make this distinction confuses ideology with the dependent political behavior that it purports to explain or influence. Unless the analysis of ideology reaches the central value system of a political process, any attempt to explain political behavior within a given historical context will be misconstrued. The link between policy and ideology depends upon an analysis of legislative or policy alternatives within the context of their intellectual antecedents. This allows the influence of ideology in the decision-making process to be determined and opens the way for understanding particular policy decisions within a broader intellectual context. Insights are also possible into evolving ideological systems developing in response to efforts to find new explanations and solutions to changing circumstances and conditions.

An understanding of American attitudes toward the military during the revolutionary era rests upon a careful distinction between ideology and dependent political behavior. This study argues that the controversy over the military in American society is understandable only within the larger context of eighteenth-century republican ideology. The often repeated charges that standing armies were a threat to civil liberties, which were leveled against both British and American regular troops between the Seven Years' War and the War of 1812, do not represent a fundamental antimilitaristic strain in American culture. Nor, for that matter, can policies and attitudes toward the military be understood simply as a belief that military power and civil liberties were incompatible. Analyzed within the atmosphere of ministerial conspiracy, moral corruption, and political oppression that permeated republican thought before 1775, the American response to the British military presence becomes part of a broader concern about constitutional balance, local political prerogatives, and the moral quality of American society. In many ways, the issue of the British military presence itself was secondary to that of what that presence indicated about the moral and political condition of American society.

During the war years and after, attitudes toward the military continued to be linked to the character and dynamics of civil society. Divergent views developed after 1775, producing conflicting ideas about the individual's responsibility for the national defense. Central to these competing visions of the military was the tension between those individuals who espoused a parochial republicanism that sought to restore virtue and unity to American society, principally through the aegis of the local community, and an increasing number of individuals who were willing to embrace a vision of society and politics similar to that expressed by James Madison in *Federalist 10*. The tension was in part the result of the changing physical and political dimensions of American society, changes which altered the sources of social order and political power as the thirteen colonies moved haltingly and hesitantly toward nationhood.

The constitutional and institutional development of America within the British Empire had left the colonies with broad prerogatives over the raising of troops for their own defense. Social order had long been the responsibility of the *posse comitatus* and the militia, both of which were also under the direct control of local officials. The expansion of national political power into both of these realms threatened long-standing lines of political authority and social control, in the process raising fundamental questions about the relationship between political power and freedom. Resolving the tension between parochial and cosmopolitan conceptions about the place of the military in American society was an integral part of the constitutional considerations between 1776 and 1789. Compounded by domestic political turmoil as well as important strategic and tactical advances in the art of war, those same concerns informed the debate over the military after 1790. At issue was not only the security of the American republic but also the viability of republicanism itself.

Since Caroline Robbins connected the thought of the eighteenth-century commonwealthmen with the political thought of revolutionary America, historians have sought to work out the dimensions of the republican ideology that served as the intellectual sounding board for the revolutionary generation. Bernard Bailyn, Gordon Wood, J. G. A. Pocock, and Richard Buel, Jr., among others, have made important contributions to understanding the ideological dimensions of American thought between the 1760s and the second decade of the nineteenth century. The traditional republican fear of standing armies and the republican preference for militia defenses have been touched on by most of these historians, but no attempt has been made to explain the place and role of the military in republican thought or to understand the influence of republican ideology in public policy discussions concerning the military. It is to this gap in the study of republicanism that this study is directed. At the same time, this study of policies and attitudes concerning the military offers insights into the broader issues of public virtue, internal unity, social solidarity, political authority, and the pervasive worry over the constancy of the nation's republican character.

Part I
Ideas and Institutions on the Eve of the American Revolution

No one concerned with the political liberties of Englishmen in the eighteenth century could ignore the relationship between military institutions and constitutional stability. Cromwell, the expanded army of Charles II, and the intrigues of James II had inspired concerns about the military structure of a free society that went to the core of English political theory. For many, though, the successes of the Glorious Revolution raised as many questions as they answered about the military needs of a free society. The accession of William and Mary to the throne had rid England of a tyrannical monarch, but had the constitutional guarantees of the Bill of Rights changed in any basic way the political theory and assumptions that had brought England to the Glorious Revolution? Was the citizen-soldier still the only certain guarantor against external attack and internal intrigue? Or were Parliament's newly won controls over the nation's regular army sufficient to prevent any abuse of the army's inherent coercive powers? Indeed, had the growing complexity of English society and the continuing threat of the French army made a standing army necessary for the security of English liberties?

Englishmen wrestled with these questions in the years before the American Revolution, seeking a better understanding of the implications of military necessity for the constitutional structure of British society. Americans, too, addressed these issues, altering their own military institutions to meet the immediate military demands imposed by the intercolonial wars of the eighteenth century. The colonists asked yet another question, though, one that had far-reaching implications not only for the institutional development of the military in America but also for the British Empire itself. How did the political rights wrestled from the crown by Parliament affect the responsibilities and prerogatives of the colonial assemblies in North America? The tensions that question provoked and the lingering concerns in America about the military's relationship to political freedom played an important role in the intellectual and political developments that produced the American Revolution.

I

The Military in American Colonial Society

[Ordered impressed for military service] all such able-bodied persons . . . as shall be found loitering and neglecting to labor for reasonable wages; all . . . [found] leaving wives or children without suitable means for their subsistence, and all other vagrant or dissolute persons, wandering abroad without betaking themselves to some lawful employment.—Virginia House of Burgesses (1757), in William W. Hening, ed., *The Statutes at Large*

As it is the essential property of a free government to depend on no other soldiery but its own citizens for its defence, so in all such free governments, every freeman and every freeholder should be a soldier.—Thomas Pownall, *The Exercise for the Militia of the Province of Massachusetts Bay* (1758)

Colonial military institutions developed in an atmosphere informed by military necessity and by a sensitivity to the implications of military power for the rights and liberties of a free people. By the middle of the eighteenth century, Americans no longer considered defense the responsibility of the entire community. The demands of the ongoing battle between Great Britain and France for hegemony in North America and the changing character of colonial society left the principal responsibility for the defense of British North America in the hands of professional British soldiers and the long-serving volunteers that filled the ranks of the armies raised in the colonies. The militia had not disappeared, but it had all but lost its military significance, becoming more a reflection of local political relationships and a lingering symbol of the responsibilities as well as the rights of a citizen in a free society. The growing reliance on military professionalism implicit in the evolution of colonial military institutions was predicated on the primacy of the colonial assemblies in military affairs. So long as military operations and policies remained a manifestation of the authority vested in the increasingly powerful assemblies, latent concerns about the political and social implications of military professionalism lay dormant. The primacy of the colonial assemblies, though, was critical. Any threat to that arrangement evoked questions about the political significance of the British army in North America as well as concerns about the viability of a free society that had ceased to include defense among the responsibilities of citizenship.

Soldiers and Militiamen

The early colonies were military outposts, replete with military men like Miles Standish and John Smith, all ready to defend their colonies against Spanish, French, or Indian intruders. But the expenses of maintaining a professional military force, the English militia tradition, and a desire, particularly in New England, for a more homogeneous community inspired every American colony except Pennsylvania to organize a militia system in one form or another during the seventeenth century. Virginia established a militia system during the 1620s that required all free white males to provide their own weapons, keep them in good repair, and attend frequent militia drills. Plymouth Plantation and Massachusetts Bay had established similar organizations by the 1630s. As it was in England, the militia in New England and the Chesapeake was functionally and organizationally a local institution. Legislative and executive committees periodically provided guidelines for military preparedness, but the internal operation of the militia fell almost entirely to local militia officers. They conducted drills and supervised local military construction. Fines for failure to attend musters or for unsatisfactory maintenance of weapons were levied, collected, and expended under their supervision.

Statutory limitations on militia service outside a unit's locality underscored the militia's role as a local institution. Exceptions were made in emergencies, but extended service away from home was usually limited to no more than two or three months. The prerogative of local militia officers to call out their units to meet civil and military emergencies further reflected the local function and responsibilities of the militia. The threat of surprise attack and the isolation of many localities made that power essential, but it also undermined provincial military authority. Though the governor was the commander in chief and the legislature held the ultimate power to call out the militia, its real power rested in the hands of the local leadership—militia officers, whether elected by militia members, nominated by local civil authorities, or appointed by the colonial governor, who were indistinguishable from the local civil establishment.[1]

Nevertheless, by the last quarter of the seventeenth century, the militia had ceased to be the principal military arm of the colonies. The development of a buffer zone between Indian territory and most of the colonial population and the inclusion of North America as a battleground for the imperial struggles between Spain, France, and Great Britain significantly altered colonial military requirements. Colonial authorities found themselves in need of military institutions able to respond to demands beyond the capabilities of the local militia. Troops had to be willing to serve for extended periods of time, capable of traveling great distances, and prepared to face an enemy, more often than not a Frenchman or Spaniard, who fought in open fields or behind fortifications. Consequently, the militia in all the colonies came to function as an organizational unit designed to arm and train individual men, but not to fight. Volunteer expeditionary forces did the fighting. These units were raised by colonial authorities for extended military campaigns or for precautionary raids into the frontier. Colonial authorities appointed the officer corps for these expeditionary forces and established regular wages for troops in the ranks. As early as the 1620s, Virginians were finding it more convenient and economical to raise volunteer units to handle troublesome Indians. During the 1670s, colonies in both the Chesapeake region and New England raised volunteers with varying degrees of success to meet the last serious Indian threat to the eastern seaboard.[2]

Expeditionary forces were the principal instrument for colonial military operations during King William's War. Virginia kept a small band of rangers in constant service on the frontier during the 1690s. This "standing force," which already had a decade of service to its credit, was the creature of the colonial assembly. The House of Burgesses assigned each unit a particular part of the frontier to guard, encouraged experienced troops to continue in service, appropriated money for their maintenance, and provided pensions for the disabled. In New York, troops were raised to meet the French threat in and around Albany County; but these were not simply militia units called into the field. Bounties from twenty shillings to five pounds encouraged enlistments, while five pounds bought exemption from possible conscription. Service under the command of British regulars also distinguished these troops from the militia. Massachusetts also turned to volunteers during the 1690s. The Massachusetts assembly granted the governor power to use the militia outside colony boundaries during emergencies, but troops needed for extended service were made up of volunteers enlisted under the threat of conscription. As in New York, a five-pound fee bought exemption from personal service. This provision allowed propertied persons to avoid service with little difficulty and left the burden of military service on those unable to purchase exemptions. Noting that those "ablest and fittest for service" usually purchased deferments, leaving expeditionary units ineffective and demoralized, the Massachusetts assembly later required each militia unit to keep one-fourth of its men in readiness for royal service. Nevertheless, the five-pound exemption was not revoked.[3]

During the first half of the eighteenth century, Massachusetts continued to look beyond its franchised citizenry to meet its military manpower requirements. The threat of Indian warfare in 1721 and 1724 moved the Massachusetts assembly to pass legislation reminiscent of that during King William's War, including enlistment bounties, pensions for the wounded, and purchasable deferments from personal service. The same legislation was passed again during King George's War, with the addition of provisions to arm destitute volunteers and to allow the enlistment of minors and servants. These provisions enlarged the pool of persons eligible to serve as substitutes, making it easier for franchised citizens to avoid military service. The legislation was revived in the Seven Years' War, but with a new twist. When sufficient volunteers for expeditions into Canada could not be raised with bounties and conscription, vagrants were ordered impressed. Service was mandatory unless those transients could provide a substitute or prove membership in another militia unit. Similar developments took place in New York. During King George's War, "sojourners" were required to attend conscription musters. New York's inability to generate enough volunteers for the Seven Years' War caused the legislature to grant pardons to persons willing to enlist from their jail cells.[4]

Virginians were particularly alert to the possibility of using drifters, the economically dispossessed, and other social undersirables to meet military manpower needs. Throughout the intercolonial wars, Virginia exempted soldiers from taxes and granted them immunity from civil suits, which included the exemption of property from all "executions, attachments, and distresses whatsoever" during actual service and for a limited time afterward, to encourage military service by the poor and financially distressed. In 1740, the House of Burgesses ordered justices of the peace to search out and impress "such able-bodied men as do not follow or exercise any lawful calling or employment, or have not some other lawful and sufficient support and maintenance, to serve his majesty, as soldiers" in the expedition against Cartagena in the West Indies. An act levying troops for the 1754 Ohio Valley expedition made the same persons available to recruitment officers. The burgesses, though, warned recruiters that no one "who hath any vote in the election of a Burgess" was subject to impressment. These acts provided troops for royal service outside the boundaries of the colony. But even when recruits were needed for service within the colony, the burgesses did not look to the landed citizenry for military manpower. Frontier military requirements in 1757 produced an order to impress transients and the unemployed. Again, no "freeholder or housekeeper qualified to vote at an election of burgesses" was to be impressed.[5]

The colonial militia, however, had not disappeared, though demographic, social, and military developments had significantly altered its original function. It still occasionally functioned in a military role, most often in a rather primitive, usually retaliatory, capacity. More characteristically, the militia served as a local police force. Throughout the colonies, militia units were used in conjunction with the *posse comitatus* to quell civil disorder. When the militia was not called out in times of domestic discord, it was usually because too many militiamen were involved in the disturbances. As John Shy has pointed out, the militia was gradually becoming less a means of defense and more an "instrument of either order or insurrection depending on the circumstances."[6] The fear of slave insurrection made the police functions of the militia particularly important in the South.[7] The New York City militia, acting within the bounds of its civil police function, was largely responsible for putting down the slave insurrection of 1741. In New England, as in New York, the militia was connected to local police functions through the institution of the night watch. Though operating under civil authority, except during emergencies, the night watch merged in form and function with the militia. In many statutes, the militia was used as the organizational base for distributing night-watch duty among the citizenry.[8] The use of expeditionary forces to meet provincial military needs reinforced the localism that pervaded the seventeenth-century militia, allowing the eighteenth-century militia to evolve as a civil institution responsible for the security of property and the maintenance of civil order. Its original function had changed, but the militia remained very much the armed embodiment of the civil constitution.[9]

Defense had ceased to be a function of the community in colonial America by the middle of the eighteenth century. The militia's continued association with the preservation of order and authority at the local level made its utilization for external defense improbable and, in some cases, particularly in the South, undesirable. Instead of a citizen army, colonists relied on special fighting forces manned by draftees and volunteers and officered by British regulars or American colonists holding commissions outside the militia establishment. The application of martial law to expeditionary troops (militiamen normally served under civil law) underscored the growing separation of the colonial military establishment from the rest of society. Indeed, the near total reliance on expeditionary forces by colonial authorities and the presence of British regulars in some of the colonies, notably New York and South Carolina, combined to give the colonial military establishment a professional cast. In their composition, at least,

8   Ideas and Institutions

colonial armies had more in common with the mercenary forces serving the monarchs of Europe than they did with the citizen armies glorified by classical republican theorists.

The separation of citizenship from soldiering reflected important social and military developments in the colonies. The same factors that made a landless poor available also made militia mobilization inconvenient, if not intolerable. The growing density of the seaboard population and the expansion of the nonagricultural sector of the colonial economy generated a social atmosphere conducive to the use of the expeditionary forces recruited during the colonial period. At the same time, warfare was becoming increasingly complex, rendering the haphazardly trained and poorly disciplined militia useful only for short-term emergency duty. Like the Englishmen of the same period, Americans faced trained regulars on the battlefield, and they looked to skilled and long-serving soldiers to meet their military needs. The disfranchised and often impoverished volunteers who were willing or could be compelled to serve in the expeditionary forces raised by the colonial assemblies both allowed most Americans to avoid military service and provided the degree of military expertise necessary for successful campaigns against the hardened regulars serving in the armies of Europe.[10]

Questions of Control

This defense establishment was supported by a fairly clear sense of the function and place of the military in the colonial constitutional order. Americans, like Englishmen, had come a long way toward recognizing the value of regular and expeditionary forces, but their appreciation was founded on the colonial legislative control that they had come to demand over troops serving within their jurisdictions. British regulars in the colonies served under the command of the colonial governors and were housed at the discretion of the colonial assemblies. Expeditionary forces were creatures of the colonial assemblies. They were paid, supplied, and often armed under the appropriation powers exercised by the assemblies. Indeed, the astute manipulation of the power of the purse had allowed assemblies to make inroads into such traditional executive prerogatives as the appointment of commanding officers, the planning of military operations, and even the deployment of forces. The colonial governor's position as commander in chief balanced the fiscal control of the legislature against the prerogatives of military command. This insured that no branch of the civil establishment could use its military powers to upset the constitutional balance of the government.

The militia also had an important role in the preservation of constitutional balance. Although it had ceased to be an effective means of external defense, it remained a basic instrument of civil control and continued to be identified with the preservation of liberty and property. A militia muster could mobilize the body politic to preserve civil order, effectively cutting off the popular basis for any movement against the established political order. On the other hand, if the citizenry supported the unrest en masse, the militia had the potential of being an armed arbiter in the resolution of domestic grievances. The militia had the dual function of maintaining civil order while ensuring that the demand for domestic order did not become a disguise for tyranny. As long as the local militia held the power to prevent the colonial authorities from pursuing a policy contrary to the public interest, the exercise of civil and military authority at the provincial level could not be abused.[11]

The whole system accentuated the assemblies' control over military operations. While the militia was largely responsible for the preservation of civil order, the local militia leadership conceded military command to the officers appointed by the assemblies to lead the expeditionary armies. At the same time, intercolonial military cooperation was virtually nonexistent. No single administrative or tactical command had the power to mobilize or direct the combined military strength of the colonies. Geography and the traditional autonomy of the colonial governments were in part responsible. The shift of power from the executive to the legislative branch of colonial government, which was closely connected to the use of expeditionary forces, also contributed to the reluctance to engage in intercolonial cooperation. The representative assemblies' military prerogatives were central to the colonists' perception of the compatibility of royal and expeditionary soldiers and the preservation of traditional English liberties in the colonies. Any attempt to undermine the prerogatives of the colonial assemblies could raise questions about the legitimacy of the regular or expeditionary forces serving in the colonies.[12]

The American response to British military policy during the Seven Years' War confirmed the importance of the constitutional arrangement that supported the colonial military establishment. When war broke out with France, Britain, despite the control the colonial assemblies had come to exercise over troops serving within their boundaries, moved to organize colonial defenses under a single commander in chief. The job began in earnest when Lord Loudoun arrived in America in 1756. As the king's military representative in North America, Loudoun held more central authority than any British general in England or on the Continent. His commission contained authority to issue warrants for the payment of money, to supply arms and stores from the American Ordnance Office, to appoint officers to every rank except colonel, to review court-martial findings, to supervise continental Indian affairs, and to control the naval officers on the inland lakes. His relationship to colonial authorities, however, was far from clear. He could ask for recruits, money, quarters, transport, and assistance from provincial troops, but what power he had to force the colonial governments to grant his requests remained unclear. In his efforts to unite the colonies into a single defense establishment, Loudoun ran headlong into colonial political establishments profoundly jealous of their military prerogatives.[13]

The quartering issue provides a case in point. During the eighteenth century, royal troops had been quartered in a variety of ways, but always at the direction of the colonial assemblies. The Bill of Rights had vested Parliament with the sole authority to quarter troops on the populace in England, but no parliamentary act had ever indicated how regulars in North America were to be quartered. Thus, in practice, if not by law, the colonial assemblies had come to exercise Parliament's right to control quartering. Despite the absence of any legal precedent, Loudoun ordered local magistrates to provide housing for troops on the move and instructed governors to persuade their assemblies to build permanent barracks, all the while threatening to forcibly quarter his men if their needs were not met. Loudoun's attempt to dictate quartering of British troops in the colonies produced angry charges that his actions represented an assault on the constitutional guarantee against arbitrary quartering. Royal instructions to obey any order that the commander in chief issued also suggested a degree of civil subordination to military authority which was disconcerting to royal governors and colonial assemblies alike. Assemblies in Massachusetts, New York, Pennsylvania, and South Carolina were particularly strident in their criticism of Loudoun's usurpation of what had become colonial prerogative. In every case, the crisis was resolved only when the colonial assembly resumed responsibility for sheltering troops, while also making the British military presence dependent upon colonial sanctions. This was not what Loudoun had in mind, but it worked, and he preferred to accept colonial legislative controls rather than force the issue of his constitutional powers.[14]

Loudoun's recall in 1757 eased tensions between the colonies and the British command in North America. The colonies reluctantly met the needs of the British army, while also sending into the field a good supply of troops under the control of colonial assemblies. Nevertheless, William Pitt's decision to seek American support for the war by reimbursing the colonies for their military expenses only encouraged colonial independence in military matters and reinforced legislative prerogatives over the power of the purse and sword. Between 1764 and 1767 colonial assemblies in Massachusetts, New York, New Jersey, South Carolina, and Georgia quibbled with the authority of Parliament to extend the quartering provisions of the Mutiny Act across the Atlantic. In each case, the colonies insisted on retaining control over appropriations necessary for the housing of transient royal troops. As long as British regulars fit the American perception of the military's place in the constitutional order, they were a welcome addition to colonial defenses. If they did not, colonists were not hesitant to raise questions concerning the legitimacy of the English military presence.[15]

The same attitude shaped the American response to the British decision to maintain regulars in the colonies after 1763. James Otis's *The Rights of the British Colonies Asserted and Proved* (1764), among the most influential pamphlets of the 1764–65 period, typified the immediate colonial reaction. For Otis, the army represented a danger only in that its fiscal needs provided an excuse for tightening parliamentary control over the colonies. Any threat to American liberties stemmed not from the British regulars—though he reminded his English readers that Pompey, Caesar, and Sulla had used armies stationed in the provinces to conquer the Roman republic—but from the schemes of royal ministers determined to increase their own political power. He was confident that the army could be kept in America without upsetting the constitutional balance within the colonies and between them and Parliament if the army were supported by requisitions on the colonial legislatures.

Nevertheless, Otis preferred to leave the defense of the colonies in the hands of the Americans. "A good provincial militia, with such occasional succors from the mother country as exigencies may require, never will attend with hazard." A militia defense, the traditional English cure-all for tyrannical intrigue, would eliminate the need for parliamentary taxation —the basis of the ministerial machinations—while also ensuring that the army would not rise up to challenge the legitimate force of the Empire. Otis believed that the British "regular troops [were] the best in the world," but a good militia would ensure the perpetuation of British liberties guaranteed in the Bill of Rights while also defending the interests and prosperity of England and the colonies. A militia-based defense establishment had the added advantage of ensuring that the control of the military forces in the colonies would be under the supervision of the colonial leadership.[16]

Theory and Policy in Conflict

The army dropped from public debate during the mid-1760s, ceasing even to be mentioned in the context of taxation by the end of the Stamp Act crisis. The location of the bulk of troops on the frontier, the customary American reliance on regular or semiregular troops for frontier defense, and the feeling of mutual accomplishment in the just-won victory over France helped to contain any widespread protests against the British presence. Business and family ties between Americans and the British army also helped sidestep a potentially sensitive issue. Besides, many Americans had come to see the British military presence as part of a partnership in arms dating back to King William's War. The "formidable fleets, and brave and disciplined armies" of Great Britain provided security from "the hostile attempts of any power in Europe." The Americans were not, however, passive partners. "The Continental Colonies too, in an emergency, are able to furnish many thousand brave men, who, when joined by any body of regular forces from England . . . would effectually shake the French and Spanish dominions, both in North and South America." The British army supplied the professional leadership, while the colonies provided, "not mercenary hirelings ready to engage in the service of the highest bidder," but rather a "fund of hardy, brave soldiers . . . ready to engage in the service of Great Britain."[17]

Americans recognized the importance of trained regulars in a military era dominated by standing armies. Yet they retained an ambivalence toward British troops that reflected a pervasive suspicion of military professionalism. Otis recognized the value of regulars to colonial defense in his analysis of British policy in 1764, but history warned him that the Roman republic had fallen under the weight of a standing army. Even the essayists cited above, who were writing to praise the advantages of union with Great Britain, clearly distinguished between colonial soldiers and British regulars. Americans served to defend liberty and order; they fought for freedom and not for hire. Despite a century of legislation designed to draw the disfranchised into military service, soldiering remained in the American mind, if not in practice, an important responsibility of citizenship. As Governor Thomas Pownall explained in a message to the citizens of Massachusetts during the Seven Years' War, a free society can "depend on no other soldiery but its own citizens for defence." "A freeholder that is no soldier" leaves the freedom and security of society in the hands of hired mercenaries unconcerned with the rights and privileges of freemen. Thus every citizen must consider "it his truest honour to be a soldier-citizen."[18]

Possibly only the governor of Massachusetts could have written those words. Massachusetts had one of the few militia systems that could be expected to perform well in an emergency. Nevertheless, Pownall's association of citizenship and the freehold with soldiering reflected the special relationship between political freedom, property, and social obligation in Anglo-American thought that would not have been unfamiliar in any of the colonies. In part, this was because the militia remained an important local institution in almost all the colonies. Its continued association with local police functions as it ceased to be an instrument of external defense reinforced the local importance of the militia and helped to keep alive ideas about individual political responsibilities and liberties that were associated with basic English liberties in the American mind. English Opposition thought, which permeated the American political outlook, also contributed to maintaining the association between the militia and a politically healthy society. Drawing upon that body of thought, Pownall was able to contrast the moral and political significance of the militia with that of the standing army, in the process suggesting that the presence of the latter represented the failure of the citizenry to meet their social obligations to the community.[19]

The suspicion of military professionalism articulated by Pownall during a war fought primarily by British regulars and long-serving volunteers drawn from outside the ranks of the colonies' enfranchised citizenry underscored the discrepancy between theory and policy that characterized American military operations in the eighteenth century. Americans met the demands of the wars for empire by consciously separating military service from the responsibilities of citizenship. Indeed, the nature of colonial military institutions reflected at least a tacit acceptance of the pro–standing army argument espoused by a majority in Parliament since the Glorious Revolution. Still, colonists remained sensitive to long-standing English perceptions of the citizen militia's significance as an expression of constitutional balance and political stability. This disparity would play an important role in shaping subsequent attitudes and perceptions about the military in the revolutionary era.

So long as the sanctity of English liberties remained unchallenged in the colonies, Americans gave little thought to the implications of their growing reliance on professional soldiers, satisfied with their effectiveness and confident that the prerogatives of the colonial assemblies in military affairs would contain any dangers inherent in the use of regular armies. Parliament's decision to tax the colonies directly and to use regular troops to enforce those taxes changed all of that. Employing a system of ideas and assumptions about political corruption and decay drawn from English Opposition thought, the colonists began to rethink their relationship to the British Empire and to place added significance on the militia's traditional role as the best and only certain guarantor of the rights and security of a free society. That development, though, laid bare the long-standing discrepancy between policy and theory. Colonists found their militia institutions to be only pale reflections of the social and political values associated with the citizen-soldier, as well as generally unable to meet the demands of a protracted war. Forced by military circumstances to impose the regimen and order of professional soldiers on their revolutionary army, Americans would find themselves faced with the need to reassess the ideological assumptions implicit in a citizen army and to come to a better understanding of the military requirements of a nation born in a world of sophisticated tactics and highly trained soldiers. In short, political and constitutional requirements of revolutionary America would demand a means to rectify military necessity with republican theory.

To understand those developments, it is necessary first to examine the significance and role of the militia and standing armies in English Opposition thought. That ideological system provides the key for understanding the development of anti–standing army rhetoric and the renewed interest in the militia after 1768. It also offers an explanation of why both played such an important part in the movement toward independence. The pro-army argument needs analysis as well. For though America took up the logic and rhetoric of Opposition theory, its view of the military in civil society during the revolutionary era was shaped as well by a body of ideas that considered military professionalism necessary for and compatible with the survival of a free society.

2

Citizens and Soldiers in English Political Theory

In former times, says our Author [John Trenchard], there was no difference between the Citizen, the Souldier, and the Husband-man; but 'tis otherwise now, Sir, War is become a Science, and Arms an Employment. —Daniel Defoe, *Some Reflections on a Pamphlet Lately Published, Entitled, an Argument Shewing That a Standing Army Is Inconsistent* . . . (1697)

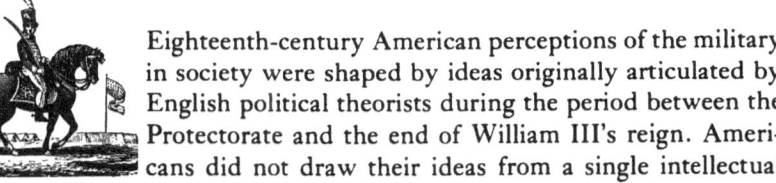

Eighteenth-century American perceptions of the military in society were shaped by ideas originally articulated by English political theorists during the period between the Protectorate and the end of William III's reign. Americans did not draw their ideas from a single intellectual tradition or ideology. Classical republican theory and more recent ideas about specialization and social interdependence both helped to mold the eighteenth-century view of the military in society. The former spoke to the constitutional significance of the citizen-soldier, while the latter emphasized the importance of trained professionals in the defense of a modern nation.

A cyclical view of history, a commitment to the militia as the only acceptable military manifestation of the body politic, and a sense that constitutional stability depended upon the willingness of freeholders to fulfill the civil and military functions of citizenship generated among Opposition political theorists, the intellectual heirs of classical republicanism, a deep distrust of any constitutional arrangement that provided government with a military force independent of the citizen militia. Their opponents, the moderate Whigs, questioned the validity of the classical model. Relying on a more progressive view of history and suggesting that the rise of self-interest had made specialization critical to the operation of any modern society, they embraced military professionalism. No less committed to traditional English civil liberties than their adversaries, they argued that the constitutional balance sought by Opposition thinkers through the revival of the citizen-soldier had been institutionalized in the revolutionary settlement of 1688. International tensions combined with Parliament's budgetary control over the army to cause these moderate Whigs to view the standing army as both compatible with and necessary for the survival of English liberties. It is within the ideological systems supporting these conflicting views of the military that one must look to understand the changing American perception of the military in civil society during the revolutionary era.

Opposition Thought

James Harrington's ideas about constitutional balance, political corruption and decay, and citizenship provided the intellectual basis for the Opposition indictment of standing armies during the century preceding the American Revolution. Although his ideas were often used in ways he might not have recognized or approved, his *Commonwealth of Oceana* (1656) provides the starting point for understanding the assumptions behind the anti-standing army rhetoric that helped shape American perceptions of the military's relationship to the civil constitution. True to the classical republican tradition of which he was a part, Harrington linked the ability to operate freely in the political arena directly to economic independence. Like the tests for citizenship in ancient Athens and Rome, his concept of citizenship rested on the possession of an inheritable freehold in land, which gave the freeholder economic and political independence. Private power became a prerequisite for public power, and the exercise of either depended upon the possession of property. The citizen lived on his own property, could hold public office, and had the right and responsibility to bear arms in his own defense and in the defense of the state. The franchise was the civil manifestation of the freedom represented by arms, and the republic stood as the embodiment of the classical unity of economic, military, and political power. An individual without land was dependent on another for his livelihood and therefore could be neither citizen nor soldier. Hence, Harrington's Oceana was a dispersed city-state in which the gathering of the citizenry was both an assemblage of the electorate and a militia muster.[1]

The citizen-soldier stood at the heart of the stable and balanced constitution, making the militia essential to the survival of free institutions. Dependence on the government for the defense of society represented a transfer of the rights vested in property and included an explicit acceptance of dependent relationships in the place of the independence that was the birthright of the freehold. Once the balance was broken between the freeholder and the government, the balance necessary for the survival of the republic was lost. Political corruption was unleashed and tyranny resulted. In Oceana, the state and the militia were one. The same criterion, property, that separated citizen from servant also separated soldier from nonsoldier. The Roman republic had thrived on a citizen militia, and in Oceana, the militia would be made up entirely of those qualified as citizens.[2]

Harrington's association of propertied independence, political personality, and military obligation with political stability provided the common ground for both classical republicanism and latter-day radical Whig thought. From that point, however, their perceptions of the origins and manifestations of military power differed significantly. Harrington understood the militia to be a relatively recent development—the end product of the land redistribution begun under Panurgus (Henry VII), which passed the inherent power of the land from the nobility to the people. He believed that this reallocation of land would eventually lead to the elimination of both the monarchy and the nobility, leaving the militia at the heart of a stable republican constitution. Military power, then, would always be associated with those who held the balance of property, that is, political power, in society. Radical Whigs, on the other hand, rejected both Harrington's view of history and his conclusion that military power could not be used at the expense of the landed citizenry. Applying their own view of history to Harrington's ideas about government, they produced a thoroughgoing critique of courtly influence and ministerial corruption that purported to explain the decline of English liberty. The nature of military institutions and their relationship to the constitutional order—both understood as a reflection of the distribution of power in civil society—played an important role in this ideology of corruption that served as the core for English Opposition thought through the seventeenth and eighteenth centuries.[3]

The radical Whig indictment of professional military institutions hinged upon a belief in the historical reality of the ancient Gothic constitution. According to these thinkers, this once free and stable Gothic institution, structurally similar to the classical mixed constitution outlined by Harrington, began to falter all across Europe about 1500. The balance that existed between the king, the nobles, and the people through a series of military tenures, leaving the king without the military power to coerce his subjects, was upset with the increase of luxury through society. The new elegance was connected with the revival of learning, the invention of the printing press, and the exploration and exploitation of new land to the east and west. This new society offered broader cultural horizons, but it also encouraged the freeman to specialize his interests at the expense of soldiering and other civil responsibilities. The nobles left their independent country seats for the convenient and luxurious life of the court. They met their new expenses by commuting the military service of their tenants for money, and in turn, they paid taxes to the king instead of fighting for him in person. As mercenary armies replaced feudal levies, the force of the state passed from the nobility to the king, giving the latter the means for introducing arbitrary power. The surrender of the various civil and military functions of the citizenry and the nobility to the salaried servants of the king created a professionalized and specialized society incompatible with the tenets of classical citizenship and unable to sustain the balance necessary to support a mixed constitution. Thus, professionalism was synonymous with corruption, and the rise of the professional standing army was inextricably entwined with the subversion of the ancient Gothic constitution by ambitious kings.[4]

The critics of the Stuart monarchy considered Charles II's army an assault on the basic tenets that made a mixed constitution both possible and superior to other forms of government. Led by Algernon Sidney, a major Opposition spokesman during the tumultuous 1680s and an author widely read in the colonies on the eve of the American Revolution, they associated a vital militia with the preservation of civil liberties and constitutional stability. The army served as a tool for royal influence in Parliament and an agent of oppression among the people. Standing armies also perpetuated dependence on wage earners for the defense of the state. But the presence of a professional military in society had a deeper significance. Opposition ideology understood corruption to radiate from the monarchy. Thus, the failure of the people to respond to the crown's standing army with a vigorous revival of the militia had a special significance. The people themselves must be corrupt, unwilling even to claim their birthright to bear arms. Popular corruption was the last symptom of decadence, and so the decline of the martial spirit embodied in the militia meant the end of the free, balanced constitution.[5]

For most Englishmen, the Glorious Revolution assuaged fears that the army would become the vehicle of political tyranny. The revolutionary settlement granted Parliament complete control over military expenditures and guaranteed every citizen the right to bear arms. Nevertheless, William III's request to keep a small military establishment following the Peace of Ryswick in 1698 sparked an analysis of the relationship between military professionalism and the maintenance of a free constitutional order that reverberated well into the era of the American Revolution. John Trenchard, John Toland, Walter Moyle, and Andrew Fletcher—who knew each other well and whose writings probably grew out of discussions among themselves—wrote the principal anti-standing army tracts. Their essays betray a naiveté about the realities of contemporary warfare and an insensitivity to the constitutional safeguards placed over the army by the revolutionary settlement. Nevertheless, their works attest to the persistence of Harrington's ideas about government and society and to the continued Opposition distrust of royal power even after the exile of James II. The end product was a series of ideas about militias and standing armies that linked the former with constitutional balance and identified the latter as among "the fittest instruments to make a tyrant."[6]

Like Harrington, the radical Whigs linked the stability of the English constitution to the continued association of civil and military power with the landed interests of society. This relationship, they believed, had been the basis of the ancient constitution. Under the Gothic pattern, "the King was General, the Lords by virtue of their castles and Honours, the great Commanders, and the Freeholders by their Tenures the Body of the Army." This arrangement made it "next to impossible for an Army . . . to act to the disadvantage of the Constitution." The ancient free constitutions of the Israelites, the Athenians, the Corinthians, Lacedemonians, the Romans, and others also proved the merit of citizen armies. In these free societies, no distinction was made between soldier, citizen, and husbandman; civil stability was guaranteed by ensuring that "their arms were never lodged in the Hands of any who had not an Interest in preserving the Public Peace." As they were under the Gothic constitutions, the sword and sovereignty were united in the hands of the people and manifested in well-trained militia units capable of preventing both domestic discord and foreign invasion. Soldiering was an integral part of the responsibilities of the citizenry. The sword served no one as a profession, and armies never remained constantly afield, because "'tis evident that would have subverted the constitution."[7]

Indeed, Rome had prospered until its citizens succumbed to the luxuries and pleasures of a wealthy society. The republic had conquered Europe on the strength of a citizen army, and the empire had fallen under the weight of professional soldiers. The same fate had befallen the Gothic constitutions of western Europe. Robert Molesworth's recently published *Account of Denmark in 1692* provided a clear example of the fate of freemen who chose to hire a standing army. The lessons of classical history and of the more recent past seemed clear to the radical Whigs: "Whenever a Nation suffers their Servants to carry their arms, their servants will make them hold their Trenchers." The presence of a standing army, particularly in peacetime, signaled an impending imbalance of the free institutions of society, which would leave the nobility a mere "ornament of tyranny . . . , the people beasts of burden," and the monarchy in absolute control.[8]

An army enhanced the power of the crown and threatened the moral character of society. Radical Whigs considered the army to be a passive instrument in the hands of a naturally ambitious monarchy. No constitution could long remain in balance if the military power of society was vested solely in the monarchy. The presence of military placemen in the Commons—placemen more loyal to their employer, the king, than to the historical independence of Parliament—furthered the coercive influence of the crown. The hierarchical arrangement of military life also bred a spirit of dependence that made military men particularly vulnerable to intrigue. If Jacobite conspirators or agents of the king of France bribed but a few key military leaders, a revolution could occur so quickly that the people would be but idle spectators. Even if the appropriation powers of the Commons could control the army, the presence of a regular body of troops constituted a constant threat to the public virtues that sustained a free society and served as the last bulwark against oppression. Professional military officers and men were totally dependent on the government for their livelihood, leaving them little in common with the independent citizenry. Their usual poverty and tendency to "extravagant living" furthered that dependence, while also creating an atmosphere of "injustice and barbarity" insensitive to, if not jealous of, civil liberties. Free institutions depended on the regular rotation of public servants, both civil and military. Men who stayed in the military too long lost their usefulness in peacetime and their sensitivity to the freedoms of civilian life. Those who never served in the military soon were willing to give up their civil responsibilities in favor of a hired mercenary force. A militia offered the constitutionally safe means of providing for the national defense. A revitalized militia would return the nation's defense to its most interested—that is, propertied—citizens, reinstating the balance between citizens and government and removing the tyrannical threat of the monarchy.[9]

The militia plans written by the radical Whigs reflected as much their concern about the imbalance of the English constitution as their determination to develop a military alternative to a standing army. Fletcher and Toland both considered the involvement of men from all classes of society to be essential to a viable militia system. Fletcher's understanding of history suggested that no nation was secure while depending on its servants for its defense. "No bodies of military men can be of any force or value, unless many persons of quality or education be among them." Toland agreed, recommending that no one under eighteen be allowed to seek public office in the future without having served in the militia. Properly organized and disciplined, the militia would also become a vehicle for the reintroduction of public virtue among the citizenry—virtue that had withered in the presence of professional military institutions. Fletcher considered militia encampments to be "as great a school of virtue as of military discipline." Camp regulation would encourage personal sacrifice and a commitment to the common good among the militiamen. Militia duty, Toland suggested, would supplement the Grand Tour in the education of the elite and serve to unite the profession of arms with those of the arts, thus avoiding an otherwise inevitable division of the nation into cowards and barbarians. Certainly mandatory militia service would be inconvenient, but the alternative was the continued dissociation of property and arms—an arrangement incongruous with the perpetuation of civil and political liberties.[10]

The militia could guarantee public virtue, but its organization could also check the concentration of power in the hands of the crown. Fletcher noted that after the barons lost the military services of their vassals around 1500, militias continued to function in most of Europe, yet they were powerless to stop the growing power of the monarchs. With "the prince having every where the power of naming and preferring the officers of those militias, they could be no balance in government as the former were." The result of the shift of the appointment power to the king was the reallocation of the power of the sword from the people to the king. Radical Whigs agreed that the key to an effective militia was that the "officers should be named and preferred, as well as they and the soldiers paid, by the people that set them out." To guarantee that the officer corps remained in the hands of those most interested in the security of the community, Toland suggested that a property qualification be required for officership and that tenure be limited to three years. As in the civil establishment, rotation in militia office would prevent a single party from gaining control and sacrificing the common good to special interests.[11]

These plans had little or no impact on contemporary political debate. William III got his standing army with the consent of Parliament, and the English militia system entered the eighteenth century in a state of general disarray. Nevertheless, Opposition ideas did not disappear. Provoked by the catastrophic political and economic upheavals of the South Sea Bubble, Trenchard and the younger Thomas Gordon, behind the pseudonym of Cato, reexamined the radical Whig arguments about political stability, corruption, and standing armies in the pages of the *London Journal* between December 1720 and July 1723. *Cato's Letters*, which probably had more impact in America than any other single Opposition effort, recalled the images of corruption and intrigue used two decades before to substantiate the dangers facing society under William III. The basic Whig thesis that power corrupts was again linked to the intrigue, influence, and patronage of royal ministers and proven by classical examples. Standing armies were attacked as instruments of royal oppression, and the militia heritage was praised as the last guarantor of liberty against the oppression of an already corrupt government. Francis Hutcheson, who taught at the University of Glasgow between 1730 and 1746 and whose ideas were familiar to many American revolutionaries, continued the radical Whig tradition well into the reign of George II. Hutcheson knew personally or was familiar with the works of the antiarmy publicists from Harrington to Fletcher, and like them, he believed that military service should be the obligation of every citizen and the profession of none.

But not all mid-eighteenth-century defenders of the citizen-soldier were associated with radical Whiggery. Lord Bolingbroke joined Trenchard and Gordon during the 1720s and 1730s in raising questions about the growing military prerogative of the crown. William Blackstone, the noted Tory jurist, was also an important advocate of the citizen-soldier tradition. Like the Opposition spokesmen with whom he otherwise disagreed, Blackstone decried military professionalism on moral and political grounds. He associated soldiering with property ownership and the preservation of the rights of citizenship. Citizens should be soldiers. Professional soldiers, because they were so easily manipulated by ambitious princes, were essential to a tyrannical constitution, but "in a land of liberty it is extremely dangerous to make a distinct order of the profession of arms." "In free states the profession, is justly an object of jealousy" for precisely the same reasons it was desirable in a tyranny.[12]

The most complete restatement of Harringtonian and radical Whig perceptions of the militia in society came in the pages of James Burgh's *Political Disquisitions* published in 1775. Burgh's analysis of eighteenth-century society and politics was inspired by the agitation that swirled around John Wilkes and the founding of the Yorkshire Association. He was not a particularly original thinker, though he can be distinguished from the radical Whigs of the 1690s and the latter-day Cato by his more pessimistic view of the extent of decadence in English society. True to the basic tenets of Opposition thought, he sought to reverse the growing domination of the crown in British politics and to revive the moral fiber of the people to ensure the preservation of civil liberties. Drawing from ancient and modern history and a theory of citizenship founded in Harringtonian thought, Burgh condemned military professionalism and looked to the citizen-soldier as the only viable instrument of national defense.[13]

Ancient history provided ample evidence that "standing armies [were] one of the most hurtful, and most dangerous of abuses." The Roman republic had survived nearly five hundred years of constant warfare without the loss of its liberties because, wrote Burgh, "it seldom happened that any number of their troops were above a year without returning to enjoy the happiness of freedom and liberty." The union of civil and military power kept the "love of liberty[,] by which alone the freedom of government can be preserved," well ingrained among the Roman populace. When the Romans gave up their martial spirit in favor of a more luxurious lifestyle, they turned to professional soldiers and soon lost their freedom. The lessons of the ancient past were clear: "A good militia will always preserve the public liberty [but] if the militia be not upon a right foot, the liberty of the people must perish." The proper footing for any militia was, of course, the classical citizen-soldier. Citing the experience of the Greek and Roman republics, the ancient Goths and Germans, the present-day Swiss, and the writings of Machiavelli, Burgh declared that a militia composed of "men of property, whose interests is [sic] involved in that of their country" can be the only guarantor of domestic tranquility and national defense.[14]

The unity of arms and property was essential to the security of a free society; yet modern history suggested the growing dissociation of property from military service. Like the radical Whigs, Burgh considered the demise of the feudal military tenures around 1500 to mark the decline of the classical perception of citizenship in western society and the concomitant rise of military professionalism in the form of the standing army. He blamed the feudal barons' desire for the more luxurious life at court for their failure to maintain the military tenures that had prevented the centralization of the power of the sword in the hands of any single person and had eliminated any need for mercenary forces. When the barons gave up the military obligations of their vassals in exchange for land rents, ambitious princes hired mercenaries with which they quickly subverted the balance that had sustained the Gothic constitutions. As had the Romans, "rich and luxurious people chose rather to pay than fight. So the sword went out of the hands of the people into those of the tyrant." Burgh did not suggest the resurrection of medieval society, but he did propose the elimination of the long-term enlistments and the unlimited reenlistment policies that were the basis of professional military establishments. Soldiers should never forget the pleasures of a free civil society. Besides, the regular rotation of citizens in and out of the army would ensure a familiarity of arms among the citizenry that would allow the elimination of the professional military structure. In short, if the ministry was bent on maintaining a regular military establishment, Burgh wanted to make the army as much like the traditional militia as possible.[15]

Neither Burgh nor his intellectual forebears feared a military dictatorship, but both considered the presence of a professional army to be symptomatic of the decline of free institutions. The professionalization of the nation's military force separated the obligation for defense from the function of citizenship, destroying the relationship between property and arms that guaranteed free institutions. Just as important, a standing army furthered constitutional imbalance by increasing the power and influence of the crown. Proponents of the standing army, argued Burgh, were only interested in increasing the number of persons dependent on the court. Since Walpole's time, military men had been dependent on ministerial connections for promotion, while military placemen could hold seats in Parliament only by cooperating with the crown. Efforts to detach military officers from their dependence on the court had failed repeatedly, while the number of military officers in Parliament continued to grow, "increasing the power of the ministry [and causing] an incurable wound to the constitution." Certainly military placemen played an important role in the ministerial intrigue that Burgh believed could "alone destroy the essence of the constitution." But it was ministerial, not military, intrigue that troubled the latter-day radical Whig. The failure of the citizenry to meet the obligation for military service combined with the ambition of princes and their ministers to make the army an instrument, not an instigator, of political oppression. The army itself had a passive, almost benign, character. "But a tyrannical prince, or daring minister might bring the kingdom into dreadful confusion by having on his side an army of only 10,000 regulars."[16]

The army was an extension of the court and therefore an agent of the executive will. The connection between the ministry and the military establishments, argued Burgh, gave the ministry the confidence to pursue policies it would not have otherwise considered. Taxes were raised, both because the standing army was more expensive to maintain and because the army stood behind the ministry's tax collectors. The army affected colonial policy too. The ministry would never have considered subjecting the American colonies to an army independent of colonial control if it had not had available the political clout embodied in the military establishment. Nor would the ministry have sought to bring Americans to trial in Britain or charged that fair trials were impossible in America. Burgh also connected the decision to end the economic dependence of colonial governors on the people of the colonies to the constitutional imbalance created by the ministerial control of the standing army.[17]

Radical Whiggery provided the intellectual link between the classical republicanism of James Harrington and the critics of George III. The military's place within this ideological construct was tied principally to considerations of constitutional balance and perceptions of citizenship. These political theorists seldom addressed the nation's armed capabilities as a problem of battlefield efficiency. The indictment of the standing army rested almost entirely on the implications of professionalism for the autonomous political personality and the impact of a military establishment on constitutional balance. Similarly, the militia was understood to represent a revival of the individual independence and balance that had sustained the ancient republics. Radical Whigs saw the militia as a viable institution for national security, but they understood security more as the preservation of the constitutional balance at home than as the defeat of invaders from abroad. Geography contributed to this, but so did history. Invasion was unlikely, the English Channel having deterred invaders since 1066. But domestic tyranny was central to their understanding of the collapse of the ancient Gothic constitutions in Europe and to their view of English history under the Stuarts and after the Glorious Revolution.

Curiously, then, the ideology that supported the militia and denounced the standing army was only indirectly concerned with the fighting capabilities of either. Civil considerations pertaining to constitutional stability and the nature of citizenship were far more important: Professionalism suggested the decay of the classical perception of citizenship, while the influence and patronage inherent in the military establishment pointed to the imbalance in the constitutional order. The army and the militia were measures of the health of the body politic, and it was in that context that radical Whigs developed their commitment to the citizen militia and their repulsion for the professional army. The same frame of mind—the concern for constitutional balance—would, for Americans, prove useful for analyzing the military issues raised by British policy after 1768.

The Moderate Whigs

The radical Whig indictment of military professionalism was not the only perception of the military in society circulating in English political and intellectual circles in the eighteenth century. After the Glorious Revolution the mainstream of English political thinking embraced military professionalism. As early as 1698, moderate Whigs, who accepted the revolutionary settlement as a guarantor of constitutional balance, argued that standing armies were both necessary for and compatible with the survival of free institutions. While radical Whigs were questioning the intent of William III, Daniel Defoe, John Somers, and others were laying the groundwork for a new understanding of the nature of citizenship in a modern society and a reevaluation of the nation's military requirements based on military efficiency, not constitutional balance.[18]

The defense of the British military establishment took form in direct response to the radical Whig attack on the standing army after the Peace of Ryswick. Secure in the revolutionary settlement of 1688, moderate Whigs argued that an army in peacetime was consistent with the constitution if the safety of the realm required it and Parliament consented. James II remained determined, with French assistance, to reclaim the English throne. The navy constituted the first line of defense, but weather and an able French fleet could render it useless. Without an adequate land force, England was defenseless—its militia being ill trained and unorganized. If the existing army were disbanded, a surprise attack by the Pretender might find Parliament in recess, leaving the king with no way to raise an army. Additionally, only a regular army could protect English interests on the Continent. The nation faced a difficult choice. It could disband the military establishment, eliminating the concern that the army would become an agent of royal tyranny, or it could maintain a standing force capable of protecting English interests at home and abroad. Moderate Whigs chose the army, asking "whether 'tis not more certain, considering all things, that HE [James II] will Invade us, or attempt to Invade us, if we have no Land-Force for our defence, than that the Land-Force we may provide for that purpose will Invade our Privileges and Liberties?"[19]

Circumstances necessitated an army, causing some of its defenders to suggest that the army could be disbanded when the current crisis with France ended. But others, Somers and Defoe among them, based their defense of the army on the constitutional prerogatives of Parliament. Defoe conceded that the army had represented a threat to English liberties during the Restoration period, but he reminded his readers that "the Mischief does not lie in an Army, but in the Tyrant." An army was compatible with free government if proper constitutional safeguards existed—safeguards provided under the revolutionary settlement of 1688. The Bill of Rights vested Parliament with the power of the purse, and with that power alone Parliament would and could raise and disband the army in accordance with the public interest. Thus, that document had transformed the army from an agent of royal influence and power into an instrument of the popular will.

The army's economic dependence on Parliament kept its coercive potential in check, and the annual review of military appropriations allowed ample opportunity to remove officers and men guilty of intrigue and conspiracy. Moderates dismissed the radical Whig charge that standing armies in peacetime were incompatible with the English constitution. "If we are in danger of being invaded by our Neighbors, and if invaded, of being conquered by them, unless we have an Army as well as a Fleet for our Defence," can it, enquired an anonymous essayist, be "inconsistent with Nature and the Laws of free Government to have an Army in time of Peace?" A simple syllogism settled the issue for Defoe: The acts of Parliament are legal, and Parliament had constitutional authority to raise an army, thus the army was constitutional because Parliament chose to create it.[20]

Questions of constitutional balance and stability, so closely connected to the army issue by radical Whigs, were for moderates resolved by the Glorious Revolution. Constitutional stability had been established at home, argued Defoe, but the foreign threat remained in the person of the Pretender and his French allies. Only a permanent regular army could guarantee external security. The issue was military efficiency. The classical model used by radical Whigs to defend the militia was incompatible with both modern warfare and the reality of English society. The militia might fare well against other citizen armies, but it was of little value against the "Troops of Veteran Experienced Soldiers" that filled the continental armies. "The whole Method of War is now such that disciplined troops must prove a very unequal Match, to much greater Numbers of Men" untrained in the arts of war, argued Somers. "War is become a Science, and Arms an Employment," wrote Defoe. If courage was once the principal ingredient of successful military campaigns, training, discipline, and professionalism —qualities attainable only with a permanent military establishment—had superseded it. Considering the classical republican perception of the citizen as soldier and husbandman, one anonymous author concluded, "The Plowman had better busie his Head in consulting of proper Grain for the Ground, and leave Military Affairs to wiser Heads."[21]

The growing complexity and interdependence of modern English society had altered the responsibilities of citizenship. Mass mobilization was both militarily ineffectual and domestically disruptive. Apprenticeships, private incomes, and national wealth assumed professionalism in arms and in the economy. Radical Whigs recognized the economic sophistication of English society, but they considered that development symptomatic of the corruption of English society. Pointing to the classical republics, they argued that only the revival of the classical foundations of citizenship could guarantee the freedoms known to the ancient Britons. Moderate Whigs rejected the Opposition theory of corruption and their view of antiquity. They argued that Sparta and Rome, the most militarily successful republics, fielded citizen armies only at the expense of the arts and learning. These were actually "military republics," in which all social and economic improvements assumed a secondary role to military considerations. Embracing a progressive view of history, Somers concluded that "these [classical] Precedents can never suit our Times, unless we change our whole constitution at home, as well as the State of Affairs abroad, and banish from us not only Luxury but both Wealth and Trade."[22]

The militia represented an unacceptable military alternative to moderate Whigs for yet another reason. Radical Whig militia proposals, they argued, could only strengthen the hand of the crown. The militia would be controlled by royal appointees and could be mobilized without Parliament's consent. The Swedish king used the militia to support an absolute monarchy. The same fate could befall England if the king had access to a coercive force independent of parliamentary control. This view, of course, denied the incorruptibility that radical Whigs had credited to the militia. But for moderates, a thoroughly organized militia was nothing more than a regular army under another name and, just as important, outside the purview of Parliament. The revolutionary settlement had assured parliamentary supervision of the army, providing the foundation for internal and external security, and the existing army had proven over the previous decade militarily effective and compatible with domestic interests. A revived militia could only threaten parliamentary sovereignty and weaken national defenses, opening the possibility of constitutional imbalance and tyranny. Political, military, and constitutional conditions had changed in England since Harrington wrote his treatise on political stability and constitutional order. "What then comes of the *History of Standing Armies*?" asked Defoe. New circumstances required new policies: "Tho' there had never been any in the World, they [standing armies] may be necessary now, and so absolutely necessary, as that we cannot be safe without them."[23]

The defense of the standing army offered by the supporters of William III resurfaced again and again during the eighteenth century. Arguments of military expediency, parliamentary prerogative, and the assumption that a revived militia would produce more chaos than order in the constitutional structure were used to defend a constantly expanding military establishment. After 1738, when the Walpole ministry won a major parliamentary debate over the legitimacy of the standing army, only political theorists like Hutcheson and Burgh continued to question the army's place in the nation's constitutional order.[24]

Still, no one offered a comprehensive justification of the army's place in English society until Adam Smith published *An Inquiry into the Nature and Cause of the Wealth of Nations* in 1776. Rejecting the insights of his own teacher Francis Hutcheson, Smith expanded on ideas used by proarmy spokesmen since 1698 to argue that a standing army was both necessary for national defense and compatible with the traditions of a free people. His thesis rested on an analysis of the economic functions and social responsibilities of citizens in a commercial society, a commitment to the efficiency of the division of labor, and an assessment of the importance of self-interest in human motivation. While his contemporary Burgh sought to revitalize the near-mythical citizen-soldier of the classical past, Smith reassessed the military's place in society within the context of recent socioeconomic and military developments. His reappraisal depended upon an understanding of history and a value system very different from those entertained by classical republican theorists from Harrington to Burgh.

Smith believed that society had evolved through a series of stages discernible by their complexity. In each phase of development, the military obligations of the citizenry declined in proportion to the complexity of society. Change, of course, had none of the sinister implications implicit in radical Whig thought. To Smith change connoted improvement. The evolution of society from the simplistic to the complex and the corresponding evolution of specialization and professionalism were not indications of moral decadence or impending political doom; instead they represented the evolution of society toward the more efficient utilization of human and material resources. For Smith the professionalism of the military was not a step toward political tyranny; it was only another expression of the complexity of society.

He believed that the function of soldier and citizen merged only in nomadic and noncommercial societies. Among the hunters, the least developed state of society, domestic and military activities were not synonymous, but the skills required for both often were the same. The mobile life-style of shepherd societies made them even more formidable than the hunters. The noncommercial agricultural societies of the Greek and Roman republics were, according to Smith, the most sophisticated cultures in which the functions of citizen and soldier could be combined. These societies had little foreign commerce and no manufacturing beyond the most basic household industries. Every citizen was a farmer and a potential warrior. The labors and pastimes of the farmer prepared him for the rigors of war, though the seasonal demands of crop production left the farmer less well trained in warlike pursuits than the shepherd.[25]

An abundance of leisure and the paramilitary activities of domestic life in more primitive societies allowed persons to train in the martial arts without undermining their economic standing in society. More sophisticated economic and social structures, however, were not so compatible with universal military training. Commercial services thrived on an efficient and effective division of labor. Military training only distracted the artisan from his craft, reducing production for society and income for the craftsmen. The same applied to farmers. A universal military obligation reduced the farmers' ability to develop and apply the more sophisticated agricultural techniques required to meet the greater demands of an economically interdependent society. In short, Smith believed that the ability of the citizenry to defend society was inversely proportional to the commercial sophistication of society itself. As a society became more complex and more wealthy, and thus more vulnerable to attack, it became less able to defend itself. This paradox would not have surprised any radical Whig. After all, their quarrel with the standing army had been only part of a larger critique of the social developments that supported a commercial society. Unlike the radical Whigs, Smith did not advocate abandoning the movement toward commercialism. He argued that when the division of labor progressed to a point that the citizenry could no longer effectively shoulder military responsibilities, the state had to assume the obligation for defense.[26]

Smith believed that an advanced society could be defended in only two ways. The state could "enforce the practice of the military exercise" on all or part of the citizenry, obliging them "to join in some measure the trade of a soldier to whatever other trade or profession they may happen to carry on," but a compulsory militia, which Smith thought to be against the "interest, genius and inclinations of the people" of a commerical society, was neither as efficient nor as effective as the second option open to the state. This was to make the profession of the soldier "a particular trade, separate and distinct from all others." The creation of a professional military establishment suggested neither moral depravity nor political tyranny, in Smith's view. It was simply the recognition that the social complexity that had necessitated various civil occupational specialities also required specialization in the military sector. Like other aspects of society, defense depended upon an effective division of labor sensitive to the interests of those participating in that division. The militia, according to Smith, was inefficient because "the character of the labourer, artificer, or tradesmen, predominated over that of the soldier." The militiaman's main economic support came from his trade, and there his loyalties lay. Supported economically by the state and trained daily in the martial arts, a professional soldier would view his trade as the craftsman did his. Among members of the military profession, though, the character "of the soldier predominated over every other," leaving the defense of society to its most capable members.[27]

The total integration of the individual into military life made the professional soldier far superior to even the best-disciplined militiamen. Like the skills of the craftsman, the martial arts could be mastered only through long apprenticeship. Regular soldiers lived their entire lives in response to the orders of their commanding officers, developing a habit of obedience essential in an age when the close-order drill took priority over the manual of arms on the battlefield. Smith cited the Prussian soldier as proof of the merits of a well-disciplined professional force. Classical history also verified the superiority of professional soldiers. Philip of Macedon's standing army defeated the Greek militias; Carthaginian regulars routed the undisciplined Roman citizen-soldiers; Rome reversed that defeat only after its militia, hardened by years in the field, attacked Carthage as a body of skilled, professional veterans. According to Smith, Rome depended on these disciplined regulars for its defense from the end of the Second Punic War to the fall of the republic.[28]

Professionalism made the Roman armies invincible. However, the integration of the Roman soldier back into civil life reduced the effectiveness of the army, seriously impairing the empire's ability to defend itself. Smith dated the beginning of Rome's decline to the decision to disperse the army among the provincial towns of the empire. The army was effectively eliminated as a unified political force—which, of course, had been the motive behind its dispersal—but the army's internal discipline was also shattered. Removed from the discipline of military encampments, soldiers became involved in the commerical and manufacturing trades of their host communities, gradually becoming as much tradesmen as soldiers. In short, the military professionals reverted to the status of militiamen. Undisciplined and disorganized, they were easy prey for the marauding barbarian militias of northern Europe.[29]

The decay of the Roman armies and the empire they defended had important implications for the survival of "civilized" nations. The barbarian hordes were superior to the semitrained, undisciplined militia of any civilized country. The close interplay of military and civil functions among more primitive cultures made them easy victors over societies attempting to mix the skills of a soldier with those of craftsmen and farmers. On the other hand, the professional army kept in constant readiness was superior to every militia. On the domestic front, it guaranteed order and stability in society, while its coercive potential made the standing army the perfect instrument for establishing the law of a more advanced society throughout conquered provinces. Thus, concluded Smith, the maintenance of a standing army was essential not only for the survival of an advanced culture but also for the extension of that culture into the more primitive regions of the globe.[30]

Smith's endorsement of military professionalism represented more than a rejection of the traditional English fear of a standing army. He embraced a commercial, specialized society organized around a sophisticated division of labor and the cultivation of special interests. This, of course, was the very society that radical Whigs rejected as inherently malevolent. Nevertheless, not even Smith could endorse a standing army without considering its implications for the liberties of a free society. He justified the juxtaposition of a standing army with civil liberties on the same grounds that he used to discount militia efficiency, that is, self-interest. A professional army was no threat to civil freedoms if the interests of the civil leadership were merged with those of the army. Admittedly, the coercive power of the army had been abused by civil leaders in the past. "But where the sovereign is himself the general, and the principal nobility and gentry of the country the chief officers of the army; where the military force is placed under the command of those who have the greatest interest in the support of the civil authority, because they have themselves the greatest share of that authority, a standing army can never be dangerous to liberty." Thus the interests of civil society and the army were unified, yielding security for the sovereign, eliminating any threat to civil order, and making the standing army compatible with the exercise of domestic freedoms.[31]

Like Defoe, Smith believed new circumstances required new policies. Permanence and professionalism in the nation's military structure guaranteed domestic order and external security, and the latter was quintessential to the preservation of English liberties and institutions. Developments indicative of internal corruption to Opposition thinkers were for moderates evidence of a positive adjustment to the international military situation and to changes in the domestic social and economic structure. In a sense the debate over the army's place in society turned on the compatibility of modernity with traditional English liberties. Professionalism and specialization, the cornerstones of Smith's view of modernity, contrasted sharply with the classical republican insistence that military and political power must be vested in the land in order to preserve political stability and civil liberties. Hence, while professionalism in arms suggested military efficiency and constitutional stability through parliamentary control to moderates, it could only be indicative of the continued decline of ancient Gothic liberties in the minds of Opposition thinkers. Still, moderate and radical Whigs did share some common ground. Neither considered the army capable of initiating its own challenge to the constitutional order. For moderate and radical Whigs alike, the army was a threat only if it could be used by ambitious princes and ministers to undermine the civil order. They parted company, of course, over whether or not the revolutionary settlement of 1688 had provided the institutional framework capable of preventing the misuse of the nation's coercive capabilities.

The virtual simultaneous publication of Burgh's *Political Disquisitions* and Smith's *Wealth of Nations* provided a poignant reminder of the conflict that swirled around the British military establishment prior to the outbreak of hostilities in America. Repeating the outspoken but passé opinions of Opposition thinkers, Burgh glorified the citizen-soldier as indispensable to the preservation of a stable and free government. Smith, very much in the mainstream of contemporary English perceptions of the army in society, looked to a permanent regular army as the most expedient means of guaranteeing national security. Neither considered his perception of the military in society to be incompatible with free institutions.

But both considered their opponents to be expounding theories of society and government that were inherently incompatible with the survival of traditional English civil liberties. For our purposes here, what is important about these conflicting perceptions of the army in society is that they both played an important role in the American response to British policy after 1768. More generally, though, these ideas were at the heart of the public debate over the military's place in American society during the entire early-national period.

3

The British Army in Prerevolutionary American Political Theory

A military force, if posted among the People, without their express consent, is itself one of the greatest griveances, and threatens the total subversion of a free constitution.
—Massachusetts House of Representatives, 7 April 1770, in William Tudor, *The Life of James Otis of Massachusetts*

A well-regulated militia, composed of the gentlemen, freeholders, and other freemen, is the natural strength and only stable security of a free Government.—Maryland Convention Resolution, 8 December 1774, in Peter Force, ed., *American Archives*

The defense of society and the preservation of traditional English liberties were issues never far from the minds of political theorists in England during the seventeenth and eighteenth centuries. The security of society was entwined with questions of political prerogative and liberty in the colonies as well. Certainly the competing English arguments over the nature of military institutions and their impact on civil society touched the consciousness of the colonists. Harrington's *Oceana* was owned by 7 percent of the colonies' public and private libraries on the eve of the Revolution, including the Harvard College Library, the New York Society Library, and the Charleston Library Society. Many of the books and tracts written by the radical Whigs during the reign of William III could also be found on the library shelves of America. This was largely the result of the efforts of Thomas Hollis. Among the most effective propagandists of radical Whig doctrine, he sent hundreds of books, tracts, and commemorative medals celebrating the revolutionary principles of 1688 throughout the British Empire during the 1760s and 1770s. The presence of *Cato's Letters* in nearly 40 percent of the colonies' libraries by 1776 also reflected Hollis's persistence and the pervasive influence of radical Whig ideas on colonial political thought. Trenchard and Gordon's concise restatement of ideas articulated by Opposition spokesmen during the 1690s influenced such important Americans as Thomas Jefferson, John Dickinson, John Adams, Henry Knox, and Benjamin Rush. These men also owned or read the works of Harrington, Sidney, Molesworth, Fletcher, Hutcheson, and Blackstone, as did Benjamin Franklin, James Otis, Josiah Quincy, Jr., John Hancock, Samuel Adams, George Mason, James Wilson, and a host of lesser-known political leaders, public orators, and pamphleteers too numerous to mention. James Burgh's *Political Disquisitions* was also widely read in the colonies. Among those receiving the first printing available in America (1776) were John Adams, George Washington, Samuel Chase, John Dickinson, Silas Deane, John Hancock, Thomas Mifflin, James Wilson, and Thomas Jefferson.[1]

Little suggests that proarmy tracts found their way into American libraries prior to or during the revolutionary era, though Smith was widely read in America after 1776.[2] Nevertheless, it is safe to assume that the colonies were aware of the intellectual justification that supported the British regulars serving in America during the intercolonial wars of the eighteenth century. After all, Smith's ideas reflected the mainstream of English political thought concerning the military. Just as important, moderate Whig ideas coincided well with the military, social, and political assumptions that helped shape military institutions in the colonies during the first two-thirds of the eighteenth century. Threatened by the hardened professionals serving Britain's enemies during the eighteenth-century wars for empire, the colonies sought through the enlistment of long-serving volunteers the same skill and expertise for their armed forces that the British and Continental military establishments achieved by relying on a core of professional soldiers. Like Parliament, the colonial assemblies dissociated soldiering from citizenship and looked to the poor and disfranchised to satisfy their military manpower requirements. And, like Parliament, they did so while exercising considerable control over both the British and colonial forces serving within their jurisdictions. Indeed, colonial military legislation through the Seven Years' War reflected a perception of the military based implicitly on an understanding of the merits of the moderate Whig view of the army in society. Ironically, the development of military institutions compatible with moderate Whig theory opened the way for the articulation of the radical Whig indictment of standing armies. The colonial reliance on regular and semiregular forces was predicated on the assumption that controls over the military granted Parliament by the Bill of Rights were the assemblies' to exercise in the colonies. When British colonial policy challenged the prerogatives of the colonial assemblies after 1763, Americans marshaled the radical Whig ideology of corruption, including concerns about standing armies, to explain and respond to the changing political environment in which they found themselves.

Conspiracy against Liberty

From the English Opposition writers Americans had come to see their society as the last sanctuary of Gothic liberties—liberties that had long since succumbed on the Continent and which were on the decline in England. The American self-image might have been comforting if Opposition writers had not also passed to their intellectual heirs an elaborate statement of the instability of free, balanced constitutions and a systematic explanation of the way in which free societies decline. The vulnerability of liberty to the aggressive and tyrannical inclinations of power as described in the works of Sidney, Molesworth, Fletcher, Trenchard, Gordon, and others, was central to the American view of politics, society, and history. It took little imagination for Americans surveying their standing in the British Empire midway through the 1760s to suspect that the decadence that had devoured liberty elsewhere had taken hold in North America. Taxes were being levied without popular consent, the royal civil list was growing and with it the influence of the crown in colonial politics, and society was increasingly taking on the trappings of European culture. As long as the British army remained on the frontier, few Americans equated it with pensioners, placemen, national debt, excise, and high taxation when they described that multi-headed monster, corruption. Whitehall's decision to move the army from the frontier garrisons to the eastern seaboard ended its innocuous standing in the American dictionary of political tyranny. From the summer of 1768 to the outbreak of hostilities in April 1775, Americans came increasingly to see the British army as exactly that "ministerial tool" that radical Whigs feared most.[3]

The arrival of British regulars in Boston in October 1768 pulled the army into the midst of the ongoing debate over the purpose and intent of British policy since 1763. But why Boston? Boston was not the first place that regulars had been used to quell civil disturbances. British troops had been called in to stop the rampages of the Paxton boys in Pennsylvania in 1764 and 1765. They had also assisted in quelling the antirent riots in the Hudson Valley in 1766. In both cases, though, the troops were requested by colonial authorities through established constitutional procedures.[4]

The circumstances surrounding the arrival of troops in Boston were very different. The troops were sent by Lord Hillsborough, the new secretary of state for the colonies, after repeated pleas from Governor Francis Bernard that they were necessary to ensure domestic order. The Massachusetts Provincial Council had not approved the request for British regulars as the law required. To many in Massachusetts this was a direct challenge to the guarantee in the Bill of Rights against keeping a standing army in peacetime without the consent of the people's representatives. The redcoats were also there to enforce the Townshend duties—duties many colonists considered unconstitutional and therefore a threat to their rights as Englishmen. This left the army in the ominous role of enforcing oppressive legislation while also infringing upon the police functions of the local community. Significantly, the army did not become an issue because professional soldiers challenged a long-standing tradition of citizen-soldiering or simply because regulars were being used to quell civil unrest. Like the moderate Whigs, many Americans considered the army compatible with civil liberties if it was controlled by their colonial assemblies. Instead, it was the growing realization among the colonists that the army's role in the colonies was beginning to fit the paradigm of political oppression and corruption outlined by radical Whigs that transformed the British army's image from that of imperial defender to that of "an unnecessary standing army . . . dangerous to their [colonial] civil liberty."[5]

Americans understood well the vulnerability of liberty to the inherently aggressive inclinations of political power. The decision to move the army to Boston without the consent of the Massachusetts assembly accentuated concerns about the growing power of the crown and Parliament and raised questions about the sanctity of traditional English liberties in the colonies. Public resolutions and newspaper editorials made the colony's position clear. The Boston town meeting called on the eve of General Thomas Gage's arrival pointed to the right of representation guaranteed to all Englishmen by the Glorious Revolution. The Townshend duties were a clear encroachment on that right, but the Bostonians also claimed that the right of representation extended to the "rights of the subjects to be consulted, and to give their free consent, in Person, or by Representatives of their own free Election, to the raising and keeping a standing Army among them." Any army brought into the colony without the consent of the people's representatives would be "an Infringement on their Natural, Constitutional and Charter Rights."

Writing under the pseudonym Vindex, Samuel Adams developed that theme further in the press during the winter of 1768. The Bill of Rights, he argued, forbade a standing army in England without the consent of Parliament because the army had historically played an important role in the transfer of the power of government from the people to the king. Rejecting Parliament's claim that it represented the colonists, he concluded that the power to raise armies in North America could belong only to the colonial assemblies. The Massachusetts House of Representatives concurred. Citing the Magna Carta, the Bill of Rights, and the colonial charter, it refused to make the appropriations necessary to meet the army's quartering expenses, resolving in July 1769 that "establishing a Standing Army . . . without the consent of the General Assembly . . . is an Invasion of the natural Rights of the people" of Massachusetts and those of all "freeborn Englishmen."[6]

Colonial assemblies had been demanding control over regulars serving within their jurisdictions since the 1750s. By the late 1760s, though, the debate over control of the army had been joined with the issue of taxation to form the basis of a widespread belief that the colonies were the victims of a conspiracy to deprive them of their rights as Englishmen. Americans now considered the presence of the British army to be symptomatic of the impending corruption of their constitutional order. In January 1768, the Massachusetts House complained that the recent infusion of revenue and military officers broadened royal influence in the colonies at a time when colonial legislative independence stood very much in doubt. "The time may come," cautioned the house, "when the united body of pensioners and soldiers may ruin the liberties of America." The fear was not that ambitious soldiers might create their own fiefdom but that the army, as James Otis had hinted in 1764, might well serve as the vehicle for the consolidation of royal power in the colonies. With the army in Boston—the result of a unilateral decision made by the king's ministers—to enforce legislation that infringed upon the rights of representation, there could be little doubt that English liberties guaranteed by the Bill of Rights were in danger in North America.

The author of the "Journal of the Times," a series of anonymous articles written in Boston and widely circulated in the colonial press between October 1768 and November 1769, believed that to be the case. The military occupation of Boston, charged the "Journal," was the culmination of a much larger plot, of which the Stamp Act and the Townshend duties were a part, perpetuated by "swarms of crown officers, placemen, pensioners and expectants, [who were] cooperating in order to subdue Americans to the yoke." The king's ministers were the chief conspirators, but Massachusetts's own Governor Bernard had played an important part in the intrigue. His exaggeration of conditions in Boston had led Lord Hillsborough to order troops to Boston, and his continued misrepresentation of colonial loyalties kept the troops in garrison. Private correspondence, too, echoed the public sense of conspiracy, furthering the perception that the army's presence was symptomatic of ministerial efforts to deprive the colonists of their rights as Englishmen.[7]

The army's mission to assist in the enforcement of the unpopular Townshend duties lent more credence to the charge of conspiracy. Town and colonial officials agreed that "the body of the people, the *posse Commitatus*[,] will always aid the magistrate in the execution of such laws as ought to be executed." Widespread civil disobedience proved its own reasonableness. "The very supposition of an unwillingness in the people in general, that a law should be executed, carried with it the strong presumption that it was an unjust law," argued the Massachusetts house. An anonymous essayist reminded the citizens of Massachusetts that no magistrate could govern against the popular will, except with the aid of "foreign Alliances, or by standing mercenary Armies; and if they can support themselves by either of these Methods, the Liberties of the People are SURELY AT AN END." The Massachusetts house put the matter more succinctly: "The use of the military power to enforce the execution of the laws is . . . inconsistent with the spirit of a free constitution and the very nature of government." That the ministry felt compelled to use soldiers to enforce the Townshend duties only confirmed their unconstitutionality. And, of course, if the only purpose of the army was to enforce unjust legislation, the garrisoning of British regulars in Boston could only be part of a plot to rob the citizens of their rights and property.[8]

New England's understanding of the significance of the military occupation of Boston hinged on the radical Whig perception of the nature and origin of political corruption. Nevertheless, the condemnation of the army as an agent of ministerial influence did not include an outright denunciation of military professionalism. The issue was not whether professional soldiers had a place in American society; instead, it was who should control the army in North America, Parliament or the colonial assemblies. Even the most vocal opponents of British policy were unwilling to condemn military professionalism as incompatible with the character of American society. The "Journal of the Times" was deeply troubled by the moral impact that the army was having in Boston. The effect of the army's presence was "daily visible in the profaneness, Sabbath breaking, drunkenness, and other debaucheries and immoralities" sweeping through the city, leaving the editor of the "Journal" to speculate that "our enemies are waging war with the morals as well as the rights and privileges of the poor inhabitants." But there was hope. If the soldiers could be given Bibles and sent to church regularly, "their morals would be reformed, whereby they would become better soldiers, and render their residence in any town less intolerable to the sober inhabitants." Sam Adams, too, shared a moral repugnance for professional soldiers. The army's distinctive life-style—

the importance of obedience and submission to authority—and its unique coercive power easily led soldiers to believe themselves "an independent body, detach'd from the rest of society, and subject to no controul." British regulars had served and no doubt would continue to serve an important function in the colonies, but, Adams believed, a sound civil policy was essential to curb the moral and political dangers implicit in an otherwise useful professional force. If the British regulars were garrisoned on the frontier or moved to quarters on Castle William Island in Boston Harbor, they would pose no danger. There they could neither threaten the moral character of American society nor be used by an "ambitious and covetous governor" to destroy the political foundation of American liberty.[9]

Repeatedly, official resolutions and newspaper essays returned to the thesis that the rights granted Parliament in the revolutionary settlement of 1688 should be extended to the colonial assemblies and to the corollary that the colonies should control troops in their environs. Antiprofessionalism, probably the most far-reaching aspect of radical Whig opposition to the standing army, remained largely undeveloped in New England during the late 1760s. Massachusetts's own use of semiprofessional expeditionary forces may have had something to do with this. The generally good rapport between Massachusetts civil authorities and the British military during the colonial wars may also have been a factor. Additionally, the citizens of Boston had managed to establish a civil, if not friendly, relationship with the soldiers garrisoned there. As long as the soldiers were not involved in an outright attack on the citizenry, no one seemed willing to condemn the standing army as an institution completely lacking in social utility.

The same situation existed in New York and South Carolina, where the army had become an important issue by the end of the 1760s. The army was linked with the intrigue of corrupt officeholders, but it was not rejected as inherently malevolent; nor was the militia cited as an alternative to the professional forces that the colonies had come to rely upon for their defense. Professional soldiers had proven necessary, effective, and convenient over the course of the previous half century in both colonies. The only issue was who would exercise control. That alone was a serious problem, but one that necessitated only a limited articulation of anti-standing army rhetoric. In the other colonies the army did not become a part of the ideological arsenal used to charge the ministry with conspiring against colonial liberties—though colonists were bombarded with news and commentary originating in New England—because the British military presence was either minimal or nonexistent. With no army, the anti-standing army rhetoric of radical Whig thought remained submerged in the more pressing concerns over taxation and nonimportation.[10]

Even the Boston Massacre did not immediately change the basic American perception of the threat posed by the British army. Accounts and commentaries of the incident denounced the army as a ministerial tool designed to extract from the colonies what was not legally Parliament's to claim. They decried the use of the army to police instead of protect the colonies. But they continued to look to colonial civil control as the best means to contain the coercive potential of the regular army. James Lovell, the first to memorialize the events of 5 March 1770, typified the reaction of many to the massacre when he argued that a free people were not necessarily those who did not have an army in their midst. A free people were only "those who have a constitutional check upon the power to oppress."[11]

The Citizen-Soldier

British regulars, even if controlled by the colonial assemblies, were professional soldiers, and professionalism, for Opposition theorists, connoted the demise of the armed citizen so important for the preservation of a balanced, free constitution. Opposition thinkers like Sidney, Trenchard, and Fletcher suspected even the rights of Parliament to raise and maintain an army in peacetime. As they viewed the issue, the standing army was more than simply a potential tool of political tyranny. A professional army was a fundamental assault on the functions of citizenship and consequently an attack on the constitutional balance that supported a free society. The problem of control was secondary to the implications of professionalism, and that made the militia basic to the radical Whig indictment of the standing army. Colonists, however, were slow to inject the citizen-soldier ideal into the ideological context developing in prerevolutionary America. The militia had assumed a secondary role in the defense of society early in the eighteenth century, while at the same time, the colonial assemblies developed their own institutional independence through the use and control of semiprofessional expeditionary forces. Put another way, the political and military history of the colonies bore out the moderate Whig claim that professionalism in arms was important to the stability of civil society. As a result, most Americans proved reluctant to link military professionalism with the constitutional uncertainties facing them until British-American relations reached crisis proportions following the enactment of the Coercive Acts in 1774.

The situation in New England was different. Official resolutions and newspaper editorials during 1768 and 1769 were primarily concerned with the right of the colonial assemblies to control soldiers serving within their jurisdictions. Nevertheless, the "Journal of the Times" and other essayists, most notably Sam Adams, had on numerous occasions suggested that the moral character of professional soldiers posed a threat to civil society. These essayists, however, generally limited their critique of military professionalism to the suggestion that professional soldiers were particularly susceptible to the intrigues of ambitious ministers. They had not gone on to recommend the militia as an alternative to the British military presence in North America. The militia entered the mainstream of public debate in New England only after the Boston Massacre.

After 5 March 1770 the threat of a British standing army was no longer hypothetical. Even though Britain removed the redcoats from Boston almost immediately, the events of that day, when added to the historical accounts that filled the pages of radical Whig tracts, confirmed the worst predictions of Opposition anti–standing army rhetoric. Consequently, the colonists began to give more consideration to the subtle aspects of radical Whig thought, particularly the place of the militia in the dynamics of anti-army rhetoric. While the rest of the colonies ignored the army issue during the uneasy truce that pervaded British-American relations between the repeal of the Townshend duties and the passage of the Coercive Acts, New England embraced the Opposition perception of the citizen-soldier both as a military ideal and as an expression of social vitality and constitutional balance. The introduction of the citizen-soldier into the ideological context supporting the American analysis of the political climate in the colonies would have a profound impact on later attitudes toward the military in society during the Revolution and the early-national period.

The radical Whigs had turned to the militia as a means to eliminate the luxury, corruption, and decadence that they found destroying English society. They had hoped to revive the economic, political, and military independence represented by the citizen-soldier and thus to reestablish the balance that had sustained civil liberties under the ancient Saxon constitution. New Englanders sought to resurrect the militia for the same reasons. Corruption had a foothold in American society. Ministerial intrigue had rendered the right of representation precarious, undermined colonial fiscal control over the royal civil list, and brought standing armies into the colonies' major cities. But the symptoms of decay were not entirely external. Americans had allowed their militia to lapse into a state of total disarray, suggesting that the citizenry had lost the will to preserve its place in the constitutional order. Where military training remained a regular feature of community life, chaos and disorder at militia musters contributed more to social discord than political stability. Even more telling, the propertied members of society had absented themselves from militia service. No free society, charged essayists and pamphleteers, had long survived when those with the greatest stake in the social order renounced their obligation to protect it. Rome fell when the martial spirit of its citizenry declined, England was presently in the throes of corruption and decay for the same reason, and now a similar fate threatened the colonies.[12]

Writing as "A Military Citizen" and "A Military Countryman," Timothy Pickering was among the first to urge militia reform as a means toward stemming the decadence undermining colonial society. A sound militia had "a natural Tendency to introduce and establish good Order, and a just Subordination among the different Classes of People in the Community." This function depended upon the participation of every member of society. The men of "Fortune, Weight and Figure" were particularly important. Their participation underscored the importance of military service, brought order and able leadership to training sessions, and ensured that the best interests of society would also be served by the militia. A vital militia officered by men of wealth and standing would secure society "against the Violence of foreign Enemies by their military Skill, and in a great Measure prevent domestic Jars, by promoting good Order, and a just sense of the Subordination, necessary not only to the Well-being, but to the very Existence of Society." The annual sermons delivered to the Ancient and Honourable Artillery Company during the interlude between the Boston Massacre and General Gage's return to Boston in the spring of 1774 emphasized the same point. Orators regularly recalled the grandeur of the Roman republic when its armies were filled with men of "property and worth." They also castigated the leading men of society for neglecting their military obligation in language drawn directly from Opposition analysis of the militia's importance to the preservation of a free society. "It is highly absurd," announced Simeon Howard in 1773, "though not uncommon, that these who have most to lose by the destruction of a state, should be least capable of bearing a part in its defence." Only with the armed will and the popular will united could the safety and stability of society be assured.[13]

Howard's sermon is of particular note. Before 1774 most essayists discussed the militia as a measure of the vitality of the social and political order without explicitly questioning the merits of regular soldiers. Howard's analysis of the militia's place in the constitutional order challenged the reliability of any military force that did not meet the classical republican definition of a citizen army. Citing Trenchard's *Short History of Standing Armies in England*, he argued that "an army composed of men of property" was the only sure defense of a free people. Their conduct in the field was reliable because they were fighting for their own property and families, and they were incorruptible because they had nothing to gain by the curtailment of society's rights and freedoms. Only pay inspired the loyalties of professional soldiers, "so that neither their temporal interests, nor their regard to virtue can be supposed to attach them so strongly to the country that employs them." "Placing the sword in the hands [of those who] will not be likely to betray their trust, and who will have the strongest motives to act their part well, in defence of their country," provided the only way to ensure that an army did not become "the means, in the hands of a wicked and oppressive sovereign, of overturning the constitution of a country, and establishing the most intolerable despotism."[14]

By the end of 1773 the basic tenets of the radical Whig endorsement of citizen-soldiers had been articulated and applied to the political and social context of New England. Nevertheless, the absence of troops in New England and the uneasy truce that prevailed between Great Britain and the colonies helped produce only a hesitant rejection of the utility of a standing army and a wavering movement toward the revival of the militia as a political and military ideal. The Boston Massacre orations, for example, seldom mentioned the militia and never questioned the premise that a professional army was compatible with colonial liberties if controlled by the colonial assemblies. Even Howard's indictment of military professionalism suggested that regulars served an important function on the frontier.[15] The Boston Tea Party and the subsequent Intolerable or Coercive Acts eliminated any doubts that New Englanders had about applying radical Whig perceptions concerning political corruption and standing armies to their own political situation. The return of British regulars to close the port of Boston provided the final evidence that the crown, as well as the ministry, sought to destroy the liberties enjoyed by the colonists. Opposition writers had warned that the chief instrument of political oppression would be a standing army. With the commander in chief of the British army in North America, General Gage, also serving as the governor of Massachusetts, the implications of the Opposition anti–standing army argument took on new urgency. Liberties in Massachusetts were no longer threatened; they were on the verge of being destroyed.

New England essayists responded by charging that professional soldiers were absolutely incompatible with civil liberties, which in the process laid the groundwork for the eventual mobilization of the militia in defense of colonial liberties. John Hancock commemorated the Boston Massacre with a vociferous denunciation of military professionalism, linking, as had Opposition theorists since Harrington, the security of society with the unity of arms and property. Owning no property, the professional soldier had neither cause for good conduct nor any interest in protecting the property of those he served. Add to that the propensity of the professional soldier to serve the highest bidder and the result was a society undermined by the very force hired to defend it. Only the citizen militia could be depended upon to protect the rights and liberties of a free society. "From a well regulated militia we have nothing to fear," argued Hancock in language reminiscent of Sidney a century before; "their interest is the same with that of the state." John Lathrop recounted for the Ancient and Honourable Artillery Company the professional army's historic role as the oppressor of free peoples and concluded with Hancock that only a militia, "composed of men of fortune, of education and virtue," could guarantee the constitutional balance essential for the preservation of colonial liberties.[16]

The most complete statement of the new urgency that pervaded the discussion of the British army and colonial militia in New England during the spring of 1774 came from the pen of Josiah Quincy. His widely read and influential tract *Observations on the . . . Boston Port Bill, With Thoughts on Civil Society and Standing Armies . . .* , recalled for Americans the arguments against standing armies that had been circulating in Opposition circles since the 1690s. Recounting the ideological significance of the citizen-soldier and the army's historic role as the perpetrator of political corruption, he concluded that only the citizenry under arms could stem the tide of tyranny and oppression that had produced the Coercive Acts of 1774.

The standing army was a monster—"a monster, to which their [human] follies and vices gave origin, and their depravity and cowardice continue in existence." Relying on Whig history's understanding of the somewhat mythical constitutional order of the ancient Britons, Quincy argued that the militia was a free society's "only and sure defense in war." In the Saxon constitution, the militia was the armed embodiment of the civil constitution. Like civil enactments, it "was raised, officered and conducted by common consent." The king served as general only at the pleasure of the citizenry, while the great council formulated military policy and appointed lesser officers. This arrangement provided for the effective conduct of military affairs without allowing the king an opportunity to use the army to subvert the civil constitution. "The freeholders, citizen and husbandmen, who take up arms to preserve their property as individuals, and their rights as freemen" filled the rank and file of the militia. The stability of the Saxon constitution depended upon the unity of citizen and soldier. The balance of command between the king and the great council was reinforced by ensuring that the power of the sword rested only with persons having an interest in the safety of society. Instead of disrupting society, the military arm of the Saxon constitution gave balance and stability to the civil order. As with the franchise, the right to bear arms was a function of citizenship, and the performance of both was central to the continued order and balance of freedom under the Saxon constitution.[17]

By contrast, argued Quincy, the history of the ancient republics and of England demonstrated that professional soldiers were the servants of "ambition and power" and the agents of political corruption and intrigue. The professional officer corps had provided placemen through which to expand royal influence and undermine the will of elected representatives. The military's awesome power had made "wicked ministers more audacious . . . in projecting the propagating schemes . . . inconsistent with the liberties, destructive of the trade, and burthensome of the people of this nation." Of course the hired soldier could have no interest in the preservation of the liberties of society. He was but a "slave among freemen," having nothing to gain by defending the rights of others. In the professional army under the control of ambitious princes, "a will and a power to tyranize [sic] became united; and the effects are as inevitable and fatal in the political, as the moral world."[18]

In short, when "the profession of arms becomes a distinct order in the state, and a standing army part of the constitution," political and civil liberties can not long endure. New England's essayists and pamphleteers had approached that argument at various times since the early 1770s. But there could now be no doubt that the once-respected British army had become the tool of a corrupt administration and an ambitious Parliament bent on destroying the basic rights and freedoms enjoyed in the colonies. The time had come to replace the professional soldiers that had defended the colonies with the citizen-soldiers that had been so vital to the glories of the Saxon constitution. Colonial liberties hung in the balance, and only the militia, mobilized as the armed embodiment of the civil constitution, could preserve the constitutional balance that sustained a free society.[19]

The Militia and Civil Liberty

Though denunciations of a professional army reached a fever pitch during the spring and summer of 1774 in New England, the debate sparked by the Coercive Acts in the other colonies remained limited largely to the issue of the colonies' right to control British soldiers serving within their jurisdictions. Resolutions and instructions from counties and legislative assemblies prior to the First Continental Congress were barren of comment on the dangers of a standing army. The press was similarly without comment on the implications of the military reoccupation of Boston. When the issue did come up, it was discussed in the context of the army's role as an internal police force or submerged within the larger question of colonial rights—a circumstance not surprising given the continued local police functions carried out by the militia in all the colonies and the American determination to protect colonial legislative prerogatives. As it had in the pre-1770 period, this situation tended to forestall an outright denunciation of military professionalism, with the result that the militia was seldom mentioned as a corrective to the problems associated with the British military presence.[20]

Thomas Jefferson's "Summary View" and Pennsylvania's instructions to its Continental Congress delegation, written by John Dickinson, illustrate this trend. Jefferson denounced the use of troops "not made up of the people here, nor raised by the authority of our laws" to enforce Parliament's "arbitrary" legislation. The preservation of civil order was the responsibility of society itself and not that of mercenary soldiers. Nevertheless, what troubled him most was that the army's presence in Boston challenged the right of the colonists, through their representative assemblies, to control the military arm of society. Dickinson, as he had in the *Pennsylvania Farmer*, also looked upon the reoccupation of Boston as an affront to the colonial right of representation. Parliament's claim to tax and create standing armies in the colonies dissolved the constitutional check against oppressive legislation, leaving the colonies the "miserable alternative of supplication or violence." That the army was also being used by the ministry to expand its political influence in the colonies also threatened to undermine the right of representation guaranteed all Englishmen by the Revolution of 1688. Like Jefferson, he avoided moralizing over the standing army or the militia.[21]

The historic reliance in the middle and southern colonies on military professionals was in part responsible for the regional differences in attitude toward the British army. The difference in rhetoric also reflected the use of the army as a police force in New England—a condition that was not present in the other colonies. Colonists outside New England were certainly familiar with the tenets of the antiarmy argument. A serialized printing of Trenchard's *An Argument Showing That a Standing Army Is Inconsistent with a Free Government* was only the most notable of many examples of New York newspaper polemic that drew heavily on radical Whig thought during the quartering disputes of the late 1760s. Newspaper essays and articles, as well as pamphlets originally published in New England, brought the concerns of that region into every colony during the late 1760s and early 1770s. The artillery company sermons and the annual addresses memorializing the Boston Massacre also kept the other colonies abreast of the growing concern in New England that the American militiaman might soon be called upon to demonstrate his commitment to the political ideals he embodied. Certainly Dickerson and Jefferson were personally familiar with the tenets of radical Whig thought.[22]

The military's role in the subversion of political liberties was clear and immediate in New England. For the second time in less than a decade, an army was being used to enforce laws directed explicitly against their freedoms and property. The other colonies shared the concerns about the precarious state of their rights and liberties, but they did not have the dreaded standing army to contend with. For them, the army was only a vehicle of the larger British policy, and it was the policy, and not the vehicle, that drew their criticism. In short, the implications of a professional army were simply more immediate in the northeast, and that played an important role in pushing New Englanders into the fore of the movement toward revolution.

The convening of the Continental Congress in September 1774 gave New England's concern over the British army a national forum. During the winter of 1774–75, while the colonies struggled to reconcile their differences with the king and Parliament, radical Whig rhetoric concerning the army reverberated in the halls of Congress and through the pages of political tracts and sermons. In the ninth article of the Declaration and Resolves of the First Continental Congress, the delegates from the twelve attending colonies restated the old claim for colonial control over military matters: "Resolved that the keeping a standing army in these colonies, in the times of peace, without the consent of the legislature of the colony in which such army is kept, is against law."

But the colonies were no longer squabbling simply over the right to control regulars in North America. By the fall of 1774 the army had come to embody the ministerial effort to destroy traditional English liberties in the colonies. Essayists and pamphleteers recounted and analyzed in light of recent developments in America the constitutional implications of a standing army officered by men dependent for their livelihood on the crown, the moral corruption inherent in the organization of a professional military, and the historical use of standing armies at the expense of civil liberties. They concluded that the army had become a principal agent of ministerial intrigue, but they also went one step further. For the first time leaders throughout the colonies began to advocate militia mobilization as a necessary corrective to the developing constitutional crisis. Colonists had long relied on radical Whig thought to define the dangers inherent in recent British colonial policy. They now looked to the militia—the guarantor of constitutional balance and stability—to right the imbalance and stem the corruption overtaking the colonial constitution. Civil liberties, private property, and the constitutional order were in peril; the citizenry had to take up arms.[23]

In September 1774 the Continental Congress endorsed a resolution from Suffolk County, Massachusetts, calling for the colonies to reorganize their militias under leadership friendly to the "rights of the people," setting in motion a series of provincial actions that made the militia the cornerstone of armed resistance to British policy through the winter of 1775.[24] Massachusetts moved first to revive the militia's ancient function as the armed guarantor of the civil constitution. In October 1774 the provincial congress instructed local committees of safety to assume responsibility for the training, supply, and mobilization of the colony's militia system. It also directed the citizens in their capacity as militiamen, and "with due deliberation and patriotick regard for the public service," to elect their own company officers. Those chosen in local voting were to elect regimental officers to command the militia at the county level. The provincial congress retained the power to appoint general officers, ensuring that the military order remained ultimately subordinate to civil authority.[25]

Resolving "that a well-regulated Militia, composed of the gentlemen, freeholders, and other freemen, is the natural strength and only stable security of a free Government," the Maryland convention acted in December 1774 to reorganize its militia under a popularly elected officer corps. Across the Potomac in Fairfax County, Virginia, local political leaders, including George Washington and George Mason, met in January 1775 to enroll county militiamen under an officer corps annually elected by the rank and file.[26] Six months later, in an effort to provide a source of manpower for the newly formed Continental army, Congress recommended that all the states adopt the republican principles embodied in the Massachusetts militia structure. Congress also urged that duty for minutemen be limited to four months annually, so that even the burden of emergency service would be equally distributed throughout the population.[27] By early fall provincial assemblies in Maryland, New York, New Jersey, Pennsylvania, Virginia, New Hampshire, and North Carolina had taken steps to comply with the congressional recommendations.[28]

The reorganization of the militia in the states was more than an attempt to infuse popular support into the patriot cause. The changes politicized the militia, making membership an expression of patriot sympathies,[29] but they also had significant constitutional implications. As the colonial rebellion still aimed only at redressing grievances with the crown, committees of safety and provincial assemblies throughout the colonies linked the reconstituted militia with the return of political stability and constitutional balance. Composed of "gentlemen, freeholders, and other freemen," the revitalized militia represented a mobilization of the independent political personalities that were the foundation of the classical republican military and civil organization.[30] The popularly elected officer corps promised constitutional balance by undermining ministerial influence in colonial government and society. Militia reorganization, commented John Adams, removed the "men who procured their commissions from a governor as reward for making themselves pimps to his tools." In their place stood the natural elite of a free people, "gentlemen whose estates, abilities, and benevolence, have rendered them the delight of the soldiers."[31]

The reorganized militia represented not only a military organization necessary to stem British oppression but also a constitutional order historically linked with the preservation of civil liberties and personal freedom. Put another way, the decision to mobilize the militia in 1774 and 1775 was predicated on the reason for mobilization itself. The call to arms was not intended to win political independence. It was designed to reestablish the constitutional balance that had historically guaranteed political and civil liberties in a free society. Informed by perceptions of constitutional order and stability passed down to the colonists by popularizers of radical Whig theory, Americans turned to the one institution that had historically been linked with the preservation of civil liberties and constitutional balance: the militia.

Part 2

Society, Arms, and the Republican Constitution

During the last months of the constitutional crisis with Great Britain, the citizen-soldier assumed a position of primary importance in the ideological structure of American republicanism. Nevertheless, the militia's renewed importance in the American mind fit poorly with the historical development of American military institutions. Indeed, the disparity between past military practices and the demands of revolutionary doctrine placed a severe strain on the ideological foundations of the American republic as independence replaced redress of constitutional grievances as the justification for armed resistance.

No one seriously advocated a reconsideration of the Revolution's republican goals, but many Americans did urge a reassessment of the assumptions behind traditional republican perceptions of the military. The exigencies of the war for independence demanded military expertise beyond the reach of the poorly trained citizen militia. But military necessity could not in itself satisfy the unavoidable tensions between ideology and policy. Independence, revolutionaries agreed, was meaningless without political liberty.

Concerns about the republic's military security only begged more basic questions about the military's place in the constitutional order. Was the discipline and military expertise required to defeat a professional British army compatible with the tenets of a republican revolution? What constitutional considerations were necessary to ensure that the coercive power of the newly formed state and national governments did not become the instrument for political corruption and intrigue? Nor did the Peace of Paris remove the need to rectify the ideological implications of the idea of the citizen-soldier with the military requirements of a nation founded in a world of professional armies. In peace, as in war, fundamental questions about the compatibility of military efficiency with the ideological tenets of American republicanism demanded resolution. Few answers emerged during the Confederation period. Nevertheless, by the ratification of the Constitution, a new understanding of the military's place in society had been articulated, if not institutionalized, laying the groundwork for new approaches in the early-national period to the ideological problems raised by regular armies and the militia.

4
The Wartime Army

[Tyranny] must be the fate of every people who have not wisdom enough to make, and virtue enough to submit to, laws which oblige every citizen to serve his term as a soldier.
—Charles Lee to James Bowdoin, 30 November 1776

The liberties of this Country . . . cannot be established but by a large standing Army.—William Ellery to Nicholas Cooke, 7 September 1776

The radical Whig indictment of standing armies played an important role in moving the colonies toward rebellion. Americans used the insights and implications of radical Whiggery to identify the British army as an agent of civil tyranny and to justify the mobilization of their own militia in defense of their political rights. When the purpose of armed resistance changed from the redress of colonial grievances to the establishment of a new republic, however, radical Whig theory proved less applicable to the American experience. Radical Whigs considered the citizen-soldier a free society's best deterrent to tyranny and its most reliable defense in war. No American committed to the revolutionary cause would deny the former, but historically the colonies had found long-serving regulars more convenient and reliable than citizen-soldiers. The poor and the disfranchised had filled the ranks of the expeditionary armies and had met the manpower needs of British regiments in the colonies for as long as Opposition theorists had been proclaiming the merits of the citizen-soldier. In short, perceptions of constitutional balance and the logic of corruption and decay used to justify the call to arms ran headlong into a military tradition more in tune with the ideas of Adam Smith than with those of James Harrington. On the battlefield Smithian perceptions of the military in society won out. But in the legislative councils of America perceptions of the military as an agent of political corruption persisted. As a result, Americans developed during the Revolutionary War a constitutional and institutional structure that reflected both a sensitivity to radical Whig suspicions of the military in society and a recognition that military expertise was essential for the preservation of republican institutions.

The Military and Society

Radical and moderate Whig ideas about the military in society were part of ideological systems founded on perceptions of society and citizenship that went well beyond soldiering itself. Adam Smith believed social and constitutional order thrived on the interdependence of persons and institutions. Thus he linked soldiering with the professionalism and specialization that he believed sustained a modern, commercial society. Embracing the classical definition of citizenship, radical Whigs associated stability with the political and economic autonomy of the individual. They remained suspicious of commerce and any other economic enterprise that threatened to separate the proprietorship of land from the responsibility to bear arms and the right to participate in the political decisions of society.

Americans were not unaware of the implications of either of these views. New England's critique of military professionalism was closely connected with the demand for a return to republican simplicity that surged through American society prior to the Revolution. At the same time, though, the reluctance of the other colonies to condemn professionalism until the very eve of the Revolution suggests that some Americans doubted the applicability of classical conceptions of soldiering and citizenship in an already complex society. The rebellious colonies could conclude that British policy enforced by an oppressive regular army necessitated militia mobilization as a means to stem tyranny within the empire, but they could not field the army necessary to win political independence without also coming to terms with the nature of the society that had spawned the revolutionary movement. Could political independence be won and a republican constitutional order established with an army drawn from the citizenry and motivated by a commitment to the common good? Were Americans capable of establishing a society patterned after the tenets of classical republican theory? Or did the realities of eighteenth-century warfare and society demand a new approach to the military requirements of a republican society? Were specialization and professionalism compatible with the social and political goals of the Revolution?

The conflicting views held by Charles Lee and George Washington about the kind of military establishment needed to accomplish the goals of the Revolution mirrored the ideological tensions that pervaded American attitudes toward the military during the war years. Both men were committed to the establishment of a republican society in America. Nevertheless, their dissimilar views concerning the nature of citizenship and the structure of society necessary to preserve republican civil and political liberties produced very different critiques of the revolutionary military establishment.

When the Continental army was organized in June 1775, Lee received one of six major general commissions. Like the other ranking officers in the nascent American army, he was well acquainted with the training, tactics, and discipline that made the British army so effective. What made Lee different, though, was his deep suspicion of military professionalism —a suspicion derived from a personal association with the English Whig opposition to George III. Even the "courtly" Blackstone, he had reminded the colonists in 1774, believed that "freedom cannot be said to exist, or she exists so lamely, as scarcely to deserve the name," in a country where military camps, barracks, and fortresses separated the daily duties of the citizenry from the responsibility to bear arms. With the support of men of "the first distinction and property," Lee was convinced that the American states could field an army both more "formidable against the external enemy, and less dangerous to their fellow-citizens" than a body of professional soldiers. The army he had in mind would be drawn directly from the state militias.[1]

Lee opposed the use of bounties to attract soldiers into the army for the duration of hostilities. The republic risked losing its freedom to the very force charged with its defense if Americans did not have "virtue enough to submit to laws which obliged every citizen to serve his turn as a soldier." Enlistment incentives and extended service discouraged the cultivation of martial arts among most of the citizenry, while they promoted the development of a "distinct profession" of arms composed of "the most idle, vicious, and dissolute" part of society. Republican society, argued Lee, depended on the preservation of the classical relationship between property, citizenship, and the right and responsibiliy to bear arms. Every citizen should serve in the militia, and there should be no provision for substitution, short of infirmity. Active military duty should be rotated among the citizenry and limited to no more than two months annually. Lee did not believe that the rotation of military service would hinder military effectiveness, because only the most rudimentary tactics were necessary for soldiers "drawn from their ploughs." "Marching in front, retreating and rallying by their colours and all firing at marks" were the only tactics required of a republican army, and those skills could be learned at locally organized, weekly training sessions for soldiers not on active duty.[2]

Lee's plan for a citizen militia was influenced by Machiavelli and was reminiscent of proposals developed by John Toland and Andrew Fletcher, but his insights into tactics were influenced by the French military theorist Marshal Maurice Comte de Saxe. Tactical simplification was part of Saxe's plan to give France a national army built upon a compulsory five-year military obligation for persons from "all conditions in life," the elimination of the cumbersome ornamental garb in favor of more functional and durable clothing, and the use of more flexible strategies designed to take full advantage of both the tactical possibilities of cavalry and artillery and the collective personality, "l'imbecilité du coeur," of the troops in the field. Saxe's plan had truly revolutionary implications for the military order of western Europe and was destined to undermine the hierarchical order of European society. The full significance of his ideas awaited the declaration of the *levée en masse*—an event Condorcet considered to have transferred the theoretical equality of democracy to the reality of life. Lee, however, did not embrace the social implications of the tactical system that he appropriated. His perception of an ideal republican society was profoundly conservative and fundamentally premodern, and would have been acceptable to political theorists ranging from Harrington to Burgh.[3]

An analysis of Lee's plan for a military colony makes that clear. Each of the ten thousand men in the colony would hold property ranging from two hundred acres for rank-and-file militiamen to twenty-five hundred acres for colonels. "For the sake of order," reasoned Lee, "there should . . . be some difference of property in the different classes of men." He clearly did not foresee his colony becoming a model for frontier democracy. Nor did he expect the colony to become a haven for land speculators or ambitious merchants. An agrarian law would restrict property ownership to five thousand acres, preventing any small faction of landholders from imbalancing the civil order. Commerce would have no place, either. Commercial employment was forbidden because it "must emasculate the body, narrow the mind, and in fact corrupt every true republican and manly principle" essential to the virtue of free citizens. The "effeminate and vile" commercial occupations necessary for the functioning of even this noncommercial society were left to the employment of women. The male citizens of the colony would devote themselves to farming, hunting, and the martial arts. The militia and the militiamen, then, became not only a military alternative to a standing army but also the reflection of a social system qualitatively different from the emerging complex commercial societies of Britain and Europe which looked to a professional military for their defense.[4]

Whereas Lee sought a return to the kind of society that Adam Smith believed was compatible with the deployment of citizen-soldiers, Washington considered the American republic to be more like the modern, commercial society that Smith had described as unable to support a citizen army. Washington had not read *Wealth of Nations*; nevertheless, he analyzed American military requirements in terms reminiscent of Smith's defense of a permanent and professional military establishment. Advocates of the citizen-soldier believed that a commitment to the common good would bring the militia out and keep it in the field, but, argued Washington, they simply misunderstood the motives of those willing to do military service in the eighteenth century. He contended that few men, even in a republic, would serve disinterestedly and that fewer still could identify their interests with a low-paying army. This fact explained the mediocrity and ineptitude plaguing the American officer corps and the difficulty of finding recruits for the enlisted ranks. To attract the men of character and stature necessary for an effective officer corps, military service had to be made economically advantageous. National interests had to be linked to personal interests, and that meant a pay scale high enough to make the officer "independent of every body but the State he Serves." The economic interests of the enlisted soldier also had to be entwined with the military success of the republic. Virtue alone had proven and would continue to prove inadequate to inspire men to suffer the hardships of military campaigns. But soldiers would be willing to serve, even for the duration of hostilities, if ample rewards in the form of land and money were provided.[5]

Washington looked to higher bounties to resolve the chronic manpower shortages faced by the American army, but he also believed that only bounties would provide the long-serving regulars that would ensure the discipline and order necessary for successful military campaigns. Militia soldiers were civilians first and soldiers second. They might be familiar with the manual of arms, but soldiering remained only a part of their role in society. Their ties with civil society also left militiamen ill prepared for the hardships of camp life and the discipline required for effective military operations. Those factors alone explained why citizen-soldiers were no match for trained regulars. Soldiering was a demanding craft, argued Washington, requiring skills and training attainable only through long and continuous service. Only when the republic separated soldiering from the other responsibilities of citizenship could it be assured of winning its independence from Great Britain.

Washington, of course, was turning upside down the radical Whig claim that the militiaman's greatest strength lay in his dual role as citizen and soldier. But for Washington, the nuances of political autonomy and economic independence were of little importance compared with the need to defeat the hardened British regulars on the battlefield. Only a victorious army could guarantee republicanism in America. His concern was for an efficient and dependable military force, and he concluded, as had the moderate Whigs, that an army composed of long-serving regulars was not only compatible with but necessary for the preservation of civil and political liberties in a free society.[6]

The Revolutionary Army

Washington's analysis of the republic's military needs suggested that neither the social nor the military theory of classical republicanism was appropriate to the environment that spawned the American Revolution. Citizen-soldiers called from the plow and motivated by public virtue may have served the ancient republics, but only an appeal to self-interest could bring out the long-serving regulars required to ensure military victory in the modern world of military professionalism and economic specialization.

Certainly private interest had proven more important than public virtue during the initial year of hostilities. The emotional and ideological fervor that brought the militia into the field in the aftermath of Lexington and Concord had not lasted the winter campaign of 1775. After serving well at Bunker Hill, the militia's performance steadily deteriorated. Hopes for creating an army of citizen-soldiers drawn from the newly reorganized state militias all but collapsed after militiamen left Montgomery's army stranded at the gates of Quebec when their enlistments expired.

By the summer of 1776 Congress was well on its way toward creating a military establishment that placed a premium on military expertise, avoided the use of militiamen whenever possible, and relied extensively on enlistment bonuses and bounties to fill the ranks of the chronically undermanned American army. Even John Adams was convinced that the states could not "reasonably hope to be a powerful, prosperous, or a free People [without] a permanent Body of Troops." "Indeed," wrote William Ellery of Rhode Island, "the liberties of this Country . . . cannot be established but by a large standing Army."[7]

During the fall of 1776 Congress substantially increased enlistment bonuses, lengthened Continental enlistments to three years or the duration of the war, and adopted articles of war explicitly patterned after the British model. A year later it created the office of inspector general with duties fashioned after the "practice of the best disciplined European armies."[8] There were those, including Charles Lee, Samuel Adams, James Warren, Benjamin Rush, and one "Caractacus," who believed that the states were exhibiting "too great a propensity . . . to trust the defence of our country to mercenary troops."[9] But a majority of the state delegations in Congress, including such important individuals as Thomas Jefferson, John Adams, and Robert R. Livingston, accepted the principle that success on the battlefield in an age of military complexity and sophistication required trained, experienced, and disciplined troops. Fifteen months of military disappointment, caused in part by the untimely departure of militia soldiers, could justify no other conclusion. At the same time, Congress recognized that the experience and discipline necessary for victory against the professional army of Great Britain could be had only by offering significant remuneration, conceding that the eighteenth-century soldier was motivated by interest and not virtue, whether he was an American patriot or a Hessian dragoon.[10]

The states, too, abandoned the citizen army that they had once considered "the natural strength and only stable security of a free government." After appeals to public virtue failed to produce a continuous supply of willing citizen-soldiers, they turned to the poor and disfranchised to meet state and continental manpower needs. The unmarried sons of farmers and artisans, transient laborers, newly freed or delinquent indentured servants, and even slaves were urged, induced, and compelled into military service. South Carolina designated "all idle, lewd, disorderly men, who have no battalions or settled place of abode, or no visible lawful way or means of maintaining themselves and their families, all sturdy beggars, and all strolling or straggling persons . . . liable and obliged to serve in one of the Continental regiments of this state." Maryland followed suit, making "every vagrant or man above 18 years of age, able bodied, and having no family, fixed battalion, or visible means of subsistence" subject to impressment for Continental army service. All the states encouraged the poor and landless to enlist with promises of land and monetary bounties that ranged from outright grants of money and acreage to tax exemptions and debt deferment. Many states also granted volunteers immunity from civil judicial proceedings. This usually meant that no land or personal property could be impounded for delinquent debts while the soldier remained in active service. Connecticut even proposed that localities use public revenues to support the families of soldiers willing to commit themselves to extended military service. Even militia drafts did not pretend to raise a citizen army. Economically secure individuals could gain military exemptions by paying fines or hiring substitutes. In many states two men could be deferred for the duration of the war if they hired a third to serve for the same period of time.[11]

The unity of property and arms embodied in the citizen-soldier and so important to the ideological precepts of the Revolution failed to satisfy the pressing demands of military necessity, creating a major discrepancy between the theory of the Revolution and the military demands inherent in the fight for independence. Enlistees did not consider military service to be a lifelong occupation, but institutionally the army had many of the trappings of a professional, if not permanent, force. The Continental command clearly aspired to model their army after the professional forces of Europe. Terms of enlistment were designed to provide the republic with a single body of soldiers for the duration of the war. The lure of bounties and the promise of bonuses also reflected a recognition that self-interest, not public virtue, motivated individuals to accept the hardships of military service. Soldiers were deliberately separated from the rights and privileges enjoyed by the civilian population, and they were punished and disciplined in a manner adapted from European military codes and manuals. Certainly, no effort was made to rotate the "best men" of society into the ranks of the army. Indeed, once Congress and the states accepted the necessity of long-term enlistments, the public apparently had no trouble relegating the principal burden of military service to the poor and economically insecure.

Constitutional Balance and Stability

The realities of eighteenth-century warfare and the apparent absence of a virtuous citizenry demanded a reassessment of the republic's military requirements. That development, however, did not compromise the republican goals of the Revolution; nor did it eliminate the need for the vocabulary of balance and stability that permeated radical Whig theory. Confronted by the failure of public virtue, Americans replaced classical virtue with constitutional structures designed to control the malevolent potential of self-interest. This modification allowed military and civil leaders to ignore the radical Whig condemnation of professionalism—which never fit American military customs anyway—without abandoning the language and logic of balance, influence, and corruption that played such a major role in propelling the colonies toward independence. Americans might have adopted the moderate Whig justification of military professionalism to explain the character of the revolutionary military establishment, but like the radical Whigs, they remained convinced that military institutions could provide the means for the subversion of the political order. The concerns exhibited by the framers of the republic's first body of constitutional law made that clear.

Every state ratifying a new constitution during the Revolutionary War, save New Hampshire, Georgia, and New Jersey, noted the necessity for the subordination of military to civil authority, proclaimed the right and obligation of free men to bear arms, and denounced standing armies as a threat to the civil liberties of a free society.[12] But such declarations were usually limited to statements of general principle; no state convention sought to imitate the ancient Saxon constitution by placing the citizen-soldier at the center of the constitutional order. Instead of limiting the professional character of their military establishments, constitutional conventions sought to ensure that the states' military capacities could not become the springboard by which ambitious political leaders could subvert the constitutional order for their own political ends. Establishing the primacy of the state assemblies in military affairs provided the principal means of achieving that goal.

In no state was the governor denied the office of commander in chief of both militia and regular state troops. Nevertheless, the real power to mobilize the states' military institutions belonged to the representative assemblies. Only in Massachusetts, where the people agreed to grant the governor broad military powers only in exchange for a popularly elected militia officer corps, did the governor hold independent powers to call out the militia.[13] Most states required the consent of an executive council before the militia could be embodied.[14] Regular troops could not be raised or officers commissioned in any state without the consent of the elected assembly. In Maryland, even after the assembly had consented to raise regulars, the governor was prohibited from personally commanding state troops without executive council approval.[15] Pennsylvania's president could not command state troops, "except advised thereto by the Council, and then only so long as they shall approve thereof."[16]

All regular and militia officers in the states served under commissions granted by their respective governors. Nevertheless, taking their lead from radical Whig insights into the origins of political corruption, Americans were careful to ensure that the prerogative to commission military officers could not be used to expand the power and influence of the governors or to undermine the autonomy of the state assemblies. Delaware, Maryland, Georgia, North Carolina, and South Carolina disqualified all regular military officers serving in state or Continental lines from serving in the privy councils of their governors. Maryland, Georgia, and North Carolina also restricted regulars from holding elective office. In South Carolina any elected representative receiving a military commission had to stand for reelection before retaining his elected office.[17] Only in Maryland, where militia field officers were ineligible to hold office "as a Senator, Delegate, or member of the Council," were exclusion provisions extended to the militia officer corps.[18]

Still, there was little chance that militia officers might become extensions of an ambitious executive authority, for in no state did the governor enjoy a free hand in appointing militia officers. The governor of New York held the power to make militia appointments with the advice of his executive council. Virginia's governor held the same power, except that all appointments were to be made on the advice of local county courts. In the other states, governors had no role in the appointment of militia officers. Constitutional conventions in Delaware, North Carolina, and South Carolina required the joint concurrence of the popular branches of government for the appointment of field and general grade officers. The same conventions vested the legislative assemblies with the power to determine how to select company-grade officers. In New Jersey and New Hampshire company-grade officers were to be elected by the rank and file, and field and general officers were to be appointed by both houses of the general assembly. Pennsylvania allowed its militiamen to elect officers through the rank of colonel, and in Massachusetts popular election extended to the level of brigadier general. In both states, however, the highest level of the militia command structure served at the behest of the popular assemblies.[19]

As it had in the prewar period, the place of military institutions in the constitutional order reflected a concern for civil political intrigue germinating from the executive branch. Few state constitutions indicated a fear that the military might itself aspire to dominate the political order. The Georgia constitution provided that no "military officer, or soldier, [shall] appear at any election in a military character, to the intent that all elections may be free and open." Delaware forbade militia musters on election day, prohibited military encampments within one mile of polling places twenty-four hours before and after an election, restricted battalion or company members from voting in succession, and did not allow arms to be brought to polling places. Maryland applied the same restrictions to the election of delegates to its state constitutional convention, but that convention did not incorporate those safeguards into the body of the constitution. None of the other states viewed the military as posing a threat that merited special constitutional consideration.[20]

The Articles of Confederation also exhibited few reservations about the professional character of the revolutionary military establishment. Article 9 allowed Congress "to build and equip a navy; to agree upon the number of land forces, and to make requisitions from each State for its quota." This article, which gave the continental government the constitutional authority to maintain a military establishment to meet national security needs, apparently evoked little concern in Congress. That the congressional power to raise an army was not limited to wartime also appears not to have troubled the delegates to the Continental Congress.[21] Congress was concerned, however, that the states might raise armies of their own, opening the way for interstate conflicts that would destroy the internal unity of the republic. The Dickinson draft of the Articles, submitted to Congress in July 1776, prohibited the raising of a "standing Army . . . by any Colony or Colonies in Times of Peace, except such a Number only as may be requisite to garrison the Forts necessary for the Defence of such Colony or Colonies."[22] The provision was more explicit in its final form: No state could maintain troops in peacetime, "except such number only as

... shall be deemed necessary [by Congress] for the defence of such State." In lieu of a regular military establishment, the Articles provided for the states to keep a "well regulated and disciplined militia." The states could organize their military on a more permanent footing only if the "danger is so imminent as not to admit a delay till the United States, in Congress assembled, can be consulted."[23]

The Articles did not prescribe a permanent continental military establishment, but the prohibition against the states raising peacetime forces and the absence of any restriction against Congress doing so suggests at least a permanent continental force to garrison the frontiers. Nevertheless, the provisions for raising land forces for the common defense reflect the recognition that the states would not allow the continental government to dominate the military establishment during peacetime or war. Transferring suspicions directed against the crown during the 1760s and 1770s to the newly formed Continental government, the states remained deeply sensitive to the possibility that the army could become an instrument for the expansion of continental power at the expense of state sovereignty. All troops requisitioned by Congress for the common defense were raised at the behest of the states. State legislatures controlled the appointment of officers through the regimental level and retained the power to fill all subsequent vacancies. Congress held the power to declare war and make peace, to direct the operation of continental forces in the field, to appoint general and staff officers and all naval officers, and to establish the "rules for the government and regulation of the . . . land and naval forces" under its control. But Congress had the power neither to commission naval vessels and raise an army nor to appoint a commander in chief without the consent of nine state delegations. The Articles may have given implicit consent to a regular army establishment, but that establishment was fashioned to prohibit any single civil power from using the coercive potential of the military to corrupt the constitutional balance of the Confederation.[24]

Despite the safeguards built into the Articles, fears persisted that the continental military establishment could corrupt the constitutional balance of the fledgling republic. North Carolina delayed ratification of the Articles of Confederation after its delegate to Congress, Thomas Burke, cautioned its general assembly not to grant extensive powers to the Continental Congress. Burke was particularly concerned that "every State [have] a right to control the Cantonment of Soldiers within their Territory." In South Carolina there was concern that federal troops could be assigned to a state "entirely independent of the command of the [state's] civil power." William Henry Drayton, South Carolina's chief justice, reminded his state's general assembly of the problems that had developed from Governor Bernard's inability to order British troops from Massachusetts in 1768. In his view congressional control over troops in the state would be "dishonorable to the sovereignty of the state, dangerous to its welfare, and inconsistent with the superiority of the civil power." He urged that the Articles be amended to give state governors control over continental military affairs within their jurisdictions. He also proposed to dilute continental military authority further by allowing the people to elect general officers and to vest the states with the power to appoint staff officers in proportion to the number of line troops provided. In Massachusetts the same suspicion of continental authority brought a demand that the power to determine war and peace remain in the hands of the people.[25]

Only five states raised official objections to the military prerogatives outlined in the Articles. Pennsylvania and Massachusetts objected that only the "white" population would be used to determine troop apportionments. New Jersey was also concerned about the manpower burden placed on the nonslaveholding states. New Jersey, though, was more concerned that the Articles be amended to "clearly" forbid the raising of continental troops in peacetime without the consent of nine states. "A standing army, a military establishment, and every appendage thereof, in time of peace, is totally abhorrent from the ideas and principles of this State," declared the New Jersey legislature, and it "wished the liberties and happiness of the people [to] be carefully and explicitly guarded in this respect." Connecticut demanded an amendment that would have prohibited continental troop requisitions except during wartime. That state also proposed that no "officer or pensioners [be] kept in pay by them [Congress], who are not in actual service, except such as are or may be rendered unable to support themselves, by wounds received in battle." The latter provision reflected Connecticut's concern that Congress not use the military to create a large body of pensioners economically dependent on Congress and thus willing to promote continental interests at the expense of the sovereign states.

South Carolina also expressed concern that the military powers granted Congress threatened the sovereignty of the states. It proposed that the consent of eleven states be required before Congress could exercise its power to build a navy, raise an army, and appoint a commander in chief. To prevent Congress from contriving to use its military power to weaken the internal defenses of a particular state, South Carolina urged that only two-thirds of the troops raised by a state be eligible for service outside its borders "without the consent of the executive authority of the same." To further ensure the autonomy of the states, it recommended that Continental army troops raised from a single state remain "under the command of the executive authority of the State in which they are so raised." Multistate contingents awaiting congressional appointment of a commanding general would be commanded by the most senior officer present, and he would be responsible "for his conduct to the executive authority of the State in which the troops are, and shall be liable to be suspended" by the same authority, according to an amendment proposed by South Carolina.[26]

All of these amendments were defeated in Congress by lopsided margins.[27] Nevertheless, along with the Articles themselves and the state constitutions, they offer some important insights into the constitutional considerations surrounding the development of the republic's wartime military institutions. The preservation of the political sovereignty vested in the state assemblies was the overriding concern informing discussions of the military's place in the constitutional order. The unity of arms, property, and the franchise that provided the foundation for political stability and balance within classical republican constitutional theory remained part of the rhetoric of American republicanism, but the citizen-soldier was clearly only an ideal superseded by the realities of eighteenth-century warfare and society. In the American constitutional order the freeholders' role in military affairs was manifest in the actions and prerogatives of the state assemblies, not necessarily through the regular exercise of arms.

Americans did not consider the military to be a potential independent arbiter in the political process. Like the Opposition theorists, they considered the military to be little more than a tool in the hands of civil power that controlled it. Thus many persons in Congress and in the states remained acutely sensitive to the possibility that the nation's military establishment could become the means for the subversion of the political and social order. That concern was shaped by the radical Whig assumption that corruption originated in the executive branch and radiated out to undermine representative institutions. Hence, constitutional restrictions made it impossible for state executives to expand their political influence and power through the agency of state military institutions.

The Articles of Confederation and the proposed amendments reflected the same pervasive concern that Congress should be able to wield little military power without the full cooperation of the state assemblies. So long as the representative assemblies faithfully reflected the will of the citizenry, the coercive potential of society could not be misused. This constitutional arrangement embodied, in a uniquely American way, the balance that classical republican theorists believed necessary for the preservation of a free society. Radical Whigs had been concerned that civil power over the military be spread along a horizontal continuum; the peculiar constitutional order of the American states led Americans to apply the same concern about the centralization of power to a vertical continuum—the state assemblies replacing the classical citizen-soldier as the guarantor of constitutional balance and stability—capable of maintaining the federal constitutional balance that supported the union of confederated states.

In another sense the constitutional structure of the fledgling republic reflected a willingness to bend the ideological dictates of republican theory to meet the practical demands of an extended war. Certainly the professionalism implicit in the institutional structure of the nation's army represented a departure of major proportions from the republican theory that had inspired the Revolution. There is, of course, some irony in that after a decade in which the colonists had moved gradually, if not hesitantly, toward viewing the militia as the only sure guarantor of the rights and liberties of a free people they should create a state and national constitutional structure far more concerned about the balance of power within the civil establishment than with the character and composition of the nation's military forces. Indeed, the state constitutional conventions and assemblies seemed to assume that a regular army would play an important role in the wartime policies of the new nation. It should be remembered, however, that the state constitutions were written after the colonists had abandoned their efforts to resolve their constitutional grievances with the crown and Parliament. That point is important for understanding both the apparent American departure from the tenets of republican theory and what would be an ongoing effort to rectify the military requirements of the republic with the ideology that had fired the Revolution.

The crisis that culminated in the mobilization of the militia in 1774 and 1775 was more constitutional than military. The state constitutions, on the other hand, were written after the debate over constitutional principles had been replaced by the war for independence. At that point immediate political ends, not theory, dictated military policy. Hence the states created for themselves and for the nation a constitutional structure sensitive to the dangers inherent in a regular army but also capable of responding to the realities of eighteenth-century society and warfare. The nation's leadership recognized that political independence would be secured by success on the battlefield and not necessarily by a close adherence to the dictates of traditional republican theory. When the war for independence ended, however, and the concerns of the nation turned from the exigencies of military campaigns to the nature of republican society and government, the military theory of republican ideology would again move to the fore, raising basic questions about the nature of the American experiment in republicanism and the military institutions necessary to ensure its success.

The Half-pay Controversy

The half-pay controversy offers important insights into the constitutional and ideological factors affecting attitudes toward the American military during and immediately after the Revolutionary War. In a very basic way the organization of the American army on a professional footing was predicated on the constitutional balance established between the states and the continental government. Conceding that self-interest had replaced public virtue as the principal motivational force in American society, the nation's political leadership nevertheless continued to view the army as a potential agent of civil political power and influence in much the same way that radical Whigs had during the eighteenth century. Not everyone, however, could accept interest as a legitimate substitute for public virtue. As the war progressed, a growing suspicion developed even among those who could that concessions to interest would subvert the Confederation's constitutional organization. The plan for a half-pay establishment, which began as an effort to satisfy the pay demands of the Continental army officer corps and ended as part of an attempt to expand the power and influence of the continental government, sparked debate that reveals the importance of the constitutional arrangement that supported the professional character of the republic's wartime army. The debate also reflects a persistent concern about the army's compatibility with the goals of the Revolution, as well as a corresponding effort to incorporate into the ideology of American republicanism a justification for a regular army establishment.

The half-pay issue originated during the long hard winter at Valley Forge. The typically low wintertime morale at army headquarters deepened in the winter of 1777–78 after the army had failed to prevent the British advance into Philadelphia. With Congress exiled in York, Washington's army faced severe shortages in matériel, experienced the usual exodus of enlisted personnel, and suffered from a depleted, disorderly, and demoralized officer corps. To resolve this latter problem, Washington reluctantly asked Congress to provide lifetime pensions at half pay for every officer who served to the end of hostilities. Congress debated the issue well into the spring of 1778, finally passing a pension of half pay for seven years for officers serving for the duration of hostilities.[28] Military and political interests, however, continued to press for lifetime pensions. They succeeded in October 1780 after the emergence of a more nationalist-minded leadership in Congress and amidst fears that the failure to revise the pension establishment would render the planned partial demobilization a difficult if not dangerous operation.[29]

Nationalist efforts to fund the half-pay establishment ran into stiff opposition after the American victory at Yorktown, however. A parochialist coalition, comprising New Englanders plus a few important antinationalists in the South, blocked efforts to fund the promised half-pay establishment during 1782, as nationalist influence in Congress steadily eroded.[30] The army's recognition that half-pay pensions might never be funded combined with pressures generated by reports of growing dissatisfaction among the soldiers garrisoned at Newburgh and by a concerted nationalist drive to add the army to the list of public creditors who would support legislation creating an independent source for continental revenue to prompt congressional action commuting half pay to five years' full pay in March 1783.[31]

From the outset, opponents of half pay viewed the pension scheme as an assault on the ideals of the Revolution and as a threat to the constitutional structure that sustained the existing military establishment. After all, lamented James Lovell of Massachusetts, "this *was* in its beginning a *patriotic* war." Henry Laurens, serving as president of Congress in 1778, considered the "total loss of virtue in the Army" a most reprehensible justification for half pay. Most of those demanding pensions had no claim to distinction beyond their ability to accumulate "immense fortunes by purloin and peculation, under the mask of patriotism." Officers motivated only by private interest had no place in a military organization founded to throw off British decadence and corruption. "Is there no danger," wondered Laurens, "that Men of this disposition will . . . accept half Pay . . . from the Enemy," if it be in their interest? Even if the motives of the officers could be condoned, the pension plan still posed a threat to the constitutional structure of the republic. Critics pointed out that pensioners and placemen had expanded the influence and power of the British crown during the course of the eighteenth century. Elbridge Gerry believed that the American "aversion to placemen and pensioners[,] whereby Great Britain is likely to lose her liberty," posed a major stumbling block to the half-pay plan. Lovell predicted that American society would soon be infested with the same kind of "haughty idle imperious Scandalizers" that had served to further corruption in England if Congress granted pensions to the officer corps.

That the pensioners would also be military officers was equally troubling. The republic's existing military structure reflected the balance between state and Continental power that informed the confederation of sovereign states. A military pension system threatened to undermine that balance by joining the interests of the officer corps to those of the continental government. Even worse, the special treatment promised Continental army officers threatened to demoralize state militias, undermining the internal security of the states and increasing the coercive potential of the continental military establishment. In short, there were those in Congress who sensed that the creation of a half-pay establishment would bring to American society the seeds of evils like those that had prompted revolution in 1776.[32]

Critics of half pay would have preferred to have left army pensions to the discretion of the state assemblies. The plan to commute half pay to five years at full pay in no way assuaged the fears of those suspicious of an expansive national government. The problem, as the parochialists saw it, was less the legitimacy of the officers' claim than the implications of commutation for the political and social order of the new republic. Continental funding of the military debt would increase the demand for a national impost. The association of a permanent revenue with a military force, according to the parochialists, was clearly contrary to the "established truth that the purse ought not to be put into the same hands with the Sword." The connection of the debt owed the army with other public creditors also troubled the opponents of commutation. Such a large body of creditors tied directly to the national government threatened "to establish & perpetuate a monied interest in the U.S." This possibility revived fears "that this monied interest would gain the ascendance of the landed interest, would resort to places of luxury & splendor, and by their example & influence, become dangerous to our republican constitutions." A constitutional balance conducive to the preservation of republican liberties, argued opponents, could be maintained only by leaving commutation to the discretion of each of the state legislatures.[33]

Outside Congress commutation provoked public debate only in New England. The Massachusetts assembly castigated Congress for enacting legislation "calculated to raise and exalt some citizens in wealth and grandeur, to the injury and oppression of others." Commutation was overly generous and "inconsistent with the equality which ought to subsist among citizens of free republican states." Rhode Island endorsed the position taken by Massachusetts, but it was in Connecticut that the real debate over commutation took place. That state's opposition to pensions dated from 1778 when it proposed an amendment to the Articles of Confederation prohibiting postwar pensions. In 1782 the Connecticut assembly ratified the 5 percent impost with the proviso "that no part of said Monies [was] to be used and applied for the Payment of any Pensions or half Pay to discharged Officers, or to any Person or Persons Whatsoever . . . not then in the Actual Service of the United States." During the summer and winter of 1783 and into 1784 a major debate over the implications of commutation occupied town meetings and filled the Connecticut press, producing, in the words of James Madison, "almost a general anarchy."[34]

Opponents viewed commutation as a ploy designed to undermine the republican institutions secured in the war for independence. Repeatedly, commutation was identified as a capitulation to self-interest. Town meetings resolved that army officers had ignored their republican obligation to serve the common good in their demand for half pay. Why, wondered the town meeting of Torrington, were the citizens and soldiers who suffered to support the patriot cause being neglected while "all these revenues of the country, [were] be[ing] heaped on the officers?" Torrington town leaders charged that the officer corps had been among the most blatant speculators in war matériel and now they were being awarded again for their effort in what everyone else considered to be a patriotic war. Considering the mutual sacrifices of the citizenry in the war effort, the citizens of Farmington called commutation "unjust, impolitic, and oppressive to the people, subservient of the principles of the republican government, and exceedingly dangerous when drawn into precedent." "Cives" echoed similar concerns. He argued that the merchants, farmers, and tradesmen had made the most sacrifices in the war effort, but now they would be taxed to support the officer corps. This in spite of the fact that "there is not a officer of the army what has doubled his interest in the war."[35]

Linked to the charge that commutation bestowed rewards upon men motivated only by private interests at the expense of the virtuous citizenry was the question of civil political corruption. Interest and influence—both sources of corruption and intrigue in the radical Whig lexicon—were repeatedly associated with the creation of a military pension establishment. In May Farmington officials charged that commutation promised to create an aristocracy wherein "the Direction & management of the state is committed to the Great & Powerful alone." The influence and corruption of just such a group of pensioners, the Torrington town leaders reminded the citizens of Connecticut, had forced the colonies to declare independence in 1776. The half-pay establishment opened the way for continental civil authorities to use the army to attain political goals otherwise outside their reach. In short, the national government might use the economic dependency of the officer corps to expand its political influence, gradually undermining the constitutional balance that supported the union of confederated states.[36]

The Society of the Cincinnati, founded in the aftermath of the Newburgh crisis, compounded the suspicions of civil corruption. The aristocratic trappings of the society, including badges of honor and hereditary membership, represented a threat to republican institutions by themselves. But since members of the Cincinnati would also be the beneficiaries of commutation, the danger was even greater. In his widely read attack on the Cincinnati, Aedanus Burke wrote that he feared that the link between the society and commutation would be fatal: "However pious or patriotic the pretence, . . . any political combination of military commanders, is, in a republican government, extremely hazardous, and highly censurable." The Middletown convention of Connecticut towns, called to protest commutation, endorsed Burke's position in its December 1783 and March 1784 sessions. Together, commutation and the Cincinnati promised a "new order of peerage and knighthood." Will the twin evils be eliminated, or, asked the March Middletown convention, will the citizens of Connecticut "tamely resign your present republican form of government for an aristocracy?"[37]

Critics bemoaned the blatant surrender to self-interest represented by half pay and commutation and worried that such concessions threatened to undermine the republican goals of the Revolution. But while opponents retreated to the rhetoric of radical Whiggery to define the dangers implicit in the pension establishment, proponents marshaled the logic of moderate Whig thought to justify the pension plan as a means to improve military efficiency and to ensure political stability in the fledgling republic.

George Washington opened his defense of half pay with an attack on the social assumptions that supported the classical republican critique of self-interest in the political arena. Interest, not public virtue, he argued, was the "governing principle of most of mankind." "Motives of public virtue may for a time . . . actuate men to the observance of a conduct purely disinterested," wrote the commander in chief, "but they were not of themselves sufficient to produce a persevering conformity to the redefined dictates and obligations of social duty." Patriotism had brought officers out during the early days of the war, but as the war continued, patriotic fervor declined, leaving the officer corps depleted, ineffective, and apathetic. The reason was simple. "Instead of gaining any thing, [an officer] is impoverished by his commission and conceives he is conferring, not receiving a favor in holding it." Only when military service became profitable would men commit themselves to the defense of the republic. No doubt half pay would be expensive, but the cost in men and matériel would be far greater if the officer corps were not soon staffed by men of merit. "Few men are capable of making a continual sacrifice of . . . private interest or advantage, to the common good," cautioned Washington, and unless there was a change in the nature of mankind, it was unlikely that the American army would long survive with an officer corps motivated by public virtue alone.[38]

Half pay also promised immediate political and military advantages. Officers' pay had been raised by 50 percent in October 1776, but that increase was quickly swallowed up by the inflationary economy. The pension plan offered a simple and, for the moment, inexpensive way to make military service more attractive without further depreciating continental currency. It also promised to improve discipline in the army and to contribute to the stability of the national government. Officers could be more easily disciplined, since the threat of dismissal would carry with it clear economic implications. The economic advantages of a military commission would also "introduce that Subordination to civil Authority which is Necessary to produce an internal Security to Liberty" because it would be contrary to the officer corps' interest not to support the civil establishment. Thus the half-pay establishment would provide an institutional structure capable of controlling the malevolent potential of self-interest. Public virtue had proven undependable, but self-interest, if properly manipulated, would preserve and protect the republic.[39]

When the war ended and nationalists found their influence waning before a growing concern about the scope and power of the continental government, the pension plan became even more important. For men like Robert Morris commutation represented the last opportunity to use the army as a means to stabilize and centralize the power of the Continental Congress. The pension plan promised to make military officers de facto creditors of the national government, adding yet another powerful and influential group to those economically dependent on Congress. Morris and others argued that without the support of these and other creditors the states would be propelled into the abyss of tyranny that anticommutation spokesmen feared most.[40]

Justifying commutation as a necessary outgrowth of the failure of public virtue to sustain the war for independence, Noah Webster linked the plan to the necessity of integrating professionalism into the nation's military establishment. If commutation catered to special interests, those special interests were essential to the success of the republican experiment in America. Dismissing the classical republican view that a militia motivated by virtue could defend a free society, Webster set forth an analysis of society that not only justified commutation but also provided the rationale for the integration of a well-paid and highly professional military into American society.[41]

What republican theorists called "public virtue" was no more than the union of private interests directed toward a common goal. Military emergencies were no exception to Webster's thesis that "self-interest is the [operat]ing principle of all mankind." In times of public danger, he reasoned, it was in the interest of every citizen to defeat the common foe. What essayists called patriotism was only self-interest. "If such a thing exists, as love to our country, aside of all private considerations, it seldom operates or at least terminates in told benevolent wishes."

Webster believed that Connecticut's conduct during the war and the commutation debates illustrated his thesis. The proclaimed passion for liberty declined rapidly among the state's militiamen as the war dragged on and as military service increasingly represented personal hardship. Enthusiasm fell to indifference, and indifference succumbed to reluctance, "till at length a soldier could not be procured without a bounty of fifty or sixty pounds." Now that the emergency had passed, there was little interest in repaying those who had served in the common defense. No doubt the officers of the army had threatened to quit the service if half-pay pensions were not promised. Nevertheless, they deserved condemnation no more than the farmer and the merchant who would provide foodstuffs and matériel only at exorbitant prices. "The truth is," wrote Webster, "no person will labour without reward—Patriotism is but a poor substitute for food and cloathing, but a much poorer substitute for Cash."

The cost of retaining the American officer corps in the field may have been high, but in Webster's view, it had been worth the expense. Militia and Continental soldiers had chronically neglected their military responsibilities, while the officer corps had served faithfully. "If the officers were bound to the service by stronger ties of private interest than the soldiers, the half pay establishment was a prudent and necessary measure." If public virtue had motivated the officer corps' conduct, and this Webster doubted, then "patriotism deserves some uncommon reward." For Webster, the revolutionary military experience confirmed the view articulated by Washington earlier in the war. The defense of a republic demanded men willing to endure the hardships of prolonged military service. An appeal to interest, not to virtue, was the only way to secure men willing and able to defend an eighteenth-century republic.[42]

The Prospect of Peace

The intellectual, institutional, and constitutional foundations of the republic's revolutionary army reflected a perception of the military shaped by ideological and historical considerations. Long-serving regulars had historically met American military needs, and it was to that kind of army that Americans turned to win their independence. But history alone could not justify abandoning the citizen-soldier. The militia was central to the political stability and constitutional balance that sustained a republican constitution. For that reason alone, men like Washington and Webster found it necessary to explain and justify what was a major discrepancy between the ideological foundations of the Revolution and military policy. The professional character of the American army was compatible with revolutionary theory, they argued, because interest, not virtue, motivated soldiers in the field and because questions of military effectiveness and efficiency were of more immediate importance than the constitutional implications of the citizen in arms.

The nation's leadership, for the most part, accepted that explanation, or at least acquiesced in recognition of the military realities of the Revolution. Nevertheless, the acceptance of professionalism implicit in the evolution of the revolutionary military establishment depended directly upon the continuing demands of an extended war. The experience of the war years in no way suggested that the professional army would become the cornerstone for the republic's peacetime security. Americans might have acceded to the logic of the moderate Whig defense of military professionalism in order to satisfy wartime military requirements, but they remained concerned about the implications of a regular army for the political stability of a free society.

Few Americans worried that the army itself would disrupt the nation's constitutional order, but its relationship to civil authority remained an issue of major importance throughout the Revolutionary War years. The army was understood to be apolitical, but its unique coercive power and its susceptibility to political patronage made it a potential instrument of political intrigue and corruption. Thus state constitutions consciously diffused civil control over state military institutions to make their misuse all but impossible. The framers of the Articles of Confederation also carefully divided control over the nation's army between the continental and state governments.

The debate over half pay and commutation underscored the importance of radical Whig axioms in shaping the institutional structure and constitutional standing of the military in American society. When nationalists attempted to use the military establishment to expand the powers of the continental government, parochialists were quick to recall the relationship between interest, influence, corruption, and pensioners outlined in English Opposition tracts. The military's civil connections with the British crown had helped corrupt the English constitution. The pension scheme wedded the military to the continental government, making it, they argued, a first step toward the usurpation of the constitutional balance necessary for the preservation of a union of confederated states. The parochialists' determined resistance to half pay also portended one of the principal problems of the postwar period: How could the new republic rectify the constitutional assumptions implicit in a union of sovereign republican states with the continuing need for national military security? Having worked out a viable institutional and intellectual arrangement to meet wartime needs, Americans now faced the task of coming to terms with the constitutional and military needs of peacetime.

5
Liberty and Security in the Postwar Period

A well regulated militia is the glory and defence of every country. They are a greater security than standing armies, who, though necessary in the time of war, are ever dangerous in peace.—Zabdiel Adams, The Evil Designs of Men (1783)

It is a flattering but I believe a mistaken idea–that every citizen should be a Soldier. . . . An apprenticeship must necessarily precede the acquisition of any trade, and the use of arms is as really a trade as shoe or boot making.
—Friedrich von Steuben, A Letter on the Subject of an Established Militia (1784)

Hence the wisdom . . . of forming the manners of the rising generation on principles of republican virtue; of infusing into their minds, that the love of their country, and the knowledge of defending it, are political duties of the most indispensable nature.—Henry Knox, A Plan for the General Arrangement of the Militia (1786)

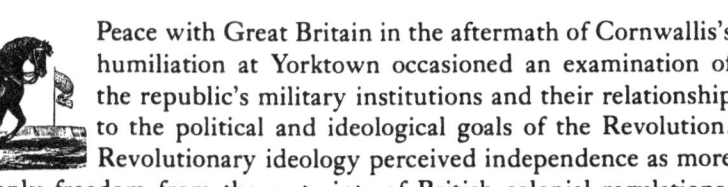

Peace with Great Britain in the aftermath of Cornwallis's humiliation at Yorktown occasioned an examination of the republic's military institutions and their relationship to the political and ideological goals of the Revolution. Revolutionary ideology perceived independence as more than simply freedom from the restraints of British colonial regulations. The rejection of royal authority was also a repudiation of moral decadence and political corruption. Hence, the American Revolution was in part an effort to recreate a social, economic, and political structure lost since the republics of antiquity—a structure in which the citizen-soldier, of course, had held an important place.[1] Nevertheless, the war years had seen the republic's military institutions evolve steadily away from the citizen army —composed of sturdy yeoman farmers, armed, enfranchised, and committed to the preservation of the common good against the intrigues of self-interest and ambition—described in the tracts and official resolutions written in 1774 and 1775. Certainly the Continental army had not been a militia force; but that had troubled ideologues who feared throughout the war years the emergence of moral and political corruption. With peace at hand and the preservation of republican liberties again representing a more pressing concern than military preparedness, these ideologues believed that the time had arrived to replace an army that was inherently dangerous to republican institutions with a body of politically and economically independent, armed, and locally organized militiamen able to resist the ambitions of an inherently aggressive central political authority. For them, only that kind of peacetime military establishment would ensure the constitutional balance and political stability essential for the survival of republican institutions.

There were, however, important discrepancies between this ideological vision and the military and social realities of the new nation. The militia had not performed well during the Revolution. The Continental army had assumed the principal burden for the nation's defense during the war precisely because the citizen-soldier had exhibited neither the public virtue nor the military effectiveness credited him by republican theorists. The structure of American society also raised questions about the viability of an army of citizen-soldiers. The social and economic qualities associated with the classical citizen-soldier might be found in the western counties of the mid-Atlantic and southern states, but they were rapidly disappearing —if they had existed at all in the eighteenth century—in the more populated regions of the United States. There, society resembled more the urban and rural landscape of industrial England than the homogeneous cultures of the ancient republics. Social stratification, fewer opportunities to own land, and economic specialization and dependence more accurately described the culture in which most Americans lived by war's end.[2] The questions raised by these developments were important for both the military and political security of the republic. Given the constitutional assumptions upon which the Confederation was founded, how could the republic guarantee its security if the citizenry could not be depended upon to serve the public good?

Warren and Ramsay

That question troubled the nation's military and political leaders in the aftermath of the war. The answer was by no means obvious.

The war years had left Americans deeply divided over the implications of the militia's proven ineffectiveness. A good example of that division is found in the popular histories of the Revolution written during the 1780s by Mercy Otis Warren and David Ramsay. Both acknowledged the weakness of the militia, but for ideologically opposite reasons drew different conclusions from the nation's wartime experience. Warren considered inefficiency unavoidable. Ramsay believed military strength through an established army to be essential to the republic's security. Their divergent views help define the issues that informed the postwar debate over the nation's peacetime forces.[3]

Warren, whose three-volume *History of the Rise, Progress and Termination of the American Revolution* reflects a thorough grounding in the fear of standing armies that pervaded English radical Whig tracts like John Trenchard and Thomas Gordon's *Cato's Letters*, blamed revolutionary military shortcomings on the erosion of republican values. She credited the mobilization of New England's citizen-soldiers after Lexington and Concord to a revival of public virtue (long dormant in America owing to the colonists' prolonged association with Britain's professional soldiers) sparked in large part by the Coercive Acts of 1774.[4] Unfortunately, she conceded, the martial spirit that had inspired American soldiers to heroic heights at Lexington and at Bunker Hill quickly evaporated, leaving the American army often undermanned and always poorly disciplined. Republicanism itself was partly to blame. "Unused to standing armies, and . . . impatient at the subordination necessary in a camp," Americans refused to enlist for more than a few months. But that was a minor factor compared with the "avaricious spirit" that crept into American society and destroyed the public virtue that had informed the initial call to arms. High enlistment bounties, the demand for half pay, and the founding of the Society of Cincinnati—all reflections of the professional character of the American army—were only the most obvious manifestations of the spirit of self-aggrandizement that had jeopardized the struggle against tyranny during the war. Well versed in the symptoms of corruption that had historically undermined republican liberties, Warren argued that strict adherence to republican principles would have eased the problems that had plagued military and civil leaders. The military effort of a republic might be "hazarded by the unrestrained license of [its militia] soldiers," she wrote, but that was a small price to pay to avert the moral and political corruption inherent in an army enlisted for "an indefinite term."[5]

Ramsay rejected the wisdom of *Cato's Letters*, arguing instead that the republic's wartime difficulties were the result of too much republicanism. He had little doubt that "the ideas of liberty and independence, which roused the Colonists to oppose the claims of Great Britain, operated against that implicit obedience which is necessary to a well-regulated army." "The principles of general liberty" used to justify mobilization had led the continental leadership to trust "too much in the virtue of their country men." At the same time, little attention had been paid to the need for "subordination and order in their army, which, though it intrenches on civil liberty, produced effects in the military line unequalled by the effusions of patriotism, or the exertions of undisciplined valour." Ramsay reasoned that the militia's successes at Lexington, Concord, and Bunker Hill had caused many civilian leaders to believe that the yeoman farmer could meet the country's military needs. They had failed, however, to distinguish momentary gallantry from the perseverance necessary for continued success. The militia had not persevered, and the shortage of adequately trained soldiers had brought the republic "to the brink of destruction" more than once before independence was won.[6]

"The result of the [revolutionary] experiment," Ramsay wrote, "was, that, however favorable republics may be to the liberty and happiness of the people, in the time of peace, they will be greatly deficient in that vigour and despatch, which military operations require, unless they imitate the policy of monarchies."[7] Assuming a sound defense to be prerequisite to civil liberty, he argued that no nation—republic or monarchy—could long endure without an army of well-organized and disciplined regulars. Warren judged the militia adequate for military emergencies; just as important, she considered the citizen-soldier a measure of the republican virtue without which a republic could not long endure, This ideological conflict between the most popular historians of the Revolution went to the core of the debate over the military during the Confederation period. When the question of peacetime security fell to the army to ponder, its leadership considered both the military lessons and the ideological heritage of the Revolution. George Washington and his advisers showed on the one hand that fears of the regular army were exaggerated but on the other that an effective military establishment could be founded on the ideologically important militia. In Congress, however, ideological differences evoked strident debate. When Alexander Hamilton proposed to leave defense to the regular army and a continental reserve, he aroused a determined opposition united behind the classical republican axiom that standing armies in peacetime were incompatible with republican liberties.

Peacetime Security

In the spring of 1783 a congressional committee chaired by Hamilton asked the commander in chief to prepare a plan for the "interior defence" of the states commensurate "with the principles of our government."[8] Washington sought the opinions of such advisers as Inspector General Friedrich von Steuben, Chief of Artillery Henry Knox, Quartermaster General Timothy Pickering, and Adjutant General Edward Hand, as well as those of General Rufus Putnam, once the army's acting chief engineer, and George Clinton, governor of strategically important New York and formerly a brigadier general. Pickering, Knox, and Steuben were well versed in the military arts, and Putnam had extensive experience in the sophisticated art of fortification. These veteran soldiers knew that independence had not left the republic impregnable. Indian nations actively contested American territorial claims west of the Appalachian Mountains, and British and Spanish soldiers occupied positions on the republic's northern, western, and southern frontiers. Nevertheless, except for approximately seven hundred regulars left over from the wartime establishment, the nation's security depended on the same state-controlled and haphazardly organized militia system that had proven ineffective during the war.[9] Certainly, nothing Ramsay was to write later in the decade would have surprised the commander in chief's correspondents in 1783. They knew well the difficulties inherent in keeping an effective army in the field.

But though the need to create a reliable military force was foremost in their minds, Washington's advisers could not and did not ignore the ideological foundations of revolutionary republicanism. Clinton, Hand, and Putnam, for example, understood the American suspicion of standing armies during peacetime. Pickering believed a "standing army would endanger our liberties." With Knox, he considered the militia the "palladium of a free people."[10] Neither could these men have failed to note the renewed political influence—evident during the recent congressional debates over officer pensions—of persons who shared a profound ideological opposition to military professionalism. Hence their analysis of the nation's military needs involved much more than a call for preparedness. Aware that any peacetime force would have to be acceptable to congressmen sympathetic to the assumptions of radical Whiggery, these military leaders sought to reconcile the ideal of the citizen-soldier with the demonstrable effectiveness of a professional army. Personal ideological proclivities naturally led Pickering and Knox to devise plans compatible with the principles of radical Whiggery. For others, most notably Steuben, a realistic assessment of the political atmosphere of the postwar years may have proven more influential. But no matter what their motives, they sought to create a military establishment that met both the ideological and the military needs of the republic.[11]

Washington's advisers all believed that the militia must remain the principal instrument of national defense. Clinton pointed out that the "modern

[European] system of military arrangements . . . would be totally inadmissable with us." More enthusiastically, Knox described the militia as an institution that embodied "the ideas of freedom and generous love of . . . country."[12] Nevertheless, the commander in chief's correspondents were uneasy with the classical republican notion that public virtue would ensure the citizen's willingness or ability to serve under arms. They also doubted that military service, unlike the franchise, should be regarded as one of the continual obligations of citizenship. Indeed, they contended that universal service was as militarily unreliable as it was socially disruptive. Steuben thought it "a flattering but . . . mistaken idea—that every Citizen should be a Soldier," for "the use of arms is as really a trade as shoe or boot making," requiring an apprenticeship like any other craft. According to him, the failure to recognize the need for uniform training and discipline was the principal cause of "that want of confidence in themselves —that reluctancy to come out—that impatience to get home—and that waste of public and destruction of private property, which has ever marked an operation merely Militia." If the American states still sought to rely upon citizen-soldiers during peacetime, the assumptions behind militia service would have to be reassessed and the institution itself reorganized. With that end in mind, Washington's counselors uniformly recommended that a national militia system be established, one designed to keep a select group of citizens constantly prepared for military emergencies.[13]

Washington's correspondents agreed that militia units should be composed of citizens, substitutes discouraged, and blacks, mulattoes, and aliens excluded. Nevertheless, they perceived the militia in terms quite different from the assumptions of classical republicanism. They insisted that only a selective approach to militia service could achieve the proficiency required for an effective force. Pickering, Putnam, Steuben, and Knox, for example, proposed that the militia be classified by age, with the burden of service falling on the young. In a limited sense militia duty would remain universal—all young men would bear arms—but the concept of universality was stripped of much of its former meaning. The general's advisers understood militia service to be an apprenticeship in arms designed to impart mastery of the martial arts rather than an expression of public virtue. "It would be otherwise," advised Steuben, "were courage the only qualification requisite in a Soldier." Indeed, he thought training would offer "no easy lesson[s] to a mind filled with ideas of equality and freedom."

The advisers also separated the citizen's economic stake in society from the obligation to serve under arms. Men aged eighteen to twenty-four, the generals reasoned, not only did not have the family and economic obligations that would make such training unduly burdensome and impractical but could be called out in an emergency without disrupting the entire society. In time, Steuben noted, "a perfect knowledge of the duties of a soldier [would be] engraved on the mind of every citizen," creating "the best possible magazine for a Republic firmly established." Nevertheless, the war years had demonstrated, at least to these officers, that the American militia should no longer be regarded as the military manifestation of the civil constitution.[14]

While these militia plans suggest one mind on the need to reassess the assumptions behind militia service, they also reveal significant differences over the ideologically sensitive question of institutional control. Washington's advisers agreed that the militia must be systematically armed and organized, but disagreed over the institutional apparatus required to accomplish that end. Historical circumstances supported decentralization, and, of course, a decentralized militia structure had long been considered an important deterrent to political tyranny. The lessons of the war, though, seemed to call for a degree of centralization theretofore unknown to the American militia.

Influenced by ideas common to the ideological position that Warren represented, Pickering proposed a decentralized militia structure. He recommended that the states have charge of officering, training, and administering the militia. The Articles of Confederation vested the states with the responsibility to maintain a well-regulated militia; only an inspector general paid and appointed by the continental government would be necessary to ensure that the states fulfilled their constitutional obligation. Pickering believed that an effectively organized state-militia system could meet the nation's military requirements while also continuing to provide a check against political tyranny. Indeed, the constitutional relationship between the continental government and the sovereign states prescribed in the Articles demanded a citizen militia devoid of all but the most basic forms of national control.

Putnam, ideologically closer to the position espoused by Ramsay, proposed a highly centralized militia structure. Regimental officers would be appointed by state governors but commissioned by Congress, giving the Confederation government the final word in determining the character and composition of the officer corps. Militia regiments would be numbered without regard to states and organized in divisions commanded by congressionally appointed major generals. These generals and their staffs would be required to reside within the geographic areas they served—a concession to local supervision—but would be independent of state control. The entire system would be headed by the commander in chief of the Continental army. The smooth incorporation of militia manpower into the Continental army had been a chronic problem during the war, and it was

82   Society, Arms, and the Republican Constitution

to that problem that Putnam addressed his plan for militia reform. He ignored the militia's traditional obligation to oppose the centralizing drive of tyranny.[15]

Steuben was probably motivated more by a careful reading of the political climate than by ideological commitment; nevertheless, his plan best accommodated the need for military efficiency to the thorny issue of militia organization. He recommended that the militia be organized into self-sufficient legions, two each for New England and the South, and three for the mid-Atlantic states. The officer corps would be appointed and commissioned by the states, with appointment of general rank officers falling to the state providing the most men. State officials would supervise training, since drill would be conducted by state-appointed legion commanders. A provision allowing militiamen to take their arms and equipment home at the end of their three years of intensive training would further strengthen the militia's local ties without detracting from the institutional integrity of the national system. The seven militia legions would constitute a dependable twenty-one-thousand-man force able to respond to any emergency.[16]

Similar differences over the desirability of centralized military institutions surfaced when Washington's advisers considered the separate matter of the peacetime army. None of the general's counselors disputed the need for regular soldiers to man frontier garrisons: The constabulary duties of frontier forces had not been considered part of the responsibilities of the citizen-soldier since late in the seventeenth century. Still, the plans for the organization and control of the regular army—like those for the militia—reflect the conflict between ideologically motivated demands for decentralization and the desire to create an effective and reliable military.

Pickering, influenced by the assumptions of radical Whiggery, never forgot that standing armies in peacetime had been used by ambitious men to oppress free people. He proposed an eight-hundred-man frontier constabulary more regional than national in composition and organization. The frontier should be divided into regions, with the states in each region supplying continental troops and officers only for their own frontiers. States needing troops to protect their coastlines would use their own forces. Pickering recommended that no staff officers be commissioned. In the wartime Continental army, staff officers had been appointed by Congress, and Pickering wanted to prevent the peace establishment from falling under the influence of officers not dependent on the states for their commissions. He reasoned that forces serving under the scrutiny of the state assemblies would be less susceptible to corruption. Just as important, a decentralized command structure represented an obstacle to the oppressive propensities of centralized authority. Pickering did not intend to allow the frontier constabulary to become the germ of a standing army that might one day destroy the liberties secured through independence.[17]

Washington's other advisers recommended a larger and more centralized force. Steuben recognized that geographic isolation made a large standing army unnecessary. Nevertheless, he believed a legion of three thousand regulars and an engineer-artillery corps numbering one thousand—all under a continental command—to be necessary to guard the seaboard and frontier and to meet the exigencies of war.[18] Putnam and Clinton were particularly concerned that Congress "preserve the great outlines of an army." Edward Hand endorsed the same approach. Specifically, he proposed that staff departments be continuously officered at wartime levels. Like the others, he wanted to ensure that the national government had a command structure able to organize and direct a large number of citizen-soldiers in the event of war. With Steuben, Clinton, and Putnam, Hand insisted that a force so conceived promised efficiency in arms without posing a threat to liberty.[19]

No matter how the peacetime army was organized, all of the commander in chief's correspondents believed that its enlisted ranks should be composed of men willing to make soldiering their occupation. Professionalism was needed in the officer corps as well. Steuben was the most outspoken on these points, arguing that the army's effectiveness depended upon the republic's willingness to view military service as a legitimate profession. Extended enlistments encouraged by attractive bounties would ensure a competent rank and file.

Washington found less unanimity among his advisers on how to develop a skilled officer corps. Pickering opposed military academies, fearing that they would become the breeding ground for the same kind of decadent military elite that led Europe's corrupting armies. He noted that the arts and sciences usually associated with military education were already being taught in American colleges, and he proposed that the republic rely on those institutions to prepare men for the officer corps. If military academies were established, he urged that they accept no more students than necessary to fill vacancies in the frontier constabulary.[20] Clinton shared Pickering's preference for a civilian education for the nation's regular officers, but he favored more formal instruction under the tutelage of professors of military science located at a civilian college in each state. These civilian instructors would be supervised by distinguished military leaders paid by the states. Under Clinton's plan only those students receiving degrees in military science would be awarded commissions in the regular army.[21]

Steuben, Hand, and Knox held that military academies could best meet the republic's need for professionally trained officers. Indeed, they believed that properly constituted academies could eliminate any need for a large standing army. Steuben's recommendations typified that point of view. He proposed founding military schools in New England, the mid-Atlantic states, and the South. Each would be organized within the Continental army command and staffed by regular officers skilled in engineering, artillery, and staff operations. The principal function of each academy would be to equip young officers to handle the problems of modern warfare. But these academies were to be more than nurseries for regular army officers. Of the expected one hundred cadets graduating each year, no more than ten would be awarded commissions in the Continental army. Ninety percent of the graduates would return to civilian life, there to lead and train local militia units. In short, the academies would provide the cement for a unified system of defense consisting of the peacetime army and the select militia. They would serve as normal schools for instruction in military skills, and their graduates would prepare the citizenry to meet the military requirements of the nation. In time, the country would have not only a well-trained corps of regular army officers but also a well-regulated and disciplined select militia led by academy-trained officers.[22]

Washington distilled his advisers' ideas into a defense plan that reflected his own understanding of American republicanism as well as his concern for military effectiveness.[23] He held indisputable the need "to put the National Militia in such a condition as that they may appear truly respectable in the Eyes of our Friends and formidable to those who would otherwise become our enemies." The histories of Greece and Rome "in their most virtuous and Patriotic ages" and the contemporary security of Switzerland, the commander in chief noted, "demonstrate the Utility of such Establishments." Nevertheless, Washington clearly had doubts about what he considered to be the "primary position, and the basis of our system," the assumption "that every Citizen who enjoys the protection of a free Government, owes not only a proportion of his property, but even of his personal services to the defence of it." Like his correspondents, he believed that a dependable militia depended upon a reassessment of the assumption traditionally associated with militia service and a reappraisal of the militia's historically decentralized organization.[24]

All citizens aged eighteen to fifty should be enrolled in the militia, but, the general noted, "amongst such a Multitude of People . . . there must be a great number, who from domestic Circumstances, bodily defects, natural awkwardness or disinclination, can never acquire the habits of Soldiers." Accordingly, while the practice of enrolling all adult males might be continued, Washington urged a classification system that placed the principal burden of training and service on volunteers willing to assume a three- to seven-year militia obligation. He considered entrusting that obligation only to "able bodied young Men, between the Age of 18 and 25" to be a viable but less desirable option. Service in the select militia would be encouraged by "such exemptions, privileges or distinctions, as might tend to keep alive a true Military pride, a nice sense of honour, and a patriotic regard for the public." This "Continental Militia" would be designed to resist "any sudden impression which might be attempted by a foreign Enemy," providing time for full-scale national mobilization.

Washington also proposed that it be organized under the same rules and regulations as the regular army, and he hoped that veteran Continental army officers would be encouraged to assume command of militia units. These provisions would assure a national orientation for militia corps that would be geographically defined by state boundaries. Washington could still accurately claim that his select militia offered a system of defense free of the dangers inherent in "the Mercenary Armies, which have . . . subverted the liberties of allmost all the Countries they have been raised to defend," but clearly the idea of every citizen serving as part of the obligation of citizenship, as in the ancient republics, did not have a part in his understanding of how best to assure national security. Nevertheless, the militia, properly organized and thoroughly trained, retained in his scheme primary responsibility for the republic's defense.[25]

The need for military effectiveness dominated Washington's counsel that Congress keep a small regular army in the field. The commander in chief conceded that peacetime armies had proven dangerous in the past, and he recognized that American geography and ideology combined to make a force capable of defeating an invading European army both unnecessary and unacceptable. He advised, however, that current "circumstances" made a small number of regulars "not only safe, but indispensably necessary." He recommended a force of 2,631 officers and men, organized without regard to the states and entirely dependent upon Congress "for their Orders, their pay, and supplies." The commanding general would report directly to the secretary of war, and soldiers would be moved regularly from garrison to garrison in order to prevent the development of local associations "which often prove very detrimental to the [national] service."

Washington proposed to staff the Continental army with long-serving regular soldiers and professional officers. Initial recruits would serve three years, with later enlistments being based "upon Terms of similarity with those of the British": Soldiers in Britain's peacetime army enlisted for life. Discipline would be strict, but the commander in chief expected few recruiting difficulties. "When the Soldiers for the War have frolicked a while among their friends, and find they must have recourse to hard labour for a livelyhood," he wrote, "I am persuaded numbers of them will reinlist upon almost any Terms." The isolation of frontier garrisons would require more officers, but Washington's suggestion of an expanded officer corps also reflected his determination to place the army's leadership in the hands of professionals. During an emergency the nation could look to these officers "well skilled in the Theory and Art of War" to fill the command positions in an expanded army, thus avoiding the confusion and delays involved in elevating untrained citizens to positions of command.[26]

Washington thought that the proposal prepared by Steuben offered the best means to train the army's officers. "That an Institution calculated to keep alive and diffuse the knowledge of the Military Art would be highly expedient," he wrote, "will not admit a doubt." Still, he recognized that academies might for the moment prove beyond the means of the young nation. "Until a more perfect system of Education can be adopted," he proposed that a number of "young Gentlemen" be trained in the art of war at posts manned by engineer and artillery corps officers. These cadets would fill vacancies in the regiments during peacetime. As "able Engineers and expert Artillerists," they would also represent an important addition to the republic's wartime capabilities.[27]

The commander in chief was not, nor for that matter were any of his advisers, recommending that the regular army replace the militia as the principal instrument for national security. Indeed, there is nothing in Washington's assessment of the republic's peacetime needs that suggests a desire to scrap the militia. His endorsement of Steuben's academy proposal suggests his interest in keeping a well-trained and ably officered militia. Even when Washington criticized himself for being guided by what "I thought *would*, rather than what I conceived *ought* to be a proper peace Establishment," his comment was aimed at his failure to recommend a more comprehensive militia system.[28] It was not an implicit endorsement of a large peacetime army. Indeed, if the country became wealthy enough to afford the luxury of "a standing Army adequate to our defence," the general thought the money would be better spent "building and equipping a Navy."

Washington's intentions in 1783, as they would be later in his career, were to provide the confederation with a systematically organized and carefully trained select militia that, together with a small regular army, could protect against surprise attack and provide the means for a quick and orderly popular mobilization in the event of actual war. Military efficiency was critical, but in the minds of General Washington and his advisers, the principal means to that end remained militia reform. As Washington put it, "Our National Militia . . . is to be the future guardian of those rights and that Independence, which have been maintain'd so gloriously, by the fortitude and perseverance of our Countrymen."[29]

Military Skills and Republican Values

Hamilton received Washington's plan, along with Steuben's recommendation for a system of military academies, during the first week of May 1783.[30] He, however, proceeded to draft a military plan that ignored Washington's serious attempt at militia reform. Acknowledging that Congress had a "constitutional duty" to ensure that the states maintained a well-regulated militia, he urged the adoption of common organizational and training systems. Nevertheless, Hamilton clearly did not intend the state militias to be an important part of the nation's defense system. He recommended that they assume only a limited obligation for service outside their territorial boundaries. Certainly, his suggesting that the militia be arranged by marital status was not designed to invigorate the institution. Single men would be required to attend six training sessions annually, and married men, four; in both categories the obligation for emergency service would extend to men fifty years of age.

This proposal was but a pale reflection of the classification system recommended by Washington and his aides. The proficiency and effectiveness that the commander in chief believed the select militia could bring to the national defense was to be provided, according to Hamilton's plan, by volunteers paid, supplied, and armed by the continental government. Conceived more as an auxiliary for the regular army than as an extension of the local militia, these units would train twice monthly as companies and once as regiments. In the event of war they would be obliged to serve three-year tours of duty wherever Congress ordered. To encourage the service of competent volunteer officers, Hamilton proposed that they hold rank on a par with regular Continental army officers.[31]

Hamilton urged that the regular army take primary responsibility for the republic's defense on the ground that it alone could provide the professionalism and the centralized organization necessary for an effective military. Indeed, his eagerness to relegate the state militia to obscurity was matched only by his determination to place the peacetime army on a national as well as professional footing. He proposed that Congress assume complete control over the recruitment of soldiers and the appointment of officers—functions left to the states by the Articles of Confederation—in addition to commanding, paying, and supplying the army. Since no state would fill an entire regiment, the appointment and apportionment of regimental officers would become needlessly complex if left to the states.

Efficiency also justified congressional recruitment. Continental control would eliminate competitive enlistment bounties that would inevitably raise the cost of national defense. To ensure proficiency and effectiveness, Hamilton recommended six-year enlistments for his three-thousand-man force as well as a highly paid and well-trained officer corps.[32]

Congress received Hamilton's proposals in mid-June 1783, at a time when the influence of Robert Morris and other proponents of expanded national power had begun to wane.[33] Four days later, without acting on the plan, Congress fled Philadelphia for Princeton to escape mutinous troops demanding back pay. The move revived a parochialist coalition led by Elbridge Gerry, David Howell, and Arthur Lee and affiliated ideologically with the position articulated in Warren's *History*. The coalition, a loosely knit group bound by a common distrust of Robert Morris and his nationalist-minded followers, had recently failed to block the commutation of half pay to regular army officers. Determined to prevent the creation of a peacetime army, it now successfully used the tensions generated by Congress's hurried departure from Philadelphia to delay action on the report. In August nationalists succeeded in inviting Washington to Princeton as part of an effort to revive debate, but Washington's visit produced only a flurry of committee meetings and a decision to postpone further discussion until October.

By September hope for passing Hamilton's plan had all but disappeared. Even the commander in chief found it wanting. Though Washington thought Hamilton's arrangement of the regular army generally adequate, he regarded the classification scheme and the proposal for a reserve force independent of the militia "not . . . well calculated to answer the object in view." He hoped Congress would organize a select militia after the fashion he had proposed. Meanwhile in Congress, parochialists pressed for the defeat of Hamilton's recommendations. They denied that Congress had constitutional authority to maintain troops in peacetime, linked the new impost proposal with the creation of a standing army, and charged that Hamilton's military plan was only another effort to expand congressional powers at the expense of state sovereignty. The October debates failed to produce a compromise, but Congress did formally agree that the vulnerability of the frontier required "some garrisons . . . to be maintained in time of peace at the expense of the United States."[34]

Congress's move to Annapolis in November 1783 marked the end of efforts under the Articles of Confederation to build a Continental army capable of ensuring the nation's security. During the spring of 1784 the mood in Congress increasingly reflected the parochialists' claim that the Articles did not sanction a national army during peacetime. Repeatedly, parochialists criticized Hamilton's plan as an attempt to saddle the republic with an oppressive standing army. If Congress were allowed to raise a few men for a short time, they argued, nothing could prevent that body from extending the term of enlistment and enlarging the number of men under arms. Power was inherently corruptive. Congressional control over a regular army and an elite reserve—the latter intended to supersede the state militias—would jeopardize the constitutional foundation of the Confederation. If no continental force were allowed, the militia would thrive, preserving that institution as the ultimate guarantor of civil liberties. "We have many brave and veteran officers to discipline the latter [the militia]," wrote Elbridge Gerry, "but if a regular army is once admitted, will not the militia gradually dwindle into contempt? And where then are we to look for the defence of our rights and liberties?"

After a stirring speech by Gerry charging that "standing armies in time of peace are inconsistent with the principles of republican governments, dangerous to the liberties of a free people, and generally converted into destructive engines for establishing despotism," Congress, on 2 June 1784, reduced the army to a handful of officers commanding eighty soldiers stationed at Fort Pitt and West Point. The next day, it "recommended" that Connecticut, New York, New Jersey, and Pennsylvania recruit from their militias a total of seven hundred men for a single year's service on the frontier. A year later, the term of service was extended to three years, and regulars replaced militiamen, but that measure was intended only to solve specific problems inherent in frontier duty; it in no way resolved the more basic question of the republic's peacetime security.[35]

At the heart of the differences over the military needs of the Confederation stood the question of the compatibility of political liberty with military effectiveness. Antagonists were asking basic but different questions —questions determined by their understanding of how best to preserve a free society. Hamilton concluded that the preservation of republican liberties depended on the ability of the national government to field a body of trained soldiers able to repel attack. Moderate English Whigs from Daniel Defoe to Adam Smith had reached the same conclusion, and it was in that tradition that Hamilton embraced a centralized and professional military establishment as necessary for and compatible with the survival of free institutions. Parochialists believed that peace had eliminated the need for regulars. Equating professional soldiers with moral decay and political corruption, they, as had republican theorists in the line of James Harrington and Algernon Sidney, looked to the local militia as an expression of republican virtue and as a deterrent to tyranny. A decentralized militia composed of citizen-soldiers was admittedly inefficient; still, it alone could guarantee a free and stable republican constitution.

Given the renewed influence of the parochialists in Congress, no peace establishment was acceptable that failed the test of classical republican theory. Had Congress considered the plans developed by Washington or Steuben instead of Hamilton's, its mood might at least have been conciliatory. The commander in chief and his head training officer understood the importance of the militia and looked to it as a primary guarantor of national security, though Congress most certainly would have questioned their insistence on a centralized command and a selective approach to service. No doubt Pickering's plan for a decentralized militia and a regionally organized frontier constabulary would have been more enthusiastically received than any other prepared in 1783. Yet even Pickering would have been criticized for not conceiving of militia duty as an expression of republican virtue. Needed was a peace establishment plan that not merely recognized the militia's role as a deterrent to political tyranny but also actually reinforced the republican virtue so important to republican theorists.

The proposal prepared in 1786 by Secretary of War Henry Knox in response to a congressional request for a system of defense compatible with the military clause of the Articles met both requirements. Knox's *Plan for the General Arrangement of the Militia* is also noteworthy because during the early-national period it became the touchstone for men—both Federalists and Republicans—committed to the republican tenets of the Revolution yet uneasy about the republic's capacity for defense.[36]

Republics, Knox argued, were inherently less responsive to military emergencies than were monarchies. Deliberative government precluded executive tyranny but often at the expense of decisiveness. That made peacetime military preparedness particularly important. In America, however, peace had undermined national security, in part, Knox believed, because Americans were again exposed to the "effulgence of wealth" and the "seducing influence of luxury" that produced "a corruption of manners, destructive to a republic." A sound peacetime military structure, Knox reasoned, should sustain the martial spirit of the citizenry and "form the manners and habits of the youth, on principles of true republican magnanimity." A properly organized militia could do that. Specifically, he intended militia service to impart the basic republican concept "that the love of their country, and the knowledge of defending it, are political duties of the most indispensable nature."[37]

Knox's view of the militia as an instrument for instilling public virtue led him to envision a system aimed at classical republican ends while yet unencumbered by the ideal of universal service. He proposed that the burden of militia service be borne by an "advanced corps" composed of young men aged eighteen through twenty—an age when youths were normally apprenticed to a trade or employed on a family farm. These young men could easily be committed to regular military training, he reasoned, since their labors usually provided their masters with excessive profits. Youths were more available than heads of households; they were also more receptive to "the splendor of military parade" because they were not distracted by family obligations. The "main" and "reserve" corps, composed, respectively, of men twenty-one through forty-five and forty-six through fifty-nine, would be required to serve in emergencies, but their main responsibility would be economic. These older men would be assessed for the cost of training, supplying, and equipping the advanced corps, as well as for supporting the families of men called to active service. "Although the substantial political maxim, which requires personal service of all the members of the community for the defence of the state, . . . is the main pillar of a free government, yet," argued Knox, the general welfare could best be served by a careful analysis of the obligations and responsibilities of the various age groups in society.[38]

Knox, however, had no intention of allowing the defense of the country to fall into the hands of politically and socially irresponsible youths. Borrowing from an early radical Whig plan for militia reform, he pointed out that an important function of the annual "camps of discipline," to which members of the advanced corps would be sent for forty-two days each year, would be to "mould the minds of the young men, to a due obedience of the laws" as well as "instruct them in the arts of war." Camps would be located near rivers and far from large cities: "The first is necessary for the practice of manoeuvers, the second to avoid the vices of populous places." Amusements would be limited to the military-related skills of running, swimming, and wrestling. Camp discipline would be designed to instill habits of industry and to discourage idleness and dissipation. Youths would be exposed to regular and concise discourses on the "eminent advantages of free governments to the happiness of society" and the importance of "the knowledge, spirit, and virtuous conduct of the youth" to such government. In short, every effort would be made to "form a race of hardy citizens, equal to the dignified task of defending their country," and to make military education "an indispensable qualification of a free citizen."[39]

Under Knox's plan the continental war office would supply arms and accoutrements which each soldier would retain at the end of his tour with the advanced corps. Actual mobilization would be directed and supervised by state officials, though militiamen would be expected to serve during emergencies anywhere in the United States for a period not exceeding one year. This, Knox believed, gave the states the means by which to prevent misuse of the militia; yet it also ensured that the continental government would have access to a body of reliable soldiers. The plan required neither a large professional army nor mass mobilization, while still guaranteeing a well-armed citizenry capable of functioning as soldiers. The ranks of the army would be filled with men familiar with the moral, political, and military principles taught in the camps of discipline. There would be no need to entrust "unprincipled banditti" with responsibility for "defending every thing that should be dear to freemen." In sum, Knox's militia plan would do what the adoption of republican constitutions had failed to do: It would "foster a glorious public spirit; infuse the principle of energy, and stability into the body politic; and give a high degree of political splendor, to the national character."[40]

Knox's proposal built upon the need—generally recognized by military planners—to reassess the classical republican idea that virtue would ensure military preparedness. The result was a bold attempt to satisfy the competing concerns for liberty and military efficiency that had informed the debate over national security since 1783. The secretary of war made the militia responsible for the nation's security, dismissing even the need for an expandable regular army. That represented an important recognition of the ideological tenor of Confederation politics. But the plan was more than simply a revival of the sensitivity to radical Whig republicanism that had pervaded military planning before Hamilton sent his recommendations to Congress in 1783. If parochialists were most concerned about liberty and nationalists were most concerned about military efficiency, Knox proposed to meet these concerns by making the militia an agency of both military skills and republican values. The plan promised an effective military force as well as a virtuous citizenry. The republic's propensity to moral decadence, as well as the growing complexity of contemporary tactics, demanded a reassessment of the nation's military institutions. Yet Knox was convinced that a careful blending of ideological and practical considerations could ensure not only a strong national defense but also the perpetuation of traditional republican values and institutions.

The congressional committee that had commissioned the preparation of the plan gave it a favorable reading during September 1786. The plan also evoked a positive response from David Ramsay, who feared only "that our governments are too relaxed to bear any system which will be attended with so much time and expence."[41] Formal debate was forestalled, however, by the meeting of the federal convention of 1787. Nevertheless, the committee's positive reception suggests that Knox's plan did offer an ideologically and politically acceptable means for transforming the state militia system into an effective and efficient military force. The problem, though, was that even his plan required that the militia become part of a national network, and that point alone made it unacceptable to republican ideologues of the stamp of Mercy Otis Warren.

Differences Unresolved

The debate over the Confederation's peacetime military requirements illuminated the deep concern in America about the viability of the new republic. No nation could be secure without the ability to protect its frontiers. At the same time, the republican ideology upon which the American states had been founded demanded the establishment of an institutional structure able to avoid the political instability and constitutional corruption that had destroyed free societies in the past. The citizen militia easily met the latter need, but it had proven during the war years to be a reluctant and ineffective defender of national sovereignty. No one questioned the effectiveness of professional soldiers, but a regular army symbolized the moral and political corruption to which republics had historically been susceptible.

Faced with the seeming incompatibility of military effectiveness and republican principles, the nation's political and military leaders found themselves forced to reassess the ideological implications of militia service. They agreed that the citizenry must continue to shoulder the burden of national defense, but militia service itself was perceived less as a manifestation of the rights and responsibilities of republican citizenship and more as a means to inspire an indifferent population to new levels of military competency. They were, however, of two minds about the institutional structure necessary to ensure an effective system of national security, reflecting the conflict between radical Whig notions about citizenship and soldiering and moderate Whig ideas and assumptions supporting the compatibility of military professionalism and institutional centralization with the tenets of a free society. While proponents of the former looked to the state controlled militia structure as the most expeditious means to meet the Confederation's constitutional and military needs, advocates of the latter position linked the preservation of domestic liberties to the creation of a dependable system of national security and urged the establishment of a truly national military structure organized around a body of carefully trained and well-disciplined officers and men.

During the Confederation period, concerns about liberty won out over the dictates of sound military policy. Nevertheless, that Americans failed to agree on the means by which the republic could both guarantee domestic liberties and prevent the assaults of Europe's most powerful armies spoke to the profound importance of the issues involved and the depth of the intellectual currents that informed the divergent opinions about the nation's military needs.

6

The Military and the Federal Constitution

It might be here shewn, that the power in the federal legislature, to raise and support armies at pleasure, as well in peace as in war, and their controul over the militia, tend, not only to a consolidation of the government, but the destruction of liberty.—"Brutus" [Robert Yates], *New York Journal*, 18 October 1787

Some gentlemen seem to have confused ideas about standing armies: *that the legislature of a country should not have the power to raise armies, is a doctrine he [Thomas Dawes] had never heard before.*—Thomas Dawes, speaking to the Massachusetts Convention, 24 January 1788, in *The Debates in the Several State Conventions on the Adoption of the Federal Constitution*, edited by Jonathan Elliot

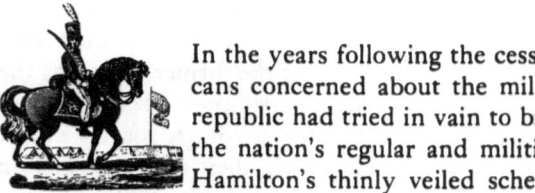

In the years following the cessation of hostilities Americans concerned about the military disarray of the new republic had tried in vain to bring meaningful reform to the nation's regular and militia forces. Whether it was Hamilton's thinly veiled scheme to replace the militia with a professional army and reserve or Knox's plan to make the militia both a viable fighting force and a guarantor of republican liberties, every proposal ultimately failed because American political leaders in Congress and in the states rejected the centralization of the American military establishment. This was hardly a phenomenon unique to the postwar period. Since the middle of the eighteenth century Americans had persistently resisted efforts to centralize the continent's military command. British efforts in the 1750s to unify the command of their North American army and General Washington's attempt to establish a truly continental army had both failed because colonial and state assemblies insisted upon maintaining some control over forces raised or serving within their civil jurisdictions.

Political jealousies, custom, and a pervasive localism had important roles in creating this organizational decentralization, but ideological factors also played a part. Perceptions of political stability, citizenship, and constitutional balance articulated by radical Whig spokesmen during the preceding century directly influenced the decision to vest the states with the power to raise soldiers under the Articles of Confederation. The object had not been to prevent the creation of a regular army, though a deep suspicion of standing armies was involved. Historically more concerned with questions of control than of the moral implications of military professionalism, Americans were willing to support a standing army if it was raised under the supervision of the state assemblies.

Proponents of the Articles contended that only the state assemblies could be trusted with that power because their members were ordinary citizens called to public office only to express the actual views of their fellow citizens. In that capacity they were not likely to sanction any abuse of the government's coercive powers. The localized militia also provided a check against the abuse of society's military potential. If the citizenry's representatives were corrupted, the militia stood ready, in its historic role as the ultimate deterrent to political tyranny, to reassert the rights of the citizenry and to return the constitution to its proper balance. To remove the control of society's military power from the immediate representatives of the people or to alter the pervasive localism of the militia, then, suggested far more than a mere institutional reordering of society's military potential. To many Americans it represented a basic threat to the constitutional balance and therefore a fundamental assault on the foundations of republican society.

Shays' Rebellion

Washington, Hamilton, and others of like mind, believed, however, that a decentralized military establishment left the nation vulnerable to foreign attack and domestic discord. Arguing that republicanism in America had failed to produce the classical citizen-soldier, they concluded that institutions dependent upon a virtuous citizenry were incapable of preserving the internal and external security of the republic. The worst fears of these nationalists were confirmed when news arrived from Massachusetts in September 1786 that armed insurgents had closed the courts of Common Pleas in Hampshire, Worcester, and Middlesex counties. Instead of rallying to defend the civil order, the local militia sided with Shays' Rebellion. Only a day after Governor James Bowdoin had called upon the citizenry to quell the rebellion, word arrived from

Worcester that "there did appear universally that reluctance in the People to turn out for the support of Government as amounted in many instances to a flat denial: in others to an evasion or delay which amounted to the same thing." From September through January reports of the militia's unreliability flowed into the governor's office. Even the militia's successful defense of the Continental arsenal at Springfield was marred when supposedly loyal militiamen joined the ranks of the insurgents during the skirmish. Resistance to constitutional authority was by no means limited to the militia's rank and file. Militia officers discouraged their companies from taking the field, prevented the distribution of powder and supplies, and actively recruited their subordinates for service with the insurgents.[1]

A joint resolution of the Massachusetts house and senate described a systematic effort in the troubled western counties to raise and organize "regular military companies properly officered" for the "express purpose of opposing in arms, the Constitutional government of the state." Certainly the militia's conduct had raised serious questions about the state government's ability to protect the liberties and property of its citizens. Bowdoin complained to the house and senate that the constitutional order depended on the fulfillment of "reciprocal duties" vested with the people and their leaders. He could only declare a state of emergency; the people had the responsibility to put it down. If the militia "refused to appear; or appearing join the insurgents, the laws cannot be executed," leaving the citizenry exposed to "all the evils, that may arise from the suspension, or prostration of law and justice." The governor believed that the crisis engulfing Massachusetts was in large part the result of the citizenry's failure to fulfill its constitutional obligation. The assumption that "a sufficient number of brave, loyal and determined citizens would always appear ready to support their government; [and] that a majority of the people would be too wise and too well informed to permit the basis of their rights and privileges to be overturned by the needy, desperate banditti" had, as Theophilus Parsons later reflected, proven erroneous.[2]

The rebellion was finally put down in early 1787 with the help of loyal local militia and a substantial body of troops raised in the eastern reaches of the states. Nevertheless, the rebellion sent shock waves through the national political community. Congress found itself helpless. Short of men and fearful that direct intervention by the continental government would only provoke more internal discord, it requested just over one thousand New Englanders for service on the western frontier, planning covertly to use those troops to preserve order if Massachusetts failed to quell the rebellion. The same factors also forced Congress to leave the defense of the Continental arsenal at Springfield in the hands of state authorities. "The imbecility, the futility, the nothingness of federal powers" were impressed upon the minds of many in and outside Congress as Continental army leaders stood by exasperated while state forces moved in to quell the rebellion. "What stronger evidence can be given of the want of energy in our government than these disorders?" Washington wrote James Madison. "If there exists not a power to check them, what security has a man for life, liberty, or property?"[3]

With the military weakness of the Continental Congress fully exposed, delegates gathered in Philadelphia in May 1787 to revise the Articles of Confederation. The federal Convention periodically debated the military weakness of the Confederation during the summer, resolving, with little apparent disagreement, to recommend to the states a new constitutional arrangement which included a national military establishment. The proposed Constitution granted Congress the power to declare war, to raise, support, and regulate an army and navy, to call out the militia for the enforcement of federal laws, the maintenance of civil order, and the expulsion of foreign invaders. Congress was also given control over the organization, arming, and disciplining of the militia. Command over all troops raised for federal service, whether regular or militia, was vested in the office of the president. Except in emergencies the states were prohibited from raising troops without congressional consent.

Nevertheless, traditional Whig safeguards against the misuse of the military arm of government remained. Congress could raise and support armies in peacetime, but appropriations were limited to two-year terms. The powers to raise and command troops were also explicitly divided between the legislative and executive branches. Federal access to the state militias was limited too. Congress could call out the militia, but only to enforce federal law, suppress insurrections, or repel invasions. The states retained supervisory authority over any congressionally prescribed militia training program as well as the right to appoint militia officers. The new constitutional arrangement did, however, eliminate the states' role in raising and supporting national troops and made significant inroads into their control over the militia. Under the new arrangement the national government held the power and the responsibility for maintaining the external security and domestic tranquility of the states.[4]

The military provisions of the new Constitution sparked a heated debate over the implications of centralized military power for the American republic. Anti-Federalists drew on the axioms of radical Whig ideology to indict the new arrangement as a scheme to undermine the republican gains secured by independence. Federalists also marshaled the familiar anti–standing army aphorisms of Opposition thought. But drawing as well upon insights derived from moderate Whig theory, they claimed that the failure to create a national military establishment would lead to the very political tyranny that Anti-Federalists feared most. At issue in the debate over the military provisions of the federal Constitution, as they had been in previous debates over the location of military power in society going back to James Harrington and his intellectual heirs, were the terms upon which a society would be both militarily secure and politically free.

Anti-Federalist Fears

Few Americans in 1787 would have quibbled with the proposition that civil government required the power to raise regular troops to meet the exigencies of extended hostilities. Neither would most Americans have rejected the idea that a republic would be secure from the abusive potential of standing armies as long as the decision to raise troops remained the prerogative of the representative branch of government.[5] The new Constitution granted the power to raise and maintain armies to Congress, but this presented serious problems for Anti-Federalists. Reviewing the terms of the proposed Constitution, Anti-Federalists were struck by what they considered to be the unrepresentative nature of the popular branch of government. Delegates to Congress would represent districts many times larger than those of state assemblymen, and their terms of service would make their contacts with constituents far less frequent. If most citizens had little or no contact with their representatives, they would seldom share common interests, rendering Congress incapable of responding to the wishes of the citizenry. To give a governmental body incapable of representing the public interest the power to raise and maintain armies at will, reasoned the Anti-Federalists, was tantamount to granting a king sole control over the military forces of his realm.[6]

This view of the nature of representation under the Constitution provided the basis for the Anti-Federalists' entire critique of the military power vested in the national government. If Congress were unrepresentative, then it would be possible to characterize the entire national governmental structure as unresponsive to the popular will. Like the despots that curtailed civil liberties in the ancient republics, the national government as a single entity, not just its executive branch, would be inherently ambitious and therefore eager to expand its power at the expense of both the citizenry and the states. Once Anti-Federalists had identified the national government as inherently corrupt, they had no difficulty marshaling the theories of balance and corruption articulated by the radical Whigs to argue that the proposed Constitution would jeopardize the balance upon which the American republic was founded.[7]

Under the Articles of Confederation constitutional balance had been ensured in part by leaving the military power of the republic in the hands of the states' assemblies. Regularly elected and often acting with the explicit instructions of their constituents, state assemblymen ensured that the military potential of the republic was not subverted to tyrannical ends. The new Constitution proposed to eliminate that safeguard, and that made Anti-Federalists uneasy. John Lansing of New York reminded his state's ratifying convention of the fate that befell the landed barons of medieval Europe after they had surrendered control over their armies to their princes. "Not possessed of pecuniary revenues, or a standing military force, he [the prince] was, whenever the barons withdrew their aid, or revolted against his authority, reduced to a very feeble situation." The allocation of independent military powers to the prince, though, destroyed the balance of the ancient constitution and rendered the barons subservient to the prince's command. Comparing the states to the barons and the national government to the feudal prince, Lansing argued that eliminating the military prerogatives of the states would lead to the demise of the republican principles secured during the Revolution.

Patrick Henry offered the same insights to the delegates of the Virginia convention. Armed with a standing army "to execute" their commands, the national leadership would "act as they think proper." Meanwhile, faced with the oppressive regiments of the national government, the states would find that "all the strength of this country" had passed into the hands of their enemies. As had been the aim of the ambitious feudal princes, "the object of all of this," bemoaned "Cincinnati," "is to fix upon you . . . a strong government that will enable a few proud, intriguing, aristocratic men, to make you the instruments of their avarice and ambition, and trample upon your privileges at pleasure."[8]

The unlikelihood of adequate representation in Congress compounded the dangers inherent in granting the national government control over the republic's armies. In every society, Anti-Federalists contended, law enforcement depended either on citizen support or military coercion. Free governments, wrote Robert Yates, "have depended for the execution of the laws on the *posse comitatus*," never doubting "that the people would refuse to aid the civil magistrate in executing those laws they themselves had made." The American states had never had reason to resort to military coercion precisely because the mechanics of representation within the states ensured that no laws were passed contrary to the public will. Under the new Constitution, however, the citizenry would have only infrequent contact with their representatives, raising doubts whether national laws would be of the people's own making. "The consequences will be, they [the people] will have no confidence in their legislature, suspect them of ambitious views, be jealous of every measure they adopt, and will not support the laws they pass." In time, national leaders would be faced with accepting their own ineffectiveness or with "establishing an armed force to execute the laws at the point of the bayonet." Anti-Federalists all agreed that when national leaders faced those alternatives, it would only be a matter of time before the nation was saddled with a standing army.[9]

If these perils needed further amplification, Anti-Federalists pointed to the Constitution's militia clause. The militia had lost its status as a viable military institution, but for Anti-Federalists it retained its symbolic role as the ultimate guarantor of republican liberties. To give an unrepresentative Congress control over the arming, training, and organization of the citizen militia, particularly if the states no longer controlled the recruitment of regular forces, represented a basic assault on the constitutional balance that guaranteed the stability of republican institutions. Tyrants had historically deprived citizens of their liberties by raising standing armies while simultaneously neglecting the militia. The Constitution would enable the national government to do both. Anti-Federalists charged that congressional control over militia armaments could leave the entire population disarmed. Patrick Henry wondered if "a single musket" would be left in the states after the Constitution went into effect.[10]

If the new government organized the militia, the result might be equally as dangerous. The citizenry might be called out on long and arduous marches, or held in service indefinitely; militia mobilization might also be used as a guise to place the population of an entire state under martial law. Many Anti-Federalists suspected that any attempt to discipline the militia would be nothing more than a ploy to better "reconcile them [the citizens] to the idea of regular troops."[11]

The prospect of a select militia system was also troubling. "Should one fifth or one eighth part of the men capable of bearing arms," wrote the "Federal Farmer," "be made a select militia . . . , and those the young and ardent part of the community, possessed of but little or no property, and all the others put upon a plan that will render them of no importance, the former will answer all the purposes of an army, while the latter will be defenceless." In short, the militia clause would ultimately disarm the citizenry—a prospect that struck at the very heart of the classical perception of republicanism espoused by the Anti-Federalists. If the new Constitution rendered the citizenry without representation in the councils of government and left them without the means to defend themselves, the balance essential for the survival of republican institutions would be forever lost.[12]

During the state constitutional conventions a decade before, gubernatorial military prerogatives had evoked considerable concern. Anti-Federalists, though, exhibited only a secondary interest in the powers granted to the national executive by the proposed Constitution. The clause allowing military appropriations to extend over two years and the presidential prerogative to command the army and navy did spark charges that the president could use his powers and influence to destroy political opposition and institute despotism behind the force of a standing army. These concerns, however, were often expressed only as asides, buried deep within more penetrating discussions of the danger represented by the national government in general.[13] Time had doubtless helped to erase memories of the military abuses perpetrated by the royal governors. The assumption that Washington would become the president probably also helped to dilute criticism of presidential military powers. Nevertheless, the failure to decry the expanded powers of the president had much to do with the basic nature of the Anti-Federalist indictment of the Constitution's military clauses. The potential abuse of presidential powers was clearly of secondary importance, given the Anti-Federalists' conviction that the unrepresentativeness of Congress would eventually cause that body to raise standing armies against the citizenry anyway.

None of the insights that Anti-Federalists offered into the dangers represented by the Constitution's military clauses was particularly original. Critics of the Constitution drew extensively from the logic and assumptions of the radical Whig anti–standing army argument, which, in its simplest terms, denounced the centralization of military power in the hands of unrepresentative institutions as inherently detrimental to the balance of a free constitution. It is worth noting that Anti-Federalists avoided the moral indictment of military professionalism that characterized much of the radical Whig rhetoric. Neither were they given to extended praise of the citizen-soldier, although they obviously believed that the citizenry would respond energetically to the threat of political tyranny.

This selective application of radical Whig theory was very much in tune with the long-standing American use of Opposition thought. During the 1760s and 1770s, Americans had looked to radical Whig theory to clarify and define threats to the civil constitutional order, while turning to the regular army to meet the military exigencies of the fight for independence. For Anti-Federalists the issue was not the prohibition of regular armies in the American republic—the realities of eighteenth-century warfare and the historical development of the states' own military institutions made that argument untenable; rather, it was to ensure that armies were raised under the supervision of the people's representatives in the state assemblies.[14]

History was filled with examples of the misuse of regular armies by ambitious men acting without regard to the will of the citizenry; the colonial experience, too, spoke to the constitutional importance of the assemblies in military affairs. Thus Anti-Federalists found the paradigm of balance and the logic of corruption articulated by the radical Whigs applicable to the federal-state relationship which they believed to be necessary for the survival of republicanism in America. Unable to accept the representative features of the new Constitution, they had no choice but to view the military clauses as a first step toward the end of republican institutions and the rise of tyrannical government behind the strength of a standing army.

The Federalist Vision

Proponents of the new Constitution did not challenge the Anti-Federalists' claim that the representative branch of government should control the power to raise and to sustain military forces in a republic. They did, however, question the assumptions behind the theory of representation that claimed that the state assemblies were the only representatives of the popular will. The Anti-Federalist conception of representation depended upon a classical perception of society in which virtuous citizens conscious of the common good designated representatives to express their views. Representatives, being inherently corruptible, required the close supervision of their constituents through instruction, regular election, or both, making the small geographic areas served by state assemblymen necessary to prevent the corruption of republican government. Federalists, however, doubted the virtue of the private citizen. They argued that private interest, not public virtue, informed the conduct of Americans. Thus, the citizenry, as well as its representatives, became a potential source of political corruption.

The intricate checks and balances woven into the Constitution testify to the persistent concern that power could corrupt the citizens' representatives. But balance alone was not enough. A new theory of representation was required to channel special interests toward a collective goal otherwise unattainable without public virtue. For Federalists the process of representation became a means to diffuse the impact of special interests on the governmental process. Thus the small electoral districts that provided the cornerstone for much of the Anti-Federalist suspicion of national powers became a basic source of corruption. The best way to ensure that a single interest did not corrupt the function of representation, reasoned Madison in *Federalist 10*, was to increase the size of the electoral district so that a delegate, by necessity, would be forced to look beyond particular local considerations. Since the citizen's role as the ultimate source of sovereignty remained intact, Federalists were able to argue, the collective will of the citizenry was best expressed in a national assembly uncorrupted by petty and particular interests. It followed then that if the state assemblies retained control over the republic's military power, the potential for abuse was far greater than if national representatives exercised that power.[15]

Combined with the new perceptions of soldiering and citizenship that had emerged in the peace establishment plans of the 1780s, this important shift in the implications of representation had a direct impact on the Federalists' defense of the national military establishment. It allowed them to use the language of corruption and balance that had fueled radical Whig attacks on standing armies for a century to support the military provisions of the new Constitution. In part, this spoke to the political acumen of the Constitution's supporters. Recognizing that the Constitution represented a significant departure from the existing American political structure, they marshaled familiar ideological axioms to outflank Anti-Federalist critics. At the same time, though, the Federalist analysis of the document's military clauses represented a serious effort to overcome what, from their point of view, was a growing division between the military requirements of the American states and the traditional ideological foundations of a republican society. Indeed, their reinterpretation of the nature of representation allowed them to argue that a national military structure was an essential guarantor of republicanism in America.

The Federalists' reassessment of the nature of representation opened the way for a challenge to the assumption that the division of military power between the states and the central government provided a check against political tyranny. Madison argued, both in the federal convention and in the press, that if the national government remained militarily dependent upon the states, the result would be "fatal to the internal liberty of all." Congressional inaction during Shays' Rebellion had forced Massachusetts to raise its own army to put down the rebellion. Similar crises in the other states, argued Madison, could transform the Confederation into thirteen disunited states perpetually on the brink of war.

Under the guise of "Publius," John Jay and Alexander Hamilton joined Madison to warn that the inability of the Continental Congress to respond to the military needs of the nation would eventually cause the collapse of the Confederation. The scenario described by Hamilton in *Federalist 8* typified Publius's perception of the republic's future if the states were left to provide for their own defenses. Fearing attack by their stronger neighbors, the smaller states "would endeavor to supply the inferiority of population and resources, by a more regular and effective system of defence, by disciplined troops and by fortifications." Other states would be forced to follow suit, making the federal-state balance embodied in the Articles meaningless. Neither would civil liberties fare well if interstate military rivalries developed. Since "it is the nature of war to increase the executive at the expense of the legislative authority," wrote Hamilton, the establishment of despotic rule in all the states would only be a matter of time. Madison concurred. In Rome "it was a standing maxim to excite war, whenever a [domestic] revolt was apprehended." The recent histories of the European monarchies also lent support to the radical Whig aphorism that "a standing military force, with an overgrown Executive will not long be safe companions to liberty." The inability of the national government to initiate and sustain military action independent of the states, then, promised both the proliferation of standing armies within the states and the destruction of civil liberties. These, of course, were the very developments that the Articles of Confederation had been intended to prohibit.[16]

Most Americans concurred with Madison's assessment that "the greatest danger to liberty is from large standing armies." Most also agreed that the best way to guard against a standing army was to make it unnecessary. Federalists argued that a national military establishment encompassing both regular and militia soldiers could do just that. A common military establishment would eliminate the potential for cataclysmic military competition between the states. Instead of thirteen states poised for war on as many fronts the Atlantic seaboard would be the home of a single nation characterized by domestic tranquility and strategic isolation from the armies of its enemies.

Britain's geographic isolation had "rendered less defence necessary, and [had] admitted a kind of defence which could not be used for the purpose of oppression." The same situation could exist in America, but as in Britain, the national government needed access to the militia as well as to a body of trained regulars. Protected by the sea from its enemies, the republic would require only a small body of troops to patrol the frontiers, to protect the principal ports, and to guard the federal arsenals. The principal institution of national defense, except during extended hostilities, would be the nationally organized select militia.

Federalists dismissed charges that the militia under federal control would only be another name for a standing army. Citizen militia units, made up of the very people with the most to lose at the hands of a tyrant, were unlikely candidates for manipulation by ambitious ministers. On the contrary, argued "The Republican," a revitalized militia structure would create "a circumstance which encreases the power and consequences of the people; and enables them to defend their rights and privileges against every invader."

Tench Coxe, too, was confident that the national militia would have a salutary effect on the liberties of the citizenry. Regular soldiers would be essential if the militia were not revived from its current state of neglect, but a national militia would "render many [regular] troops quite unnecessary" and provide a "powerful check" upon their activities. Hamilton echoed the same sentiment in *Federalist 29*, concluding that a national militia establishment "appears to me the only substitute that can be devised for a standing army; and the best possible security against it, if it should exist." Thus the Federalist campaign for a national military establishment confronted the long-standing fear of a centralized military directly. Instead of undermining the principles of republican government, Federalists argued, the establishment of a militarily independent national government was essential for the survival of republican institutions in America.[17]

All of this is not to say that the Federalists believed that a national military establishment was incorruptible. They conceded that the military was susceptible to the intrigues of ambitious politicians, but they contended that the proposed Constitution contained every safeguard included in either the English Bill of Rights or the American state constitutions. The purpose of the Bill of Rights, reminded the Federalists, had been to ensure that the army did not become a tool of an aggressive executive. The Bill of Rights did not prohibit raising regular troops in peacetime; rather, it guaranteed that no army would be raised without the consent of Parliament. The same restriction was incorporated into many American state constitutions. Instead of prohibiting peacetime armies, argued Madison, the constitutions "only provided that no armies shall be kept without the legislative authority; that is, without the consent of the community itself."

No Federalist quibbled with the advisability of such restrictions. Alexander Hamilton considered them militarily and politically sound. "When they referred the exercise of that power to the judgment of the legislature, they had arrived at the ultimate point of precaution, which was reconcilable with the safety of the community." Since the new Constitution left the legislative discretion over the army intact, Federalists found absurd the Anti-Federalist charge that a national government with the power to raise armies in peacetime would degenerate into a political tyranny. James Wilson, Pennsylvania's leading Federalist, was willing to concede "that it might be dangerous, were the army kept up without the concurrence of the representatives of the people," but Congress, like Parliament, was elected by the citizenry.

The assessment by Thomas Dawes of Massachusetts of the safeguards built into the constitutional order was typical of persons puzzled by charges that the army could be used to tyrannical ends. How, he wondered, could the army be misused by a legislature biennially elected by the people, particularly if its military appropriations were limited to the same two-year period? If representatives served for seven years, as in England, placing the same congressman in a position to renew the military's requests, "an acquaintance might exist between the representatives in Congress and the leaders of the army as might be unfavorable to liberty." But the two-year term of office eliminated that danger. Any new military appropriations would have to be reviewed by "representatives, who, at the time, [would] have just come fresh from the body of the people." Thus, as in the state constitutions, the real power to raise and sustain regular troops under the proposed Constitution would continue to rest ultimately with the people themselves.[18]

If Congress did abuse its military prerogatives, Federalists argued, the militia would always be available to defend the public interest. Far from eliminating the militia, the new Constitution promised to put it on a more respectable footing. Congress was charged with organizing and arming the militia—prerogatives that Federalists claimed could be exercised by the states if the national government failed to fulfill its responsibilities—while the states retained the authority to administer training and to officer their militia establishments. "Before a standing army can rule," argued Noah Webster, "the people must be disarmed," and that was unlikely as long as the states retained a hand in the training process. Even if the national government did raise a large standing army, the people and the states would still have a sizable force with which to defend themselves. Madison argued in *Federalist 46* that the national government could create an army of no more than twenty-five or thirty thousand men, given the current size of the American population. The state militia establishment had available a combined force of five hundred thousand men. Even a regular force of thirty thousand would do poorly against five hundred thousand armed militiamen, officered by men of their own choosing and fighting for their common liberties. The federally organized militia system would also help to keep the state governments involved in the defense of the republic. Second only to the constitutional and military importance of the armed citizenry, Madison believed, was "the existence of subordinate governments, to which the people are attached and by which the militia officers are appointed, [which form] a barrier against the enterprises of ambition, more insurmountable than any which a simple government of any form can admit of."[19]

Federalists also contended that the geographic domain of the new government would also reduce the danger of a standing army. If the states were the only depositories of military power, the people might come to neglect the supervision of their representatives, allowing them to usurp the public trust. Small areas being easier to conquer than larger ones, the conquest of a state might take place before the people realized their predicament. Hamilton argued in *Federalist 28* that the national military establishment would remove the threat of usurpation by ambitious state politicians without adding to the possibility that the national government might destroy the liberties of the citizenry. The national military establishment would naturally raise the jealousies of the states and the citizenry, ensuring that a close eye would always be kept on the military activities of the national government.

Just as important, the country would simply be too large to allow the national government to dominate it with military power. "The army . . . may usefully aid the magistrate to suppress a small faction, or an occasional mob, or insurrection," wrote Hamilton in *Federalist 8*, "but it will be unable to enforce encroachments against the united efforts of the great body of the people." Even if the national government harbored a desire to dominate the republic, it would be without either the manpower or the resources to do so. For the Federalists, the national military establishment was far safer than the decentralized military system under the Articles. The expanded republic enabled the leadership of the national government to avoid the influence of special interests that might seek to abuse the military power of the government, and the sheer size of the area to be governed combined with the federal organization of the militia made the abuse of the government's military power practically impossible.[20]

Although Federalists regularly used the fear of standing armies to defend the national military establishment, they did not want to centralize the military power of the republic only to prevent the proliferation of armies within the states. A national military establishment was politically sound, but it was also militarily necessary. Repeatedly, Federalists reminded the American citizenry that regular troops had been required on the frontiers before the Revolution and that they would continue to be needed there as long as British and Spanish troops, to say nothing of Indian warriors, were stationed along the republic's perimeter. The militia, if properly reformed, could be depended upon to fill the expanded ranks of a wartime army, but historically the militia had proven unwilling to meet the day-to-day military requirements of frontier defense. Only a national army of skilled professional soldiers could effectively defend the republic along its long and diverse frontier. And only the national government, Federalists believed, could be trusted to use its military strength in the best interests of the nation.[21]

The need for professional soldiers on the frontier, however, was based on more than just the historic failings of the militia. Even if the militia were willing to serve, wrote Hamilton, the cost would be prohibitive: "A frequent rotation of service and the [resulting] loss of labor, and disconcernation of the industrious pursuits of individuals would form conclusive objections to the scheme." This claim reflected the assumption that fundamental changes in the social and economic order of society had made professional soldiers necessary even in a republic. Paraphrasing Adam Smith, Hamilton argued that military professionalism had not developed in the ancient republics of Greece because their economic orders were conducive to the support of nations of citizen-soldiers. Employed in subsistence farming and only marginally involved in commerce, the Greek citizenry was free to train in the martial arts and to pursue its economic interests. During the seventeenth and eighteenth centuries, though, "the means of revenue . . . , the arts of industry, and the science of finance" had significantly altered the economic and military requirements of society. "The industrious habits of the people of the present day, absorbed in the pursuits of gain and devoted to the improvements of agriculture and commerce, were incompatible with the condition of a nation of soldiers," argued Hamilton.

William Corbin of Virginia developed Hamilton's thesis further. Specialization, he contended, was the key to the economic and military success of a modern nation. "If some of the community are exclusively inured to its defence, and the rest attend to agriculture, the consequence will be, that the arts of war and defence, and of cultivating the soil, will be understood." To depend on the citizen-soldier, however, would lead to the "ignorance of arms and negligence of farming." The choice was simple: a republic could have "good farmers and soldiers," or it could "have neither." Governor Randolph shared this point of view. The men of the militia were needed for agriculture, and "if it be neglected, everything else must be in a state of ruin and decay." This economic justification of regular troops included no pejorative connotations. For Federalists it was merely a recognition that classical perceptions of soldiers and citizenship did not meet the requirements of a republic involved in the commercial economy of the eighteenth century.[22]

During the Revolutionary War nationalists had defended the use of long-serving regulars on grounds similar to these. Washington's advisers, particularly General Steuben, had also pointed to the need to incorporate into the American military establishment a body of professional officers and men. Nevertheless, the Federalists were the first explicitly to integrate arguments for military professionalism into the ideological context of American republicanism. Relying on arguments drawn from the moderate Whigs, they suggested not only the wartime necessity of regular soldiers but also their importance to the peacetime security of an eighteenth-century republic. In short, they were moving toward a tacit recognition that the traditional republican perceptions of the citizen in arms were inapplicable in a modern, free society. The citizenry retained an obligation to support the military needs of the republic, but that obligation was more economic than personal, the reflection of economic expediency and specialization, not the result of public virtue. Federalists perceived the military strength of the nation as a consort of special interests, both civil and military, directed by a national government toward a common goal—a goal most efficiently attained through the separate and unique contributions of those interests. The military arm of the republic might still be considered an expression of its civil constitution, but that constitution had assumed a form neither intended nor envisioned by the republican theorists of the Harringtonian mold.

Part 3
Creating a Peace Establishment

In June 1789, Thomas Barnard advised the members of Massachusetts's Ancient and Honourable Artillery Company that the United States had the opportunity to prove that "communities of men are capable of deliberating upon forms of government, chusing those which are friendly to all the rights of which men can enjoy in society, and yet of establishing an AUTHORITY which shall controul their actions destructive to the social state." Whether or not the newly reconstituted nation would succeed depended upon its ability to balance liberty against the authority needed to prevent the instability that had destroyed republics in the past; and that ability, suggested Barnard, hinged in large part on the nature of the republic's "military arrangements."

He did not expect war to be a common occurrence, but the nations of Europe, envious of the liberties and wealth of the American people, might eventually turn their armies against the new republic. Historically, republics had proven vulnerable to domestic disruptions, and that concerned Barnard as well. Internal discord had only recently threatened republican government in Massachusetts, and insurgency might again raise its head to challenge the stability of the republic. Additionally, "our own government might become proud and tyrannical, and aim at prostrating the rights and liberties of this people before them." The vulnerability of republican institutions made military preparedness essential, for though "tyrannical power is established by arms, . . . a people [cannot] defend their territory, or resist an assuming government but by arms."

The government of a free society required the power to enforce its authority, but since both liberty and tyranny depended upon arms, the character and composition of the nation's military forces were particularly important. Barnard conceded that the militia had long since lost its function as the principal defender of American society. Nevertheless, he still believed that an armed and disciplined citizenry remained the only means of guaranteeing the security, order, and liberty necessary for the preservation of republican liberties.*

Few Americans would have disagreed with Barnard's conclusions. For over two decades the interrelationship between arms, tyranny, and liberty had informed the American effort to create a political environment able to withstand the social and political pressures that had destroyed free societies in the recent and ancient past. How best to structure the military arm of the civil constitution, however, remained a matter of considerable disagreement. As Barnard had suggested, military effectiveness could both preserve and destroy republican society; hence, constitutional stability was as important as military efficiency in any discussion of the military institutions necessary for the success of the American experiment in republican government.

Therein lay the fundamental issue around which Americans disagreed. Nationalists and their successors, the Federalists, linked the preservation of American liberties to the maintenance of external security and the ability to prevent internal discord from fracturing the fragile political order created in the aftermath of independence. They rejected as incompatible with the realities of the American republic the theories of corruption and political stability that had been borrowed from English Opposition thought and used to denounce British military policy in the years before the Revolution. Instead, they argued that a national political structure supported by an effective and efficient military establishment promised the only means for providing the national security and domestic tranquility necessary to sustain a republic that stretched from the Atlantic to the Mississippi and from Spanish Florida to British Canada.

Simultaneously, parochialists and later the Anti-Federalists continued to see the republic's institutional and political development in terms drawn from the rhetoric of classical republicanism and radical Whiggery. They assumed the nation's constitutional order to be vulnerable to the intrigues of those who sought to centralize political power at the national level. When considering the military affairs of the nation, they consistently placed constitutional balance ahead of military efficiency and effectiveness. An army officered and controlled outside the purview of the state assemblies might be more responsive to military emergencies, but it could also serve as a vehicle for the expansion of national influence and power.

---

*Thomas Barnard, *A Sermon Preached at the Request of the Antient and Honourable Artillery Company*, 24–26.

Plans to organize the militia on a footing outside the control of the states evoked the same concerns. Taking their lead from the radical Whigs, they understood the citizen in arms to represent the last deterrent to the intrigues and ambitions of tyrants, and thus the locally organized and controlled militia remained an important guarantor of the constitutional balance necessary for the preservation of republicanism in America.

The tensions between these conflicting perceptions of the republic's military needs continued into the early-national period. The new constitutional arrangement gave the national government total control over the nation's regular forces. It did not, however, end concerns that the army might become the means for the proliferation of national political power and influence. Neither did the Constitution contribute significantly to defining the function and status of the militia in the nation's military and constitutional order. The federal government was empowered to organize, arm, and discipline the militia and to call upon it to enforce national law, suppress insurrections, and repel invasions. The states, though, retained the prerogatives to conduct training and to appoint all officers. The organizational structure necessary to make the militia a viable instrument of national policy, however, awaited legislative consideration. Between the ratification of the Constitution and the War of 1812 the demand for militarily effective institutions repeatedly confronted concerns about the sanctity of the constitutional order.

7

Policy and Ideology in the Washington Administration

An energetic national militia is to be regarded as the capital security of a free Republic.—Henry Knox to the Speaker, House of Representatives, 18 January 1790, in *The Debates and Proceedings in the Congress of the United States*

The United States ha[s] nothing to do with the Militia until in actual service.—Robert Rutherford, speaking to the House of Representatives, 21 February 1797, in *The Debates and Proceedings in the Congress of the United States*

Federalist spokesmen had argued during the ratification debates that the growing complexity of society and the sophistication of modern warfare had rendered classical republican perceptions of citizenship and soldiering inapplicable in America. In the process they had borrowed many of the concepts used by moderate Whigs to assert the compatibility of military professionalism and the institutions of a free society. Federalists had not, however, placed the necessity for military efficiency within the institutional framework outlined by Adam Smith and others. The American intellectual commitment to the citizen army, the republic's impoverished fiscal condition, and the nation's geographic isolation from Europe would not allow the institutionalization of a permanent, professional army of the size and scope known in England. They had contended that a nationally controlled militia system, founded on a new understanding of the citizen's obligation to national defense, could meet the needs of national security without burdening the republic with a standing army. Properly organized, it could also control the internal discord that had destroyed free societies in the past. A national militia could solidify the power of the newly constituted government, reform the moral character of the citizenry, and satisfy the lingering fear that political centralization would lead to a tyrannical government supported by a standing army.

Drawing on these arguments used to justify the military provisions of the Constitution, the Washington administration sought to make the militia the cornerstone of the new government's peacetime establishment.

The Call for a National Militia

Soon after Congress convened in 1789, Washington requested implementation of the Constitution's militia clause. When no plan was forthcoming, he forwarded to Congress a proposal calling for a nationally controlled, well-organized, and thoroughly trained militia able to respond instantly to foreign attack or domestic insurrection. The plan was a revised version of the 1786 plan submitted to the Continental Congress by Secretary of War Henry Knox. Like its earlier version, it was predicated on the assumption that classical republican perceptions of soldiering and citizenship were inapplicable amidst the complexities of American society and the sophistication of modern warfare. As the commentary that Knox sent along to Congress made clear, the plan also represented an attempt to create a peace establishment that reflected perceptions of government, the military, and society articulated by Federalist spokesmen during the ratification debates.[1]

The secretary's plan to class the militia by age, to require annual month-long training sessions, and to place the burden of training and actual service on the nation's young men under twenty-one years old was founded on several basic assumptions. Every government had an "indispensable duty" to provide for its defense—a duty even more important to a government whose actions must be the result of "multiple deliberations." "That every man . . . is firmly bound by the social compact to perform, personally, his proportion of military duty" was a principle equally essential to the security of a free state. Indeed, Knox believed that the right to participate in political affairs should be predicated upon prior service in the nation's militia. Of course, the citizen's ability to fulfill his military obligation depended upon "a competent knowledge of the military arts." In more primitive republics the domestic activities of the citizenry provided ample opportunity for familiarity with the martial arts. The "present state of society," however, made acquisition of military skills by most citizens difficult if not impossible without "establishing adequate institutions for the military education of the youth." This last assumption stood at the heart of Knox's militia plan. It also reflected the administration's perception of the militia's continued importance to the military security and constitutional stability of the republic.

Knox believed history had given America an "invaluable opportunity" to create "institutions as shall invigorate, exalt, and perpetuate, the great principles of freedom." As had the proponents of the Constitution, he also believed sound institutions, not public virtue, would provide the basis for a "dignified national character." Thus he recommended to Congress "a [militia] system which shall not only produce the expected [military] effect, but which in its operations, shall also produce those habits and manners which will impart strength and durability to the whole Government." A small corps of artillery and engineer troops plus a contingent of regulars would be required during peacetime to defend the frontiers and protect the federal arsenal. But these garrison troops, warned Knox, should be rotated back to the "mass of the citizens" at regular intervals. While noting that "even philosophers, and the advocates of liberty" had recently embraced the necessity of standing armies in some circumstances, he contended that "whatever may be the efficacy of a standing army in war, it cannot in peace be considered as friendly to the rights of human nature." "An energetic national militia is to be regarded as the capital security of a free Republic; and not a standing army, forming a distinct class in the community."

A select militia designed to concentrate the burden of military training and service on the young would ensure the military and moral goals that the secretary hoped to achieve. Within a generation, the republic would contain a population thoroughly trained in the martial arts. Just as important, it would do so without disrupting the economic activities important to the nation's welfare. Knox considered the current practice of placing the burden of militia duty equally upon all adult males ineffective, unnecessary, and even undesirable.

Existing militia law attempted to compensate for the complexities of the American economy by providing liberal substitution provisions. But such legislation, he argued, imposed upon society the same dangers inherent in a standing army. Militia substitutes most often came from "the most idle and worthless part of the community." As a result, the wealthy and middling families of the community held militia service in contempt and the republic's defense became the responsibility of those least concerned with its preservation. In time, feared Knox, "a standing army will be introduced, and the liberties of the people subject to all the contingencies of events."

Personal military service remained an important "pillar of a free Government," but that could be instituted most effectively by involving only the nation's youth in all but major national emergencies. "The head of a family, anxious for its general welfare, and perhaps its immediate subsistence, will reluctantly quit his domestic duties for any length of time." Periodic militia service posed few economic hardships for young men under twenty-one, reasoned Knox, since they usually had no dependents and were involved in employment profitable to either parents or masters.

Moreover, military service for established members of society might discourage industry and undermine economic security, in the process disrupting the moral character of American society. Knox's select militia plan would have just the opposite effect. He envisioned military camps charged with inculcating discipline, discouraging idleness and dissipation, and imparting to the nation's youth a clear understanding of "the eminent advantages of free Government." Carefully organized and rigorously conducted, the military encampments were the heart of Knox's plan to provide the American people with a force able to silence domestic insurgency, discourage foreign invasion, and "effectively oppose the introduction of [domestic] tyranny." They would also provide the nation with a virtuous, productive, and industrious citizenry. In short, the national militia plan promised for America the political and moral stability that had eluded the republics of past ages; it envisioned "an institution, under whose auspices the youth and vigor of the constitution would be revived with each successive generation, secur[ing] the great principles of freedom and happiness against the injuries of time and events."

Knox's goals were Harringtonian, but his perception of the institutional constraints required for an effective militia force reflected a recognition of the realities of an increasingly complex and sophisticated social and economic structure and of a citizenry motivated by self-interest, not public virtue. Knox also understood that the military needs and the constitutional peculiarities of the American republic necessitated a reassessment of the decentralized organizational structure usually associated with the militia's function as guarantor of constitutional balance. He linked the preservation of political stability with the ability of the federal government to marshal the militia in support of national priorities and policies. Nevertheless, the ideological implications of local control and the states' traditional role in militia affairs could not be ignored. The states' constitutional prerogative to appoint militia officers ensured that any national militia system would have an officer corps responsive to the patronage and influence of the state governments. Knox himself proposed to organize the militia by legions within each state as a concession to the decentralization long associated with militia institutions. He also proposed to allow each state to consider local climatic and economic conditions before scheduling summer training encampments.

At the same time, though, the secretary of war recommended numerous structural and organizational features designed to ensure that the national system did not degenerate into a confederation of state militias. Knox urged that the national government be given the power to mobilize the militia on its own authority. He also recommended that every member of the militia be subject to conscription by the national government during wartime. Each state would appoint a general staff consisting of an inspector general, an adjutant general, and a quartermaster general. But the general staff would report to and be paid by the national government. Making the militia dependent on the national government for weapons and matériel would also guarantee a level of "uniformity, economy, and efficacy" throughout the system. Arming the militia from federal arsenals and supplying it from national stockpiles would limit the militia's potential as a source of disorder within the republic as well. Federal remuneration of officers serving in the annual training camps would also provide a degree of national influence in the state-appointed officer corps. All officers and men mobilized for national service would be paid and supplied by the federal government.

Knox urged, too, that the states select Continental army veterans for key militia commands. Experienced officers would provide much-needed expertise. Veterans were also men with previous ties to the national governmental structure, and their appointment would help to assure that the militia did not become the special province of state political patronage and influence—no small consideration at a time when the new government was seeking to establish a truly national stature. The proposal to make the youthful "Advance Corps" available for service anywhere in the republic was also designed to undermine local attachments that might prove detrimental to national security and domestic tranquility.[2]

Knox's militia plan received a cool reception in Congress. Despite military setbacks, in part the result of manpower shortages and inadequate training, two years passed before Congress sent the president a bill for the uniform organization of the nation's militia. The debate was amorphous and nonpartisan, ranging from practical questions of cost and convenience to political and ideological issues concerning the responsibility of every citizen to bear arms and the constitutional implications of a centralized militia establishment. The secretary's proposal to class the militia by age found little support in Congress. Georgia's James Jackson spoke for many congressmen when he charged that a select militia "would prove as great a burthen as a standing army." "In a Republic," argued Jackson, "every man ought to be a solider, and prepared to resist tyranny and usurpation, as well as invasions, and to prevent the greatest of all evils—a standing army." A modified select militia plan recommended by a congressional committee a year later received only lukewarm support even from congressmen who considered classical perceptions of the citizen-soldier to be incompatible with the military needs and the social realities of the American republic. Thomas Fitzsimmons of Pennsylvania argued that "subjecting the whole body of the people to be drawn out four or five times a year was a great and unnecessary tax on the community." Still, he feared the proposal would prove disruptive to the economic endeavors of apprentice and master mechanics and craftsmen. Few congressmen were willing to accept James Madison's claim that extensive training was essential so that the militia "might speedily be taught the military art, and be enabled to defend their country, if her situation called for their aid."[3]

At the heart of Congress's failure to provide the new government with a national militia system, though, was an unwillingness to accept Knox's contention that a militia responsive to the needs of the national government was compatible with the constitutional balance necessary for the preservation of republican institutions. Congressmen rejected classing by age, federal control over arming and exemptions, and a proposal to give the president power to call out the militia, because each provision challenged the primacy of the states in militia affairs. The states, of course, had historically controlled militia organization and discipline. But the perpetuation of this arrangement was important for reasons that went beyond historical precedent. The local foundation of the English militia system had served as the focal point of the radical Whig claim that constitutional balance depended upon the militia's ability to prevent the usurpation of civil liberties and political freedoms by more centralized authority. Despite the general state of disorganization in their militia, many Americans continued to perceive it in much the same way. In this context the suggestion that the state militias be merged into a single nationally controlled force violated fundamental ideological tenets concerning the balance necessary for a stable republican constitution. Identifying the new and largely untried federal government with the central authority feared by radical Whigs, congressmen preferred to leave control over the militia to the states' representative assemblies.[4]

The result was legislation that hardly resembled Knox's original proposal. Pushed through a reluctant Congress only after the collapse of General St. Clair's militia-supported army on the western frontier made action unavoidable, it dropped the plan to class the militia by age and eliminated both fines and administrative organization intended to assure compliance with federal training standards and plans to arm the militia from federal arsenals. The Uniform Militia Act of 1792 required every "free able bodied male citizen" aged eighteen through forty-five to enroll in local militia units and to provide their own arms, ammunition, and accoutrements. The tactical organization outlined in the law was left to the state assemblies to implement when "convenient." The militia was to be trained in accordance with procedures developed by General von Steuben during the war years, but no uniform training schedule was prescribed.

The federal government had no power to enforce compliance with even these weakened provisions; nor was a system established to keep the president or Congress informed of the militia's readiness. An attempt to give the president the independent power to call out the militia to execute laws, suppress insurrections, and repel invasions was also stricken during the last hours of debate, leaving the national executive dependent upon the cooperation of the state governments if it wished to call the militia to arms. Congress had fulfilled its constitutional obligation to organize the militia, but it had done so without giving the national government a military force capable of meeting its broader responsibilities to ensure domestic tranquility and provide for the common defense.[5]

The Whiskey Rebellion

Federalist militia policy was predicated on the need to transform the existing decentralized system of state institutions into an effective reflection of national policies and priorities. To meet national security requirements, the militia could be nothing less than a well-trained and reliable military institution. The significance of Congress's failure to create such a force became apparent during the last years of the Washington administration. During the summer of 1794 civil discontent that had been brewing in western Pennsylvania for nearly two years erupted into a full-scale insurrection against the authority of the federal government. The discord spread quickly into the adjacent regions of western Maryland and threatened to extend across the Alleghenies into the Ohio Valley. The Whiskey Rebellion provided the first opportunity for the national government to test its ability to maintain civil order and enforce federal law. The results were less than comforting. The insurrection was put down, but not without verifying the potential dangers of a militia system tied to the localities and unresponsive to the will of the federal goverment.

The magnitude of the problem in western Pennsylvania became clear during July and August 1794 when reports arrived in Philadelphia that insurgents had assaulted federal revenue agents in the area. More troubling was the news that the rebellion was being led by militia officers and organized through the local militia structure. Supreme Court Justice James Wilson confirmed a flurry of reports that armed rebels controlled the civil and judicial structure in Allegheny and Washington counties in a communiqué to President Washington announcing that the "laws of the United States are opposed, and . . . obstructed by combinations too powerful to be suppressed by the ordinary course of judicial proceedings or by the powers vested in the Marshall of that district." The local militia having proven unreliable and its civil manifestation, the *posse comitatus*, having gone over to the rebels as well, the Washington administration found itself confronted with a situation that Attorney General William Bradford believed had the potential "to dissolve all the bonds of society and to destroy all property and government too."[6]

Even before Wilson's report arrived in Philadelphia—the Militia Act of 1792 required verification of an insurrection by the judiciary before the president could mobilize the militia against domestic disorder—Washington had sought the advice of his cabinet about how to proceed against the insurgents. Knox urged immediate action to forestall "the deluded people from entertaining hopes of a successful resistance." Pennsylvania's governor, Thomas Mifflin, should be consulted to determine if the state's militia could end the rebellion. If it could not, he called for the organization of a "superabundant force" from the neighboring states capable of demonstrating "the power of the government to execute the laws." Hamilton believed the only issues to be resolved were the number of militiamen to be called out and the states from which they should come. He, like Knox, advised the mobilization of approximately twelve thousand militiamen, half coming from Pennsylvania and the remainder from Maryland, New Jersey, and Virginia. Attorney General Bradford also urged the president to call out a substantial militia force: "The militia—drawn out in support of the civil authority, seems the proper posse in a republican government and in such great emergencies as this."[7]

Secretary of State Edmund Randolph was more cautious. The events in western Pennsylvania clearly threatened the authority of the federal government. Nevertheless, Randolph was troubled by the willingness of some in the administration to resort to military force. Many of these men, he noted, once would have considered such a plan inherently tyrannical. Now they justified mobilization on the premise that "a government can never be said to be established until some signal display has manifested its powers of military coercion." That maxim, he warned, would undermine the republican tenets of the nation's government and permanently estrange the people from national authority. The unjust use of military force could, as it had during the 1770s, spawn political revolution. The government of the United States had the authority to call the militia to arms, but that power lacked the support of history, tradition, and custom. Indeed, the citizens of western Maryland, Pennsylvania, and Virginia were more likely to support each other than the laws of the new republic. A call for soldiers from the neighboring states might be rejected by the citizenry, further damaging national prestige and authority and possibly spreading the rebellion to the south and west.

Randolph was also concerned that intrastate loyalties might also undermine the domestic peace. "Is nothing to be apprehended," he wrote Washington, "from a strong cement growing together [illegible] all the militia of Pennsylvania, when they perceive that another militia is to be introduced into the bosom of their country?" Randolph urged that Washington send commissioners into the western counties to seek a peaceful resolution of the problems that had spawned the rebellion. Only when all efforts at negotiation had proven futile should the militia be called out. At the same time, though, Randolph agreed with the other cabinet officers that any military strike against the insurgents would have to be decisive; failure could destroy the republic itself.[8]

Washington responded to the counsel of his cabinet and to the report from the western counties by ordering thirteen thousand militiamen readied for possible national service. Half of the force was to be raised in Pennsylvania and the remainder in New Jersey, Maryland, and Virginia. Threatened by the same internal discord that had destroyed many ancient republics, the administration had recourse only to a poorly trained and potentially disloyal militia. Even had the army not been preoccupied with the Indian war in the Ohio Valley, Washington lacked legal authority to use regulars to put down domestic rebellion. Just as important, he recognized that any attempt to use the army to restore order would fuel Republican charges that the army had been raised as an instrument of domestic oppression. The federal militia force would be serving in its traditional republican role as a guarantor of civil order, but it was, for the first time, being asked to function as a national and not a local institution.

At the same time, Washington sent three commissioners west in hopes of negotiating the peaceful reestablishment of national authority. Hopes that the crisis could be resolved without resort to armed force disappeared by the end of August when the commissioners reported that the determination to resist federal authority had not subsided. A basic reason, they contended, was the widespread belief among the insurgents that popular sentiment would prevent the militia from marching. On 5 September the commissioners advised that the militia should be called out if only because it would forever dispel the idea that the militia would not come out. Indeed, the long-term implications of mobilization loomed above the immediate need to end the rebellion. Mobilization would discourage "future attempts to oppose the laws." It would also provide the militia an opportunity to prove its ability to suppress insurrections and its willingness to support federal authority. A successful show of force would demonstrate as well the government's ability to enforce federal law in the furthest reaches of the republic.[9]

While the federal commissioners were urging that the militia be called into the field to demonstrate the power and resolve of the national government, efforts to ready the state militias for duty were proving, as Randolph had predicted, difficult at best. The president's call to arms caught the state militias entirely unprepared. The militia had been allowed to deteriorate in most states after the Revolution—the Militia Act of 1792 having provided little encouragement to establish institutions able to fend off invaders or ensure domestic order.

Attempting to raise their quota from units located closest to Pennsylvania, militia officials in Virginia reported that inadequacies in the state's militia law and popular support for the insurgents were hindering mobilization. One frustrated militia commander reported to Governor Henry Lee that Virginia's quota could not be met unless militia officers were "armed with *Authority* and *Means* to enforce obedience to the requisition." Too often, men called for duty paid fines in lieu of personal service or simply disappeared into the hinterland. Proinsurgent sentiment threatened both the authority of the national government and the state's ability to maintain order within its own boundaries. The situation was so serious in western Virginia that Daniel Morgan, commander of the Virginia contingent, found himself requesting arms from the state arsenal both to train his soldiers and to prevent the civil and militia leadership in the Winchester area from disrupting preparations for the march into western Pennsylvania. Virginia filled its quota by mid-September, but only after the militia draft was supplemented with a substantial number of substitutes and volunteers. Similar difficulties were reported in New Jersey, but it was in Maryland and Pennsylvania that the nation's decentralized militia structure was put to the greatest test.[10]

Insufficient training among artillery and cavalry units and the absence of legal authority to provide supplies for militia requisitioned for national service slowed mobilization in Maryland. Militiamen also proved reluctant to serve. As in Virginia, a propensity to pay fines in lieu of service or to disappear when threatened with conscription significantly reduced the militia pool in many areas.[11] In western Maryland the reluctance of the militia to come out reached crisis proportions. Armed resistance in Washington and Allegheny counties forced Governor Thomas Lee to mobilize a company-size militia guard to protect the state arsenal in Frederick and to order the distribution of two hundred stands of arms and accoutrements among "such of the militia of . . . [Allegheny] County as can be thoroughly relied upon."

By the middle of September the western counties were in open revolt. Militia company and field officers had refused to conduct the draft ordered by state officials, and they had used force to discourage others from carrying out the law or in any way supporting the national government's call for troops. Reports also indicated that the rebels had associated themselves with the insurgents in western Pennsylvania. Pressured by Alexander Hamilton, Lee mobilized seven hundred militiamen, drawn intentionally from units located some distance from the troubled counties, to put down the state's own insurgency. He also added units from the eastern part of the state to the militia contingent intended for federal mobilization at Fort Cumberland because, in his judgment, the western militia might prove unreliable. Maryland met its quota and reestablished order in its own western counties, but the crisis was deeply troubling to state authorities. Insubordination had rocked the newly formed and fragile militia structure. The inability of state authority to control the militia, warned Governor Lee, could "produce the most injurious effect and ultimately render all dependence upon our militia in the moment of danger equivocal and precarious."[12]

In Pennsylvania the government's ability to call out the militia was questionable from the beginning. To avoid a near certain affront to governmental authority, Governor Mifflin made no effort to call out the militia in the rebellious western counties. Nevertheless, Pennsylvania met its quota only with considerable difficulty. On 10 September the state senate received word that quotas had not been met in the counties of Philadelphia, Bucks, Chester, Delaware, and Dauplin. Montgomery County had raised its quota, but only with great difficulty. The low pay provided by the state's militia law was responsible in part for the militia's reluctance to come out, but so was the unwillingness of militiamen to bear arms against their fellow countrymen. In Chester County, some militia officers had already resigned, and others threatened to do the same if they were forced to march against the western insurgents.

The situation forced Mifflin to conclude that the very survival of the republic was in doubt. Judicial authority had proven helpless in the face of the armed rebels. Now the power of the executive branch was being called into question by the failure of the militia to respond. "A free republic," he wrote the adjutant of the state's militia, "can only be established by the will of the people; [and] it can only be perpetuated by their affection and attachment." If the citizenry proved unwilling to put down domestic insurrections, it faced the alternative of being consumed by anarchy or of entrusting its liberties to the "protection and support of a standing army." Speaking to the Philadelphia militia, Mifflin called for volunteers to assist in meeting the state's militia quota. "For the honor of the militia, for the sake of our laws, and for the preservation of Republican principle," domestic order and the authority of the national government had to be reestablished in the western counties.[13]

Despite the difficulties faced by the state authorities, all the states met their quotas, and the militia was prepared to march when Washington decided to use force to end the insurrection. The militia that followed Washington and Hamilton into western Pennsylvania, however, hardly resembled the citizen army so often glorified in political rhetoric. Composed for the most part of substitutes and volunteers drawn from the young and dispossessed, the militia proved unruly and destructive during its march into western Pennsylvania. Similar problems plagued commanders during the militia's brief stay in the western counties. All of this despite a host of general orders issued at various command levels advising of the symbolic importance of the militia's role as a guarantor of civil order and instructing that the "strictest attention . . . be paid to sobriety and regularity of conduct."[14]

Having met little or no resistance, the militia withdrew from western Pennsylvania in mid-November, leaving behind a small contingent "to suppress unlawful combinations and to cause the laws to be duly executed." If, as some Federalists had suggested, a demonstration of military power was necessary to establish the authority of the national government in the American political structure, the Whiskey Rebellion had provided an opportunity of monumental proportions. The new government had overcome a significant challenge to its authority, and it had proven its ability to marshal the states' militias to enforce national law.

Writing from Fort Cumberland, Washington contended that the citizenry's willingness to support the "law and gov[ernmen]t" guaranteed that future attempts to "sow the seed of distrust and disturb the public tranquility will prove equally abortive." He described the militia's role in ending the insurgency as having done "nothing less than to consolidate and to preserve the blessings of the Revolution." Here and elsewhere Washington ignored the fears and anxieties that had come with the mobilization of the state militias. In an address to Congress delivered immediately after his return from western Pennsylvania, Washington claimed that "it has been a spectacle, displaying to the highest advantage, the value of Republican Government, to behold the most and least wealthy of our citizens standing in the same ranks as private soldiers; pre-eminently distinguished by being the army of the constitution."

The militia's performance may have demonstrated, as he claimed in the same address, "that our prosperity rests on solid foundations," but the president also believed that the events of the past months provided ample evidence that the militia should be placed on a better footing. The militia structure established in 1792 had proven able, only with the greatest difficulty and confusion, to support the authority and prestige of the national government. The experience had been less than satisfactory in reality if not in the rhetorical flourishes offered in retrospect. The militia tradition was strong in America. But the local foundations of that tradition, as the

Whiskey Rebellion clearly demonstrated, had the potential to destroy the fragile character of American republicanism. Politically and fiscally unable to maintain a sizable body of regulars, the national government required direct access to a military force responsive to national needs and authority. In the aftermath of the Whiskey Rebellion the Washington administration still believed that a national militia system could meet that need.[15]

Indeed, the last troops had not yet left western Pennsylvania when the Federalists renewed their efforts to incorporate the states' militia into a reliable national force. Citing the militia's poor performance during the Revolution and the recent Indian wars, its questionable conduct during the Whiskey Rebellion, and the current chaotic and disorganized condition of the state militias, they moved in February 1795 and again in December 1796 for the creation of a select militia corps. Their message was simple: "The Government must either have a good [national] militia or a standing army." Republicans remained unconvinced. Increasingly suspicious of Federalist motives, they viewed the select militia proposals as infringements on the state's constitutional prerogatives to train the militia and assaults on the ties between citizenship, property, and militia duty that defined a republican militia. Republicans argued that a militia capable of fulfilling its military and civil responsibilities could be established simply by enforcing universal militia service. That change, of course, would in no way threaten the decentralized character of the nation's militia force. It also fell well short of satisfying the Federalist claim that the republic's militia could fulfill its function as a guarantor of civil order and national security only if its training and organization were centrally controlled and supervised. In February 1797 the House of Representatives discharged its committee vested with the responsibility to consider militia reform because, in the words of one Republican representative, "the United States had nothing to do with the Militia until in actual service."[16] A look at the Republican reaction to the Whiskey Rebellion provides some insights into their continued reluctance to embrace militia reform.

For months the Republican press had predicted that the oppressive taxes necessitated by Hamilton's financial program would evoke domestic dissent that could only be ended by a standing army. Hence many opposition leaders viewed initial recommendations to mobilize the militia to be part of a not very well disguised plan to raise a regular force that could be used to silence opposition to administration policies and programs. "Militia-men are citizens," argued the Philadelphia *Aurora*, so "it cannot be supposed that they will turn their arms against themselves; but as regulars are devoted to their chief, they will have all the *instrumentality* necessary to enforce obedience." Federalist efforts to link the rebellion with the partisan activities of the democratic-republican societies made

Republicans particularly fearful that their loyalty would be called into question. Still, congressional leaders, for example, James Madison, considered the insurrection a serious threat to the legitimacy of the national government and were anxious to reassert lawful authority. They, however, urged negotiations and not armed force as the best means to reestablish the government's authority in the area. When the government did choose to use force, Republicans were greatly relieved that the militia responded. The willingness of the militia to support the government, argued one Republican essayist, should at last "shut up the mouths of the sticklers for a standing army. In the future, . . . such men should be considered as whiskey boys, alike enemies to a free government."[17]

Although pleased that the rebellion had been put down, other Republicans found the militia's performance troubling. The militia had only reluctantly taken up arms, and then only after the infusion of a large number of substitutes and volunteers. The force that went into the field in no way resembled a military manifestation of the civil constitution. Such a militia force could not be expected consistently to put down threats to the political stability and constitutional order of the republic. Federalists had recognized the same general problem, arguing that the militia's effectiveness depended upon the success of efforts to transform the militia from a local to a national force. Taking their cue from the paradigm of corruption and political intrigue articulated by the radical Whigs, Republicans advocated a return to a militia structure that would accurately reflect local political and social configurations. The *Aurora*'s editor, Benjamin Franklin Bache, expressed concern that the veterans of the whiskey campaign would become a significant constituency for the extension of federal executive power into the local constituencies. Others suggested that the institutional integrity of the local militia would always be undermined as long as the widespread use of volunteers and substitutes was allowed.[18]

William Findley, a leading Republican in Pennsylvania, echoed this concern in his assessment of the militia's conduct during the insurrection. The militia had come out, but it had left a path of disorder and destruction in its wake. That development alone evoked fundamental questions about the viability of the militia as the republic's principal guarantor of civil order. The problem, Findley believed, was that the militia was no longer a military reflection of the civil constitution. Most of the disorder associated with the militia's march into western Pennsylvania was the result of the force being "so great a proportion composed of substitutes, or persons induced to enlist by bounty." The wealthy could avoid military service by paying a small fine, and as a consequence, military service had become identified with the "lower order of citizens."

Militia laws had to be altered to make the militia a true reflection of the body politic. After all, the militia "are as much the representatives of the citizens, when they are called to support the laws of their country, as the members of Congress are their Representatives to make those laws." If substitutes were allowed only under extraordinary circumstances, and if those serving as substitutes were required to come from the same social rank as the persons they replaced, the militia would quickly shed its image as an "undisciplined band of substitutes, induced to undertake the service by the receipt of bounty and the expectation of plunder." Properly constituted, the people would see their militia "as their fellow citizens, discharging their duty in obedience to the laws, on the same principal with a court, jury or sheriff."

A reorganized militia, based on the classical vision of the citizen-soldier, would transform the militia's composition and reinforce its local character, cementing it clearly to the social and political hierarchy of the local constituencies. That was a consideration of no small importance to opposition leaders increasingly concerned about the extension of national political power. Findley summed up his assessment of the militia's performance in the Whiskey Rebellion on an ominous note. Order was required for republican government. Unless the militia was reorganized to ensure tranquility in the body politic, the republic faced the necessity of raising a standing army to maintain order in peacetime.[19]

The Frontier Army

The debate over the nation's militia structure reflects the pervasive influence of ideas about government and society infused into the ideology of American republicanism during the revolutionary era through the writing of the radical Whigs. It also suggests the existence of an important body of thought concerning the military requirements of a free society first explored by moderate Whigs a century before. The controversy sparked by the expansion of the regular army to counter mounting Indian unrest in the Ohio Valley further reveals the influence of these competing perceptions of the military in society on the American effort to create a military establishment compatible with the republic's military and constitutional needs.

The Revolutionary War and the military frustrations of the Confederation conditioned most national leaders to accept the necessity of at least a small regular army during peacetime. With little debate Congress continued in force the infantry regiment and artillery battalion that had existed under the Confederation and in 1791 added a second regiment of infantry in order to provide the regular soldiers needed to garrison the western frontier.[20] During 1792 and 1793, as the atmosphere in the halls of Congress became increasingly partisan, the size and composition of the regular army became an increasingly controversial subject. At issue were basic ideological disagreements over the implications of regular military institutions for the liberties of a free people.

Early in 1792 the Washington administration, shocked by St. Clair's humiliation at the hands of the Indians, asked Congress to expand the existing army by five regiments. Proponents of the plan pointed to military expediency, arguing that the nation's security depended upon the creation of a larger regular army. Congress had yet to pass legislation placing the militia on a national footing, and if they existed at all, militia units were poorly equipped and ill trained. At the heart of this argument, though, was the contention that regulars were indispensable for the eradication of the Indian threat on the frontier. Rangers and militia soldiers had had little success in engagements in Kentucky and Virginia, clearly discounting the claim that their familiarity with frontier conditions made them the best Indian fighters. Once regular soldiers gained experience in the field, argued backers of the expanded army, they would be "found infinitely superior to any militia upon earth." The militia had already demonstrated a reluctance to furnish men as well as a propensity to break and run when even slightly pressed. Only regulars could provide the discipline and skill required of soldiers serving on the frontier.[21]

Opponents of the plan questioned both the necessity of the Indian war and the method by which the administration had proposed to fight it. Sufficient land existed within the more settled regions of the republic to meet the needs of the citizenry. Government policy should be directed toward the defense of existing frontiers, argued congressmen opposed to enlarging the army, not the invasion of Indian territory. If more soldiers were needed, the administration should look to local militiamen who knew the terrain and were accustomed to the irregular tactics employed by Indian forces.

Other opponents of the plan believed something more than poor judgment accounted for the administration's interest in an expanded army establishment. Military costs had tripled to $300,000 annually with the addition of a second infantry regiment in 1791. The current proposal would increase the annual cost of the army to $1,250,000. Opposition spokesmen expressed concern that "extravagant" cost might produce domestic discord, opening the way for a British attack on the divided American nation.

Maryland's John Mercer placed the army's cost in a slightly different though more sinister context. He charged that the administration's call for an expanded army was part of a plan to lay the groundwork for a perpetual tax supported and enforced by a standing army. Occasional essays in an increasingly partisan press echoed Mercer's concern and established a pattern that later Republican denunications of Federalist military policy would follow. "Observer" speculated that the Indian war had its origins in the administration's desire to expand its power with the support of military garrisons and standing armies. Knox was specifically charged with attempting to broaden the importance of the War Department through the use of federal military patronage.

Writing after Congress had approved the additional regiments, Philip Freneau expressed fear that the new army legislation would lead to domestic discord and expanded national power. Loans had provided the funds to meet the immediate cost of the army, but new taxes would soon be required to service an ever-expanding national debt. Those taxes, he predicted, would spark domestic discontent, which in turn would provide the opportunity for the government to use the army to enforce federal law. Without an expanded army, the government posed no threat to American liberties. With it, however, its power and prestige were unlimited: "A standing army . . . will increase the moral force of the government by means of its appointments, and give it physical force by means of the sword; thus doubly forwarding the main object." [22]

The same concerns informed the debate over the army's size during the winter of 1792–93. Now, however, the debate was intensified by the development in Congress of clearly discernible partisan blocs.[23] Federalists increasingly identified national security with military expertise and the expanded military power of the federal government. Relying on the assumptions of moderate Whiggery, they defended the regular army as necessary for the assurance of national security. The soldiers under Harmar and St. Clair may have been raw and undisciplined, argued Connecticut's Jeremiah Wadsworth, but they stood their ground against Indian attacks, while "the militia, who were the advanced guard, ran and threw away their guns." Regular army units, composed of young men without families or economic obligations, promised an effective force with neither the economic nor the social disruption inherent in militia mobilization. Furthermore, militia mobilization was not only disruptive but also costly —"the interruption given to the agriculture of the country by calling away [militiamen] from their business . . . is a thing beyond the power of calculation," argued one Federalist congressman. Besides, enlisting regulars for frontier service would disperse the burden of military duty through every region of the country. It would also ensure that the Indian campaigns were conducted according to federal policy objectives. The national government might have only marginal control over the actions of the local militia, but regulars would be commanded by officers appointed by the federal government, giving it firm control over the conduct of the war.[24]

Republicans denied the effectiveness of regular army soldiers and charged that the Federalist administration was acting contrary to the republican principles of the people by "keeping up standing armies." The persistent growth of the military establishment was particularly troubling. Despite the antiarmy sentiment of 1776, the declarations of the various state constitutions, and the recently ratified Bill of Rights, the United States found itself burdened with a regular army whose size and composition evoked concerns about the security of American republicanism. Republicans charged that growth of the American military establishment had assumed the same pattern that had brought despotism to the governments of Europe. Unless the growth of the army was stopped, the results would be the same. The American Revolution was fought, argued Republicans, by "the substantial freeholders of the country." Such men were available in the militia, but they would not enlist in a regular army, "nor will any one who had the disposition or the constitution of a freeman." As a result the coercive power of society was being placed in the hands of soldiers "collected from the stews and brothels of the cities, and [who] had none of the spirit or principles of the honest yeomanry, who composed the militia during former wars." Republicans argued repeatedly that the current military policy was intended to separate the citizenry from the military arm of the republic, and that development had clear and foreboding implications to a political opposition intellectually attuned to the radical Whig critique of corruption in a republican society.[25]

Turning aside Republican attempts to reduce the size of the army, Federalists successfully defended their perception of the regular army as the best defender of the nation's frontiers. Simultaneously, Federalists, frustrated by an inability to organize the nation's militia, also began to look to the army as the backbone of its peacetime military establishment. That became clear after the victory of General Anthony Wayne's regular troops over the Indian forces at Fallen Timbers in August 1794. Again overcoming Republican opposition, Federalists passed legislation in March 1795 to maintain just under five thousand men on the frontier. The legislation was significant, as Richard Kohn has pointed out, because the army's existence was no longer tied to the Indian war. Federalists argued that the unsettled condition of the frontier caused by the recent deterioration of British-American relations as well as the threat of renewed Indian unrest justified the legion-size force. But more to the point, regulars were more effective and less costly than a comparable band of mounted volunteers and far more reliable than the local militia. Regulars also ensured close federal supervision of occasionally restless and troublesome inhabitants along the frontier.

For Republicans, though, the administration's military policy resembled more and more the pattern of political abuse and corruption outlined by the radical Whigs a century before. "A Calm Observer" spoke for many Republicans when he suggested a sinister link between the administration's fiscal policy, the growth of the nation's military establishment, and the expansion of executive power. "So true it is," he wrote, "that, in some minds, the idea of governing, through the medium of a public debt, a standing army, and great and energetic powers in the executive magistrate, forms the only rule of political conduct [despite those policies being] . . . subversive, no less of the principles of the federal constitution, than of the general and sacred principles of liberty and republicanism."

A year later, William Giles of Virginia restated the Republican position in its simplest terms: "Government would be better without an army, as it was always better for Governments to rest upon the affections of the people than to be supported by terror." Nevertheless, the place of the regular army in the American peace establishment was reaffirmed during the 1796 congressional session. Though Republicans succeeded in reducing the authorized strength of the army by two thousand men—the army had been understaffed, so it actually lost little of its active strength —they, too, conceded the principle of using regulars as frontier police and as an intelligence and security force.[26]

The debate over the size of the frontier army reflected the growth of partisan divisions in Congress, but it also revealed the ideological schism that informed debate over the nation's military establishment beginning in 1792. Republicans founded their opposition to Federalist military policy on an understanding of the evolution of political tyranny derived from radical Whig thought. They seldom suggested that the army might itself come to dominate the civil establishment, and though suspicious of the army's size in peacetime, they never questioned the necessity of regular army soldiers in the event of an actual war. They were, however, deeply concerned that access by the national government to the republic's military power would endanger political and civil liberties. Fearing that the regular army would become an instrument of an ambitious national government, they looked to the local militia as the best means to counter a potentially tyrannical policy. The militia was an inexpensive and decentralized force outside the corrupting influence of the federal government and incapable of military action except that fully supported by the republic's citizenry. Hence, Republicans opposed not only the creation of a larger regular army but also the establishment of a centrally organized militia. Both positions became cornerstones of the Republican opposition to Federalist policy during the remainder of the decade.

Federalists, on the other hand, linked national security to the government's ability to mount an effective military campaign. Drawing upon moderate Whig insights into military needs and a realistic assessment of the nation's social structure, they urged the development of a military establishment responsive to the needs of the federal government and sensitive to the growing complexity of American society. Unless the militia could be organized into an effective military force, Federalists were prepared to look to the regular army as a necessary institution to ensure the political stability and national security required to guarantee republicanism in America.

8

The Crisis of Ninety-Eight

But the grand engine, the most useful instrument of despotic ambition would be a standing army. —Thomas Cooper, "Address to the Readers of the *Sunbury and Northumberland Gazette*," 29 June 1799

The position, therefore, is illustrated, that, even in times of greatest danger, we cannot give to our militia that degree of discipline, or to their officers that degree of military science, upon which a nation may safely hazard its fate.
—James McHenry to the Speaker, House of Representatives, 31 January 1800, in *The Debates and Proceedings in the Congress of the United States*

When George Washington left the presidency early in 1797, the constitutional significance of the nation's military institutions remained unresolved. The reasons were as complex as the ideological and historical traditions that had shaped American discussions of soldiers and society since British troops had arrived in Boston to enforce the Townshend duties some thirty years before. Political liberty was inseparable in the American mind from the citizenry's right to control in person or through its representative assemblies the coercive power of society. But the manifestation of military power represented far more than simply an extension of the rights of representation. It was also a reflection of the viability of republicanism.

The problem, of course, was that perceptions of effectiveness and efficiency on the battlefield in the second half of the eighteenth century conflicted sharply with classical republican ideas about constitutional stability and balance. Americans resolved early in their struggle for political independence that the discipline, order, and military expertise required for military success during wartime could be had only by imitating the structural and organizational patterns long associated with Europe's standing armies. But in reaching that conclusion, American leaders also felt compelled to explain why regular military institutions were compatible with the political and constitutional tenets of a modern republic. Still the citizen in arms remained an important part of the American understanding of the stability of their own constitutional order, particularly in discussions of the republic's peacetime military needs. That the classical unity of political, economic, and military power emerged whenever Americans felt their civil and political liberties in danger confirmed that fact.

The Washington administration understood full well that the national government's prerogative to maintain a regular army did not imply an abandonment of the ideologically significant militia soldier. Federalist leaders in the executive branch and in Congress believed that a regular army was necessary to garrison the frontier and to meet the exigencies of wartime service, but they still considered a sound militia central to the political stability and military security of the republic. That the nation's militia never assumed that role was not the result of a half-hearted commitment to transforming the states' disorganized militia structures into a viable citizen reserve. Federalists fell short of their goal because they failed to overcome the localism that underlay the ideological implications of the citizen-soldier.

Ironically, their efforts to fashion the militia into the first line of national defense were largely counterproductive. Increasingly suspicious of the intentions of Federalist economic and diplomatic policy, Republicans came to see Federalist demands for a national militia as nothing more than a guise by which to establish a standing army and, with it, political tyranny. Republicans accepted, albeit reluctantly, the necessity of a limited frontier constabulary. They blocked, however, every attempt to make the state militias an effective instrument of national policy, in the process making it clear that they understood both the expansion and centralization of the nation's military establishment to be symptomatic of political corruption and tyrannical intrigue.

By the time of the inauguration of John Adams, Federalists were prepared to seek new answers to the old question of how best to ensure the security of the republic. Deteriorating relations with France and growing concern over domestic political dissent infused a new urgency into their long-standing effort to create a military establishment capable of repelling foreign attack and of suppressing domestic insurgency. Concurrently, a deepening distrust of Federalist policy in general evoked among Republicans a penetrating critique of military policy that raised old but fundamental questions about the stability of republicanism in America. The result was a detailed examination of the constitutional implications and ideological assumptions behind the nation's military institutions that was rivaled in intensity only by the public outcry provoked by British policy in 1774 and 1775. Federalists and Republicans alike believed the nation's military institutions to be a measure of the viability and vitality of American republicanism. Their differences, shaped by partisan and ideological considerations, reflected the tensions generated by conflicting perceptions of how best to avoid the pitfalls that had destroyed republican governments in the past.

The Seeds of Tyranny

During the summer of 1798, amid rumors of a French invasion and domestic insurrection, Congress passed legislation creating the provisional and new armies. That legislation provided the catalyst for a public debate over the relationship between military institutions and republican liberties that lasted well into the election year of 1800. The Provisional Army Act authorized the president to appoint line and staff officers, organize a command and training structure, and recruit soldiers for a term not to exceed three years for a ten-thousand-man reserve army subject to military service in the event of imminent or actual invasion. The same measure empowered the chief executive to commission officers and accept into immediate federal service self-supplied volunteer companies. Volunteer corps units were to be organized into battalions with the appropriate line and staff officers, trained and disciplined under the authority vested in the president as commander in chief, and have access "at a reasonable rate" or by loan to the small arms, artillery, and accoutrements stored in the public arsenals; moreover, their members were to be exempt from militia duty during the length of their service as volunteers. The New Army Act tripled the size of the nation's regular army, adding twelve regiments and over ten thousand men. The provisional army represented a conscious effort to provide the national government with a reserve military force uninhibited by the restrictions and inadequacies of the state-dominated militia system. The new army was intended to give the government the ability to withstand at least the initial assaults of an invading army. In short, both acts were designed to remove the responsibility for the peacetime security of the republic from the state militia and to centralize and expand the coercive power available to the national government.[1]

The Republican opposition considered the Federalist-sponsored military legislation to be symptomatic of a larger effort to reestablish the same system of goverment that had plagued the American colonies during the last days of British rule.[2] Expanded royal patronage, a burdensome fiscal program, and military centralization were important components in the radical Whigs' paradigm of corruption that had informed the ideology of the Revolutionary War. Republican partisans in the press, in Congress, and at public assemblies in the nation's counties and towns drew on the same logic to accuse the Federalists of seeking to undermine both the representative and federal qualities of the American government. High taxes, the Hamiltonian funding system, extensive patronage, and the alien and sedition acts fit easily into the radical Whig perception of political corruption. Federalist efforts to alter the character of the nation's military establishment provided the crowning evidence that the American republic was in danger. While comparing themselves to the patriots of 1775, Republicans charged that the Federalists supported "a Standing Army—a Navy—heavy Taxes—high Salaries—numerous officers—and instead of a Republican, they were anxious to have a Monarchical government."[3]

Implicit in the Republican critique of Federalist policy was a thorough reexamination of the implications of military institutions for the constitutional stability of a republican society. Republicans seldom suggested that the republic could depend on militia soldiers alone to meet the demands of extended wartime service, but they repeatedly charged that the unnecessary recruitment of regular soldiers during peacetime threatened the vitality of republican society. Dependence on standing armies forged a false sense of security which encouraged the decline of the military order among the citizenry. Looking to regulars for their defense, citizens quickly forgot their own republican obligation to protect "their private property and political rights." Concurrently, the armed might of society fell into the hands of men unfamiliar with the rights of a free people. Republicanism depended upon the critical balance of right and responsibility embodied in the citizen-soldier. Without that balance, the republic was ripe for moral corruption, political intrigue, and tyranny.[4]

An anonymous essayist from Poughkeepsie argued that the "free born sons of America" would never yield the rights of citizenship, the prospect of property ownership, and the possibility of elective office to "become slaves for the trifling considerations of a Soldier's pay." Recruits would come from the lowest orders of American society, leaving the nation's defense in the hands of those least committed to its preservation. What was the nation to expect, he asked, "from an army . . . composed of thieves, drunkards, idlers and vagabonds of every name?" William Duane editorialized in the Philadelphia *Aurora* that the expanded regular army would be composed "to a great extent of bankrupt merchants, [and] men of dissolute habits." The citizens of Rutland, Vermont, summarized the fears of many Republicans in a resolution which argued that "a regular Standing Army raised at this period in the United States, will be principally composed of the refuse of society, who are destitute of property, and whose idleness and dissipation denies them existence in any other way." The republic would be better served, resolved the citizens of Dinwiddie County, Virginia, by readying the militia while keeping its young men involved in the productive labor of the community. There they could support their own families and contribute toward the reduction of the burdensome public debt. Heavy taxes would have to be levied on the "industrious" to support an army that would quickly become *"an asylum for all who do not chuse to labor."*[5]

Republican theorists had long identified an army of "hirelings" as among the principal means for undermining republican government. And the Republican opposition was quick to associate the new and provisional armies with the corruption of the constitutional order and the rise of political tyranny. Partisan essays, speeches, and resolutions charged again and again that Federalist military policy would destroy public morals and undermine the existing militia structure, creating a society susceptible to domination by a standing army. Republicans, however, did not generally fear a military coup d'état. Radical Whiggery understood corruption to radiate from the crown, and it was in that context that Republican spokesmen attacked the expansion of the military establishment. The issue at hand was the corruption of the constitutional order by civil authority, specifically the expansion and usurpation of power by the Federalist administration. Military force had a potentially important part in that corruption, but only as an agent of an ambitious and oppressive executive branch.[6]

Standing armies, Republicans charged, had "a manifest tendency to aggrandize Executive authority." An army recruited and commissioned under the supervision of the secretary of war was dependent on the executive branch for its "honors and emulments" and will always be "subservient to the views of the executive department." The constitutional and political implications of an executive army were obvious. It was the policy of all tyrannical governments, charged "A Republican," "to procure an armed force . . . to provide some lucrative and honourable places for the '*well-born*,' and to have that force in readiness to quell their own people in case of opposition to oppressive measures." In particular, the army provided an instrument of patronage and influence through which the executive branch could expand its influence over Congress and through the states.

Thus the standing army not only represented the centralization of military power but also implied the centralization of civil power at the expense of Congress and the states. The agents of this expanded federal power were the officers of the army and those of the revenue service, which no doubt would have had to have been expanded to support the costly military establishment. John Taylor of Caroline warned the Virginia assembly that an expanded army and revenue service would provide the executive branch with "swarms of officers civil and military, who can inculcate political tenets tending to consolidation and monarchy, both by indulgencies and severities, and can act as spies over the free exercise of human reason." Writing in the Boston *Independent Chronicle*, "Democritus" summarized the logic of corruption included in numerous tracts, essays, and resolutions. "We all know full well that the executive branch of every Government has a natural tendency to Despotism." The tendency toward arbitrary executive power had taken numerous forms, he wrote, but the lessons of history left little doubt that "the establishment of a standing army is a favorite scheme among Government." Only a few troops would be raised at first, lulling the public into a false sense of security and undermining the popular interest in the military arts. In time, though, their number would gradually be increased until "the patronage and strength of the executive are so extensive and formidable that it breaks the feeble barriers of the national constitution, forc[ing] a groaning people to pay enormous taxes and finally [to] riot in luxury, dissipation and blood." "A CITIZEN OF THE UNITED STATES" warned in the pages of the Philadelphia *Aurora* that an expanded military establishment, even if later reduced, created legislative precedents and personal allegiances that could in time undermine the republic. The patronage that supported the military and revenue services would create a network of individuals sympathetic to the goals of the federal governments "all at hand for the internal interprises of ambition." Edmund Pendleton of Virginia, paraphrasing James Burgh's comments of twenty-five years before, offered a scenario which reflected the fears of many Republicans: "An army of 50,000 mercenaries, at the devotion of some future enterprising President, aided by a sedition bill and accumulated terrors, with the influence of hope from an enormous patronage will subject America to executive despotism, instead of a representative republican government."[7]

If an expanded regular army establishment was not evidence enough of the Federalist determination to destroy the nation's republican constitution, the provisional army and the volunteer corps made that conclusion unavoidable. The Republican leadership in Congress considered the provisional army as nothing less than a scheme to extend the power and influence of the executive branch by circumventing and undermining the existing militia structure. The detachment of eighty thousand militiamen authorized during the emergency session the previous year would be both more effective and less threatening.

Assuming a prominent role in the Republican opposition to Federalist army legislation with James Madison's departure from the House of Representatives, Albert Gallatin, along with numerous other Republican partisans, charged that the provisional army was patently unconstitutional. "Undoubtedly, the Constitution has foreseen, that in cases of imminent danger, the United States would need a standing army, but," argued Gallatin, "it makes Congress the judge of that necessity." The transfer of the legislative power to raise armies to the president represented a dangerous precedent which could only enlarge the power of the executive branch and threaten the intricate balance that kept political tyranny at bay. Nevertheless, the transfer of power within the national government was only the most obvious threat to the republic's constitutional order.

Joseph McDowell argued that the army's provisional nature would be short-lived. The enlistment of soldiers and the appointment of officers would soon follow. He reminded his colleagues to recall "how much the appointment of a great number of officers in the army would increase the influence of the Executive, and consequently the dangerous effect it would have upon the liberty and independence of the country." If the officer corps might well become the agents of executive corruption, certainly the rank and file had to be considered a threat as well.

W. C. Clairborne and others feared that "if this army was now embodied, it would consist of the refuse of society—of men who might wear the garb of soldiers, but possess few, perhaps none, of their virtues." Supporting that contention, Gallatin argued that its proponents were misled in believing that the provisional army would be reminiscent of the patriotic force that had won independence. Men of property and responsibility would join the army only when the danger was real. He warned that to enlarge the military when the possibility of attack was remote would visit upon the republic all of the dangers historically associated with the establishment of a standing army in peacetime.[8]

Republicans in Congress considered the volunteer corps as only another manifestation of the ongoing effort "to give the President of the United States a standing army." The volunteer corps provided the president with a private army drawn exclusively from that part of society able to arm, clothe, and equip itself. There were no restrictions on the number of units that could be organized, and the president was free to deploy the force as he saw fit. Not only was this kind of force not envisioned by the Constitution but it also effectively bypassed the constitutional restraints intended to prevent the executive branch from using the military as an instrument of political tyranny. The nation's fiscal ability to support a standing army limited even the most determined despot's power to use regular soldiers to subvert the constitutional order. The self-supplied and self-armed volunteer corps eliminated that restraint. Volunteer corps members were also exempt from militia service, a clear indication, Republicans argued, of the Federalist intention to destroy the local militia's ability to protect republican liberties from the machinations of would-be tyrants. With the militia in shambles and the president backed by a handpicked army, the republic was clearly in peril. Gallatin, for one, could envision no purpose for such a force "unless, indeed, it was the intention of gentlemen to suppress political opinion."[9]

Outside the halls of Congress the opponents of Federalist policy concurred with Gallatin's assessment. The citizens of Northampton County, Pennsylvania, lumped the volunteer corps, "influenced by party spirit and . . . officered by presidential discretion," with the standing army as among the institutions that have always been "the favorite object of every prince who wished to extend his power." Quoting Henry Knox's warning against accepting volunteer companies "composed of disaffected persons . . . desirous to intrude into the army, under the pretense of Patriotic Association," "A VIRGINIAN" charged that critics of the Adams administration were systematically excluded from volunteer service. "Every man and every officer 'especially,' must undergo a political inquisition . . . before he shall be permitted to serve his country, or be trusted with arms in his hands." The volunteer corps could hardly be considered a citizen army. To the contrary, its composition ensured that it must be intended as an "instrument of PARTY PERSECUTION." "Humanus" believed the plan to organize and arm volunteers in lieu of the regular militia was "ingeniously and systematically devised [to] supercede the constitutional militia." Soon the nation's military establishment would consist of "a well-armed Party corps . . . and tens of thousands of hired army, on the one hand; and a neglected, difuse and un-armed militia, on the other." With a partisan volunteer corps in reserve and an enlarged military establishment in the field—all equally dependent on and devoted to the executive branch—the Federalists would hold unlimited power with which to corrupt and destroy the sensitive balance that guaranteed republican government.[10]

Concerned that their civil and political liberties were in danger, Republicans, as had Americans since 1768, turned to the militia as the surest deterrent to foreign attack and as the only guarantor of republican government. The citizens of Louisa County, Virginia, resolved "that a well regulated and well organized militia, as immediately connecting the duties of citizens and soldiers, are the surest safeguard to the rights and liberties of the people." The same sentiment echoed through public resolutions and across the pages of the Republican press from New England to the South. Glorifying and idealizing a militia structure that had long ago lost its similarity to the armies of classical Greece and Rome, Republicans, nevertheless, described the militia as the "proprietors of the soil," alone capable of serving both as "defensive soldiers" and "useful Citizens." "After exhibiting their discipline in the field, they return to their respective occupations," contrasting sharply with standing armies that "remain as locusts upon the land, eating up the earnings of others."

None of this was meant to suggest that extended enlistments might not be necessary in the event of an "actual invasion." Still it was the militia, with its local tradition and political allegiances that, in the minds of the Republican opposition, should provide the basis for any republican army. Anxious to return to civilian life and independent from the patronage and influence of the national executive, militiamen could be depended upon to resist and defeat enemy incursions while not becoming a threat to the domestic constitutional order. The message was old and well-known in America. Nevertheless, as "Democritus" reminded the readers of the Boston *Independent Chronicle*, it must be repeated "till every American is convinced of it, that the man who is happy and fights for his property is always a formidable soldier," and the only soldier compatible with republican liberties.[11]

A Foundation for National Security

Federalists equated constitutional stability with the national government's ability to field an effective and dependable military force; thus they considered the provisional and new armies a necessary corrective to the inadequacies of the existing militia structure. The militia's poor showing during the Whiskey Rebellion—one congressman claimed that fewer than one in five militiamen had proven willing to serve during the crisis of 1794—demonstrated the militia's unresponsiveness to national needs. The decentralized structure of the nation's militia made it particularly susceptible, some Federalists feared, to the rumored French effort to destroy the republic from within. "If the militia was wholly under the authority of the United States, and under the command of officers appointed by them," lamented one Federalist spokesman, then "they might be more relied upon." At best, the militia as presently officered and organized might successfully repel the initial thrusts of an invading army, but it could not be expected to withstand the strains of an extended campaign.[12]

The militia's ineffectiveness, Federalists believed, stemmed from more than just its decentralized organizational structure. The performance of citizen-soldiers during the Revolutionary War provided ample evidence that "men who leave families behind them will not continue contentedly beyond the time for which they are called." The constant rotation in the ranks contributed to the military ineffectiveness of the militia soldier, but it also disrupted economic activities essential for successful military engagements. "You may occasionally call the militia," argued one Federalist, "but it would be immensely inconvenient to be constantly calling the husbandmen from the field, and the mechanic from his labors, and to have the whole country marching and countermarching." Most important, though, militia soldiers were no match for the carefully trained and highly disciplined regulars that made up the armies of Europe.

Robert Goodloe Harper maintained that Americans were still committed to personal service in defense of their rights, but that the success of a modern army depended on "something more than a disposition" to serve. Certainly the classical republican claim that the union of arms and property was the principal ingredient of a victorious army had proven erroneous in America. "Though composed of persons who had the greatest stake in the country," the militia had too often "wanted discipline, and was far from being prompt in obedience to orders." Modern armies must be skilled, "and what is more important, they must have commanders." The provisional army would meet both of these needs without burdening the republic with an expensive peacetime army. Led by an effective officer corps and composed of well-trained troops, it promised a reserve army able to respond to national emergencies and capable of staying in the field for the duration of hostilities. The provisional army would also be drilled, led, and mobilized at the behest of the national government, eliminating any doubt about the dependability of the republic's reserve forces.[13]

The volunteer corps, too, was intended to enhance the government's ability to respond to short- and long-term military crises. It would also contribute toward the overall competency of the nation's reserve forces. Organized, officered, and trained under the supervision of the federal government, it, along with the provisional army, promised to fill the void left by Congress's failure to create a national militia system. Volunteer units would provide the nation with experienced officers and men, all well qualified to lead and instruct local militia companies when their tours of national service ended. If the militia, as Republicans often claimed, had become ineffective because actual service had become the obligation only of the poor, the volunteer corps offered a means to draw the nation's propertied citizenry back into military service.

Certainly no better force could be conceived for a republican nation than a body of well-trained units composed exclusively of "men possessing the property which is the strongest and dearest bond of their connexions with the community." Men motivated by bounties and the hope of personal gain had threatened the security of the republic when the militia was called out in 1794. If the militia had proven wanting in performance and composition in the past, the volunteer corps was ideally suited to take its place—"they will fight, not like slaves for pay, but like freemen for their rights." Where the militia had proven weak, the volunteer corps would be formidable: "To the invaders of our country—to the turbulent and seditious—to insurgents—to the daring infractors of the laws." Using language that recalled the classical definition of the citizen-soldier, Federalists described the volunteer corps as an armed manifestation of the rights and liberties of the republic's properties citizenry—a force committed to the national defense and the preservation of republican liberties. In short, the addition of the volunteer corps to the military establishment represented for Federalists the "admission of a body of patriotic, respectable, generous youth, into the public service, who will form a firm phalanx against any internal or external enemy."[14]

Since Congress had repeatedly expressed its reluctance to consider significant militia reform, Federalists considered the Provisional Army Act a means to ensure a level of peacetime preparedness compatible with and responsive to national needs. Put another way, the legislation promised an institutional structure through which the national government could exert control over and improve the skills of the nation's reserve military force— goals that had eluded Federalist leaders since the ratification of the Constitution. The provisional army's chief proponents, including Alexander Hamilton, Secretary of War James McHenry, and Secretary of State Timothy Pickering, discussed it in just those terms on numerous occasions late in the 1790s. Certainly if President Adams had exercised his authority to organize the provisional army, it would have provided the government with a politically and militarily dependable infrastructure of men and matériel similar to the militia proposals backed repeatedly by the Washington administration beginning with Knox's select militia plan of 1790. In an important way, then, the provisional army and its successor, the eventual army, reflected not only the Federalists' frustration and disillusionment with the existing militia structure but also their continuing adherence to the principle that a republican government must found its coercive power on popular support.[15]

The provisional army could overcome the political and military shortcomings of the state-controlled militia system—a system most recently weakened, many Federalists feared, by the infiltration of Republican Francophiles. It could also be depended on to put down domestic insurgencies and to serve as a deterrent to foreign attack. It could not, however, be expected alone to carry the nation's banners in the event of an actual war. Arguing that the formidable French citizen army depended at its core on a well-organized body of regular soldiers, Federalists looked to the new army as the cornerstone of the nation's defense.[16] Only an expanded regular army could contain an invading force. Of course, the new army would also solidify the government's as well as the Federalists' control over the nation's armed forces. George Washington spoke for many Federalists when he suggested that enough politically dependable Federalists were available to fill the ranks of the officer corps, making it unnecessary to appoint Republicans, who "will leave nothing unattempted to overthrow the government of this country."[17] Nevertheless, the new army legislation was founded on more than simply the need to serve immediate political and military ends. The army was necessary because military professionalism was necessary for the survival of the American republic.

Though congressional Republicans had disputed the necessity of an expanded military establishment at various times during the 1790s, they had seldom rejected the premise that a regular army was essential during wartime. Their opposition to the new army was concerned far more with the motivation for raising the army than with the desirability of such a force in the event of an actual invasion. Leading Federalists, however, considered the regular army essential for the security of the republic during peacetime as well as war.

Speaking after the French crisis had passed and against a Republican attempt to demobilize the army, Harrison Grey Otis advised the House of Representatives that the United States could not long expect to avoid the affairs of Europe. Rumors persisted that Spain would soon sell Louisiana to France, and that development would significantly alter the nation's need for military expertise. "Of all the arts and science now understood and cultivated in Europe . . . , the military art has attained to the most considerable degree of perfection." But in America, the "art of war is least understood." That discrepancy, he warned, could prove crucial during any prolonged contest with foreign soldiers. National security demanded at least "a few men" well trained in the rudiments of war to instruct, lead, and encourage the body of new recruits raised to meet a national emergency.

Henry Lee argued the same point. The American militia equalled any army in courage and fidelity. But in the end, "they want method, patience, obedience, and combination, without all which attributes, no man can be a good soldier." Military success required accomplished soldiers. He was not suggesting that the United States should rely on mercenary or foreign soldiers. "We want our brothers, our own sons, taught to be patient, to obey, to retreat, to act in concert," and that could be accomplished only through regular and extended military service. The new army alone could ensure the long-term security of the republic.[18]

Secretary of War James McHenry expanded on the arguments offered in Congress in a series of letters written to the speaker of the House early in 1800. The issue at hand was a plan for a military academy, but the overriding concern of the secretary of war was the need for a reassessment of the assumptions supporting the republic's peacetime military. Using the logic and insights long associated with the moderate Whig defense of standing armies, McHenry urged Congress to create a military establishment founded on the compatibility of military professionalism with the tenets of a free society. The growing sophistication of the military arts and the increased complexity of the republic's social and economic structure made it inconceivable that the citizen militia would be deployed either to garrison the frontier or to repel a foreign invasion. The militia was simply inadequately trained to meet the tactical and technological demands of regular service. Recent history abounded with evidence that "the perfect order, and exact discipline" of regular troops gave them "a decided advantage over more numerous forces composed of uninstructed militia, or undisciplined recruits." "The arts of war, which gives to a small force the faculty to combat with advantage superior numbers, *indifferently instructed*, is subject to mechanical, geometrical, moral and physical rules." Theory, principles, and details had to be learned and then applied with precision and care to quickly developing circumstances to secure victory on the battlefield. Part-time militia officers and soldiers could neither master nor apply these techniques with the precision required in the heat of battle.

Proponents of militia reform, argued McHenry, ignored the social, economic, and military realities of American society. "To qualify and keep our citizens . . . prepared to take the field against regular forces, would demand the most radical changes in our militia system, and such an uninterrupted series of training, discipline, and instruction, to be applied" that the nation would lose more "by the abstraction from labor or occupation" than it would cost to maintain a modest regular army. Making every citizen a "master of the several branches of the art of war" made no more sense than employing every man in the community in the construction of houses while expelling "as useless, architects, masons, and carpenters." Neither, argued McHenry, did the past service of the American militia suggest that it should retain a central role in the nation's military establishment. The Continental army had been ineffective against British regulars during the Revolutionary War until Congress extended enlistments to three years, allowing time to transform raw recruits into trained regulars. The militia had occasionally served brilliantly, but it was "universally felt, that regular and disciplined troops were indispensable, and that it was utterly unsafe for us to trust to militia alone the issue of war."

McHenry recognized the political impossibility of maintaining a peacetime force large enough to meet any potential emergency. Hence, it was doubly necessary to cultivate "military science . . . with peculiar care." He was not the first national leader to arrive at that conclusion. But always before, calls for the establishment of schools for formal military training had been associated with efforts to make the militia the principal instrument of national military policy. Conceding that the militia was unlikely ever to become an institution responsive to national needs, McHenry urged Congress to create a military academy in order that the regular army could assume the primary responsibility for national defense. "Military schools [were] an essential means . . . to prepare for . . . the United States, at a very modest expense, a body of scientific officers, and engineers, adequate to any future exigency, qualified to discipline for the field, in the shortest time, the most extended armies, and to give the most decisive and useful effects to their operations."[19]

McHenry's plea for a military establishment founded on military professionalism capped the evolution of Federalist perceptions of how best to provide for the nation's defense. From the founding of the new government they had based their approach to the nation's military needs on assumptions about the military and society derived from the moderate Whig defense of standing armies. What changed over the decade of the 1790s was their assessment of the institutional requirements necessary to provide the republic with a force trained in the increasingly sophisticated arts of eighteenth-century warfare. Washington and Knox had seen the select militia as a means to that end. The political developments of the 1790s, though, shattered hopes of shaping the amorphous state militias into a viable instrument of national security. At the same time, fiscal and political realities prevented Federalists from aspiring to create a regular army comparable to those in Europe. Nevertheless, the United States had maintained a small regular army since the Confederation, and by the end of the Adams administration the Federalist leadership had determined that only that force could provide a reliable institutional base for the nation's military requirements during peace and war. For them, a professional military establishment was compatible with the growing complexity of the republic's economic and social environment. In the field during times of peace and regularly drilled in the technical and tactical skills of modern warfare, it could provide the critical infrastructure necessary to lead and train the expanded forces needed during wartime. Just as important, it offered the national government the means by which to secure the power and authority it needed in a political environment historically dominated by colonial and state governments.

Federalists succeeded neither in establishing a military academy nor in maintaining the new army as the foundation for transforming the nation's regular army from a frontier constabulary to a skeletal professional force vested with the primary responsibility for the nation's defense. Improved relations with France, President Adams's suspicion about the intent of the expanded army's chief proponents, his disenchantment with Alexander

Hamilton's role in the organization and internal politics of the new army, and the election to the House of a group of Federalist congressmen, mostly from the South, sensitive to public opinion in constituencies that usually sent Republicans to Congress led first to the curtailment of enlistments and then in May 1800 to the demobilization of the new army.[20] When the Sixth Congress convened its second session in the nation's new capital on the banks of the Potomac the new army no longer existed. Nevertheless, it had left its mark on the political and intellectual history of the late eighteenth century, laying bare attitudes toward the military in the nation's political and constitutional order that paralleled those articulated in England a century before. The critical difference, though, was that while radical Whigs were a politically unimportant quantity in England, their intellectual heirs in America were not. As the eighteenth century came to a close, the Republican opposition stood on the verge of political power.

9

Jeffersonian Victory and Defeat

[The] safety of a republic depends as much upon the quality of arms and discipline among its citizens, as upon the equality of rights. —William Henry Harrison, "Militia Discipline, No. 2," in the Washington *National Intelligencer*, 1 October 1810

There seems to be a deplorable supineness and local jealousy that act as a dead weight against every attempt that is made for the amelioration of the militia system.
—unsigned essay, Washington *National Intelligencer*, 17 October 1811

Thomas Jefferson considered his election to the presidency a "revolution" as important to the history of the republic as the events of 1776. Jeffersonian partisans certainly considered it a major turning point in the republic's history. The election of Jefferson meant an end to the intrigue and corruption that had threatened, in their view, to transform the nation's republican constitution into an engine of oppression. Republicans had charged repeatedly during the campaign that the Federalists aspired to model the American government after the oppressive, corrupt, and tyrannical British constitution. "The great object with them," wrote Benjamin Austin, was "to obtain a war establishment—and, under this patronage, to riot in luxury . . . ; to live on the toils and fatigues of the industrious; to increase the public burthens; augment LAND-TAXES; and, after throwing the community into convulsions, to employ a STANDING ARMY to force the people into a compliance with their arbitrary mandates."

Oppressive taxes, an ever-expanding executive branch, the alien and sedition acts, and the unnecessary expansion of the nation's military establishment fit a pattern of corruption only too familiar to a political opposition united behind the rhetoric of radical Whiggery. The demobilization of the new army during the early summer of 1800 may have suggested to some that the Federalists were "at length convinced of the futility of attempting to raise an army of mercenaries," but most Jeffersonian partisans remained unpersuaded. Federalists, wrote an anonymous Jeffersonian essayist in the midst of the crucial New York state electoral campaign, believed "that standing armies are the pillars of society." Republicans, on the other hand, understood that "standing armies have ever proven the bane of industry, of social and moral virtue, and the destruction of liberty civil and political." A Federalist victory at the polls would only ensure the continued proliferation of regular army soldiers and volunteer troops, all officered by Federalist partisans eager to serve an ambitious administration.

Put in those terms, the election of 1800 was a struggle between proponents of military professionalism and the supporters of the traditional republican system of defense, the citizen militia—a struggle easily and often translated by the Republican press into a battle between tyranny and liberty. William Duane editorialized in the *Aurora* that, fortunately, "the people of this country . . . have become generally sensible [to the dangers of an] Executive power, with the dispensation of the public money in its hands, and the army and navy under its direction." For him, Republican successes at the polls during 1800 confirmed a growing popular feeling that the national government could "only be checked and balanced by the *inviolability* of our [state] constitutions, and *the order* and *efficiency* of the Militia." The Revolution of 1800, then, promised both a return to the federal balance that ensured republican government and a revival of the citizen militia upon which all republican societies had been based. In the end, concluded Duane, "*the two* (The Constitution[s] and the Militia) are the real bulwarks of our *domestic peace*."[1]

But if the Revolution of 1800 signaled the return of the militia to a position of primacy among the republic's military institutions, it did not imply that regular soldiers had no place in American society. Joseph B. Varnum, among New England's leading Republicans, might celebrate the demobilization of the new army with the claim that "the militia composed of the citizens, . . . comport[s] with the fundamental principles of our government, and must be scrupulously regarded if we would support and perpetuate it." Similarly, Virginia's Edmund Pendleton might mark the Republican victory at the polls with a call for the elimination of standing armies and the restoration of local military prerogatives as a means to erect barriers "against folly, fraud and ambition." Nevertheless, as Thomas Jefferson made clear in his inaugural address, his elevation to the presidency meant a commitment only to the belief that "a well-disciplined militia, [is] our best reliance in peace and for the first moments of war." As a governor of Virginia during the Revolution he had learned well the inadequacies of militia soldiers during wartime. Repeated calls to arms undermined the citizens' economic and social responsibilities to society and added little to the military capabilities of the states. Certainly Benedict Arnold had found Virginia's militia no deterrent to his campaigns through the Piedmont early in 1781—a situation that had led Jefferson to ask the Virginia assembly to consider raising regular troops for the state's protection.

This position did not, of course, contradict the recent Republican indictment of Federalist military policy. Even during the height of the crisis of 1798, Republicans avoided any suggestion that regular soldiers would not be important during wartime. Since the ratification of the Constitution, Republicans had supported, though at times reluctantly, the necessity of regular soldiers to garrison the frontier and for wartime service. They questioned the expansion of the army only when they suspected that that policy was associated with Federalist efforts to subvert the federal balance of the new constitutional order. Only so long as the republic remained at peace, then, did the Revolution of 1800 promise the perpetuation of the militia as the principal instrument of national security.[2]

The Jeffersonians would discover, however, in the years between 1801 and the declaration of war against Great Britain in 1812, that their commitment to the militia as the principal guarantor of national security until the "first moments of war" would leave America entirely unprepared to fight what some historians have called its second war for independence. In a world increasingly dominated by military forces trained in sophisticated technologies and complex maneuvers, the Jeffersonians had created for themselves an ideological dilemma. Any argument that regular soldiers might play an important role in the nation's peacetime establishment had been rendered untenable by the premises that had shaped the partisan political battles of the 1790s. Therefore, any sense that the republic's peacetime defenses required levels of military proficiency previously unknown in America had to be adaptable to long-standing republican perceptions of the citizen in arms. Those same ideological premises, however, also made it unlikely that the existing militia structure would ever be altered to make it a viable instrument of national policy. Ironically, the ideological tenets that had informed Republican critiques of Federalist policy over the previous decade would render the republic in the years preceding the War of 1812 virtually defenseless—this despite a clearly discernible sense that the nation's peacetime forces required significant reform. Federalists resolved a similar dilemma by urging the compatibility of military professionalism with the institutions of a free society. The Jeffersonians found that approach unacceptable. Preserving a military structure long associated with the security of civil and political liberties, they left American republicanism vulnerable to the same political and military force from which it had been won in the years after 1776.

The First Administration

If, as William Duane had suggested, the Revolution of 1800 held out the promise of an end to the nascent military professionalism and institutional centralization that had characterized the last years of the Adams administration, the Republican leadership in Congress and in the executive branch disappointed few supporters during their first years in office. In his first message to Congress, Jefferson urged a reduction in force intended to leave the peacetime army with only enough engineers and regulars to garrison the federal arsenals and a handful of strategically important frontier posts. The only force capable of repelling enemy intrusions along the diverse and extended American coastline and frontier, intoned the president, was "the body of neighboring citizens as formed into a militia." Congress agreed and quickly reduced the authorized strength of the regular army from just under fifty-five hundred officers and men—of whom only slightly more than four thousand were actually on duty—to just over thirty-three hundred regulars.

In December 1802, Jefferson called for a review of the nation's militia institutions based on the premise that the militia should be "our general reliance for the great and sudden emergencies." Congress responded with legislation providing for state adjutants general to submit annual returns to the president and expanding the militia's administrative staff within the state, but it did not tamper with the basic organization of the militia system. As a House committee explained, the Militia Law of 1792 "embraces all the objects of a militia institution, delegated to Congress; the principles of that law lay the foundation of a militia system, on the broad basis prescribed by the Constitution, and are well calculated to insure a complete national defence." Any inadequacies lay not in the powers vested in Congress "but from omission on the part of the State governments." Consequently, the House recommended only that the president remind the states of their obligations to "carry into effect the militia system adopted by the National Legislature [in order to] render the militia a sure and permanent bulwark of national defence."[3]

Sensitive to the recent Federalist attempt to centralize the military power of the republic in the executive branch, Congress was in no mood to consider any militia reorganization that challenged state militia prerogatives. Legislation passed in March 1803 authorizing the president to require state executives to hold in readiness up to eighty thousand militia spoke to the prevailing congressional perception of the nation's military requirements. The militia was to be the first line of national defense, but it was also not to lose its standing as a state institution. Congress granted the president discretionary powers to call the militia into service, but it was up to the state governors "to organize, arm, and equip," as well as appoint the officers for, the units drawn from their states. The president could also permit volunteer companies to enlist in lieu of militia soldiers. Nevertheless, the terms of the legislation made it clear that the volunteer corps were not to become a means, as they had under the Federalists, of circumventing state control over the nation's peacetime forces. The volunteer corps was to be "officered out of the present militia officers, or others, at the option of and discretion of the Constitutional authority in each state respectively." Congress perceived the militia as the principal institution of the nation's peacetime military establishment, but it also remained determined to ensure that that force not become an agent of political and military centralization.[4]

The axiom that the citizen in arms was a free society's best defense seemed to define and describe the Jeffersonian perception of the nation's military needs at the end of the first term. The regular army had been reduced to a numerically insignificant force spread along the nation's western frontier. The militia, long the cornerstone of Republican military thinking, had once again been vested with the principal responsibility for meeting both civil and military emergencies. Nevertheless, the institutional structure of the peacetime military establishment belied significant disagreements concerning the republic's military needs. Jefferson's repeated requests for reform of the existing militia structure and Congress's decision to provide for a small military academy in the 1802 "Act Fixing the Military Peace Establishment of the United States" suggested that at least some Americans recognized, as David Humphreys noted in 1803, that "the military art . . . is not so simple and easy as to come instinctively without practice."[5]

Indeed, the military development and international tensions spawned by the French Revolution and the Napoleonic Wars evoked a wide variety of opinions within Republican circles concerning the republic's military requirements. Though devoid of the partisan innuendos that had characterized discussions of the nation's military institutions since early in the 1790s, these critiques nevertheless reflect the persistence of ideological divisions long part of American political thought. The theses concerning national defense posed by Joseph Priestley, John Taylor of Caroline, William Duane, and other lesser-known commentators suggest the enduring influence of classical republican theory, the growing recognition that institutional compulsion must supersede public virtue as the motivational force in any citizen army, and the continuing effort by some to bring American political thinking to the point reached by the mainstream of English political thought a century before. In addition, these insights into the military requirements of a free society suggest the parameters of the political theory that shaped the Jeffersonian approach to national defense on the eve of the War of 1812.

Proposals for Peacetime Security

Jefferson had been in office only two years when Joseph Priestley published a revised American edition of his *Lectures on History and General Policy* (1803). Priestley had been associated with the Jeffersonian opposition since his arrival in America early in the 1790s. Nevertheless, his analysis of the military needs of a modern republic suggested the need for a major reassessment of Republican military policy. Like Adam Smith, Priestley cited national life-style as a primary determinant of national military needs. Geography was also important. Island nations required the least military protection, while nations with frontiers unguarded by natural barriers necessitated the largest military forces. Geography determined size, but it was life-style that determined the character and composition of a nation's land forces. Historically, Priestley argued, a nation had proven militarily powerful in proportion to its ability to keep forces in the field. The paramilitary social organization of the nomadic Tartars made them the scourge of Europe. Mounted and constantly in the field, they were always prepared to commit the full strength of their society to military campaigns. Economic specialization and the division of labor in more complex societies impeded military mobilization and thus placed special military burdens on nations that had more sophisticated social and economic structures. Nations that thrived on manufacturing and commerce were best defended, Priestley contended in language reminiscent of Adam Smith, by professional soldiers "who have no other business besides that of fighting."[6]

Priestley was a dissenter in the mainstream of the English opposition tradition, and he knew full well the dangers inherent in standing armies. They were expensive, and historically they had proven to be the principal instrument of tyrannical oppression. Certainly if every citizen were required to train in the militia, civil liberties would be more secure, and the nation, if attacked, would benefit from having an army composed of soldiers motivated by the defense of their own liberties. Nevertheless, Priestley considered a citizen army counterproductive in a wealthy and economically sophisticated society. Citing numerous examples from ancient and modern history, he claimed that inexperienced militia soldiers had always proven easy prey for more confident and disciplined regulars. Professional armies were more effective, and they were also less expensive than citizen armies "for the same reasons that we have our shoes and clothes made at less expense by employing shoemakers and tailors." Professional soldiers would burden society with individuals "idle and useless for any other purpose." Still, "the occasional practice of arms by the whole community," wrote Priestley, "would produce a greater sum of idleness, and on the whole would take the more from the mass of useful labour." To guarantee constitutional balance and preserve civil liberties while enjoying the benefits to be derived from a force "far more effectual for defence or offence" than the citizen militia, care only need to be taken to ensure that "the officers in standing armies be of the body of the people," enjoying the same privileges and sharing similar interests with the citizenry.[7]

For Priestley, a regular army properly conceived offered the most effective and efficient foundation for national security. He stopped short, however, of suggesting that a modern society could depend during wartime solely on the expertise of its professional army. A virtuous citizenry committed to the common good was also necessary to meet the exigencies of war. Priestley's sense of the virtuous citizen's responsibility for national defense, however, hardly resembled the classical republican perception of the landed citizen called from the plow to bear arms in the republic's defense. In his mind, a citizen contributed to the national wealth through his own specialized economic activity and benefited from the national power derived from that wealth. Farming, commerce, and manufacturing had equal stakes in the nation's defense; thus each could be expected to assume a role in assuring national security.

Classical republican theorists had long argued that the transfer of the responsibility for national security from the landed yeomanry was symptomatic of the deterioration of the constitutional balance that sustained a free society, implying, of course, the incompatibility of modernity and republicanism. Priestley rejected that implication as a misperception of the strength inherent in the complex social and economic structure of a modern commercial society. He argued that agricultural nations could ill afford to depend upon their citizens during military crises because mobilization drew farmers from their fields, leaving the land uncultivated and the nation imperiled from within as well as from without. Only societies founded upon a division of labor could meet the demands for men and matériel that accompanied extended military campaigns. A nation already accustomed to feeding the portion of its population involved in commerce and manufacturing with foodstuffs from its farms could easily mobilize those "being employed about superfluities" to meet emergency manpower needs without seriously damaging its ability to feed either its armies or its remaining civilian population.[8]

Neither Priestley's understanding of the need for military professionalism nor his insights into the military capacity of a modern society were original with him. Both arguments had been important to moderate Whig perceptions of the military requirements of a free society since early in the eighteenth century. Nevertheless, their restatement in the midst of the early-national period provided an important reminder for Americans faced with the difficult task of fitting the realities of their nation's social and economic complexity into visions of national security and defense which often had their origins in ideas founded upon the simplistic agrarian societies of classical republican theory.[9]

John Taylor of Caroline was also sensitive to the growing specialization and complexity of American society. But in sharp contrast to Priestley, he considered professionalism symptomatic of political and moral decay. Economic specialization connoted the proliferation of special interests and the concentration of power, both historic enemies of republicanism. The security of the republic did not depend, as Priestley had implied, on the recognition and integration of the advantages of economic specialization into the nation's military establishment. Rather, it depended upon the willingness of the American citizenry to reaffirm the values and principles of classical republican societies. Borrowing from radical Whig ideology, Taylor identified the growing national debt, the proliferation of federal patronage, mounting taxes, the enactment of protective tariffs, and the expansion of the military as evidence of a pernicious transformation in American society that threatened to turn the republic into an oppressive tyranny. If republicanism was not to meet an early demise in America, the ever-expanding power of the national government had to be reduced, economic and political power had to be wrested from the nonproductive special interests and returned to the productive, agricultural sector of society, and the militia had to be revived as the principal instrument of national defense.[10]

Taylor was a republican of the classical mold, associating the militia with propertied independence and the stability of the civil constitution. The danger of a standing army was less that it would lead to a military coup d'état than that it would become the means by which ambitious leaders could corrupt the civil constitution. The army was no more "cruel, avaricious or tyrannical than priests, stockjobbers or nobles." But it was dangerous to civil and political liberties because, like those others, it represented an avenue for executive patronage and influence. Being a "separate interest" apart from the citizenry, it was also a natural ally of other groups seeking to "cut up the general interest, for the sake of its own safety or aggrandizement." Only the militia, "being nearly the nation itself," could guarantee the constitutional balance necessary for the preservation of republican government.[11]

"Let us suppose," wrote Taylor, "a nation to [hold] both a civil and military sovereignty, one by election, and the other by an armed and trained militia." If, in time, the latter were transferred to the government "by disarming and disorganizing the militia, and raising a standing army," the essential balance of the civil constitution would be destroyed. With the government in control of the nation's military sovereignty, popular control over the electoral process became meaningless. The "naked permission to keep and bear arms," warned Taylor, was "an insufficient ally of election or civil sovereignty." Only a "real militia" was capable of preserving the civil constitution. In America the state governments were best constituted to prevent the usurpation of military sovereignty by the government. "The state governments [have] withheld from them that of raising mercenary armies." The same guarantees were omitted from the Constitution, and consequently special interests have looked to it as a means to fulfill their ambitions. Only constitutional amendments requiring that all citizens be armed and dispersing the immense military patronage power presently controlled by the president and his cabinet could eliminate the threat of usurpation by the national government. For the moment, the stability of the American republic depended, wrote Taylor, on the perseverance of the states and their determination to ensure the balance of power and prerogative upon which republican societies rested. "As no government can exist without military protections, and as a militia constitutes that, to which alone the state governments can resort, they must make it [the militia] adequate to the end or perish."[12]

Taylor's defense of the militia was profoundly conservative in both its social and political implications. It embraced a social, economic, and political structure long associated with the ancient republics and the prehistoric society of Saxon England. Taylor was uncomfortable with the forces of modernity in much the same way that the popularizers of classical republican theory during the late seventeenth and early eighteenth centuries had been. For both, manufacturing, government financial manipulations, and the growing commercial tone of society represented assaults on existing political and social relationships which were then translated into threats to the basic freedoms upon which their societies were based. Hence the growing importance of commercial and manufacturing interests in government circles, the proliferation of professionalism in all sectors of society, and the related emergence of banking and financial manipulation as an important component of modern business and government were associated with the neglect and decline of the one institution that symbolized their vision of a free society, the militia. It embodied the political values, social relationships, and economic independence that had been at the core of the republican theory articulated in English-speaking circles since the seventeenth century. Preserving the militia meant far more than the maintenance of a military force capable of preventing the usurpation of power by the national government. It also meant the preservation of traditional political and social relationships in the face of the growing professionalism and centralization associated with national government.

Not all Jeffersonians perceived the militia as a guarantor of social and political conservatism. Joel Barlow, whose essays concerning the militia were written in the heat of the French Revolution, used a curious blend of democratic radicalism and Harringtonian republicanism to offer the militia as an instrument of social revolution. Barlow, like James Harrington, associated standing armies with feudalism, particularly the functions and prerogatives of the nobility: "The military system has created the noblesse, and the noblesse the military system." Titles, pensions, and a monopoly over the functions and prerogatives of war ensured their political and social preeminence. The French Revolution dismantled the nobility, in the process transferring political sovereignty and military power to the people.

His perception of the social and political revolution that swept through France was strikingly similar to the transfer of political and military power from the nobility to the people described in *Oceana*. Certainly Barlow's political theory borrowed heavily from Harringtonian thought. "You will ... have removed the *necessity* of a standing army," he wrote, "by the organization of the legislature and the *possibility* of it by the arrangement of the militia; for it is as impossible for an armed soldiery to exist in an armed nation, as for a nobility to exist under an equal government." The popular assembly and the citizen army were synonymous in *Oceana*, and Barlow noted the critical importance of the same relationship for modern republics. The danger was not that the army might become involved in an offensive war or that it might be turned against the people. Rather, the presence of the army would breed an unhealthy sense of dependence. The principle was simple: "A people that legislate for themselves ought to be in the habit of protecting themselves; or they will lose the spirit of both."[13]

Barlow's dependence on Harrington and not the latter-day radical Whigs for his understanding of the origins of standing armies and the means for their demise was critical for establishing the revolutionary tone of his defense of militia forces. Harrington was concerned with the establishment of republican institutions, not their revival from a lost republican past. So, of course, was Barlow. Nevertheless, the most radical implications of Barlow's perception of a republican army lie in his dissociation of citizenship from property ownership. He argued that "it is the person, not the property, that exercises the will [and] for whom government is instituted, and by whom its functions are performed." Making militia service the responsibility of all citizens ensured a sense of individual independence and community interdependence critical for inspiring a dedication to the common good. "Every citizen ought to feel himself to be a necessary part of the great community," wrote Barlow, and "he should feel the habits of citizen and the energies of a soldier, without being exclusively destined to the function of either." Founding the strength and wisdom of government upon all the people irrespective of propertied status promised for a republic "a perpetual defence against the open force, and the secret intrigues of all possible enemies at home and abroad."[14]

Proponents of classical republicanism like John Taylor must have found Barlow's analysis both pleasing and suspect. The militia's relationship to the stability and balance of the civil constitution fit well into their vision of republican society. But blatantly to dissociate militia duty from property ownership was as much a threat as the growing power of nonagricultural interests in governmental circles. American militia units had historically included citizens from all economic classes, but property ownership had played an important role in the selection of the militia leadership. Barlow's dissociation of citizenship from property might indeed generate a new sense of community, but it might also be a community well beyond the scope and control of the local political elites that had historically dominated the command structures of American militias. In short, Barlow's ideas had the capability of providing an intellectual justification for dismantling the historic localism of the American militia. And that was the very thing that republicans like Taylor feared most.

The radical implication of Barlow's analysis of the militia was well outside the mainstream of American political and military thinking. The preservation of republican liberties, not the overthrow of aristocratic institutions, had always served as the principal political motivation behind American discussions of military preparedness. Nevertheless, the French Revolution did have an important effect on American perceptions of the republic's military requirements during the first decade of the nineteenth century. The military campaigns that enveloped Europe in the aftermath of that revolution saw the widespread adoption of light infantry tactics as a principal element of military strategy. That the light infantry had previously represented only a small part of the organizational structure of European armies had allowed, William Henry Harrison noted in 1810, the American strategy of "avoidance" some success during the Revolutionary War. The revolution in strategy and tactics that had accompanied the political transformation of France after 1789, Harrison and others argued, had also profoundly changed the military needs of the United States. Now, the "safety of a republic depend[ed] as much upon the quality of arms and discipline among its citizens, as upon the equality of rights."[15]

"An improvement in tactics, which gives a great superiority to the professional soldier who fights for conquest over the citizen who bears arms only in the defense of his country, is perhaps to be regretted," Harrison thought, but at the same time, it left free citizens with no alternative "but to perfect themselves in the same arts and discipline." Unfortunately for America, Harrison wrote, the commitment to an effective militia was largely confined to political rhetoric. "There is no political axiom more generally diffused amongst the people of the United States, than that which declares a militia to be the only proper defence of a republic." Still, few militia brigades existed capable of performing even the most common tactical maneuvers—exceptions being in the republic's larger towns where volunteer military associations inspired an interest in the martial arts entirely independent of the militia law.

Others concurred with Harrison's assessment of the nation's vulnerability. Thomas Baldwin reminded the Ancient and Honourable Artillery Company that a free society's liberties depended upon a "suitable posture of defence." "When a standing army is not kept," he told his audience, "it becomes more indispensably necessary, that the most vigorous and active part of the community . . . should be embodied, placed under the direction of proper officers, and instructed in the knowledge of military tactics." Baldwin's remarks were a call for reform, not a description of the nation's existing militia structure. Indeed, an anonymous essayist writing in the *National Intelligencer*, one of the most influential Jeffersonian newspapers of the day, wondered whether the ideological foundations of republicanism had not produced in America a military system incapable of guaranteeing national security. Founded upon a political ideology that looked to an armed citizenry to serve the nation during "emergencies," the United States found itself in a world where patriotism and numbers were no longer sufficient to win more than an occasional skirmish. "Experience shews every where whole nations falling an easy prey to troops inured to war, and led on by science as well as valor." A nation "attacked by disciplined and powerful invaders, or threatened by sedition" must be able to turn "its militia . . . into a regular army, or its independence and constitution are at stake."[16]

Essayists and pamphleteers agreed that the United States could not again, as it had during the Revolution, leave its defenses to a "militia serving in rotation or levies enrolled on short inlistments." The realities of modern warfare demanded new levels of discipline and order. "In our times," wrote David Humphreys in 1803, "armies are, in a certain sense machines—their action, reaction, momentum and effect, are subjects of calculations." Modern societies, argued Humphreys, "improved as they now are in the arts of attack and defence, [have] no alternative but a *standing army* or an *organized militia*."[17]

At least one essayist, writing in the aftermath of the Chesapeake Incident when rising Anglo-American tensions threatened a declaration of war, urged Americans to consider the former. Maximillian Godefroy, a veteran of the French army, used language reminiscent of Adam Smith and Joseph Priestley to argue that American security depended upon a recognition of the compatibility of military professionalism with the institutions of a free society. Godefroy believed that the republic's land forces held the key to an effective national defense system. Plans to expand the navy and to build a fleet of gunboats and a system of fortifications to protect the seacoast were militarily inadequate, too expensive, and too time consuming to meet the current national emergency. Nor, he argued, was the existing military establishment capable of repelling an invading European army. Part of the problem was the pervasive and illusory American belief that they, like the citizens of ancient Greece and Rome, could depend upon armies "composed of citizens suddenly enrolled, and led to action almost as soon as assembled." American citizens, warned Godefroy, neither resembled their ancient counterparts nor faced a comparable military threat. The Greeks fought barbarians unskilled in tactics and strategy, and Roman citizens were "neither mercantile, maritime, nor peaceful." A Roman was "restless, ambitious and ferocious, and from the very nature of his government, education, and amusements a soldier." The reverse was true in America. There, wrote Godefroy, "military talents are repulsed, and military ideas rejected, as useless." American political and social values simply discouraged military expertise.[18]

The irony, of course, was that the American republic now found itself in a world characterized by the growing sophistication of military skills. The "courage and good intentions" of the citizen militia would no longer suffice if America were again invaded by a European army. "At present, a war with certain European powers would as little resemble the war which terminated in your independence, as that war resembles those of Attila." The citizen-soldier may have played an important role in the defeat of the British armies after 1776, but since that time American society and war itself had changed dramatically. Developments in the deployment of light artillery and the bayonet and the growing sophistication of tactics and strategy made war a science "not [to] be guessed at by the ignorant, nor yet acquired by men of sense, without study and experience." American cities had grown, too, and the population had dispersed further into the countryside, making the former more difficult to defend and the latter more difficult to mobilize. If Americans continued to rely upon their militia to repel the "methodical maneuvers of enemies accustomed to war, and profoundly skilled in tactics," Godefroy feared that the republican foundation of their government might well be imperiled.[19]

America, urged Godefroy, should look to its militia only as a force of last resort. The nature of warfare demanded that and so did the structure of American society. "It can never be wise or politick, except in cases of the last extremity, to devote to the sanguinary field of Mars, a body of men, composed chiefly of heads of families, and persons attached by useful occupations to a fixed residence, whose loss to their families and to the community, no victory can remunerate." Specialization in the civil sector of society required the same in military affairs. A "free corps"—a body of professional soldiers organized as a skeletal legion so as to be easily expanded to full size by drafts from the militia during emergencies—could provide the military professionalism required of soldiers in the Napoleonic era. Encamped on the frontier and along the seacoast, it would provide a first line of defense cheaper than a system of fortification and more reliable than the untrained and inexperienced militia. Constantly afield, the corps would also serve as a training ground for the tactical and technical skills so important to modern warfare. In short, the free corps would provide the republic with "a body of troops, formed by discipline and habit, for dangerous, toilsome, secret and distant expeditions," and capable of becoming the core of an army able to defeat any force of professional soldiers in a long and arduous campaign.[20]

Most critics of the American military establishment during the first decade of the nineteenth century backed away from Godefroy's endorsement of military professionalism. While recognizing that the structure of modern society and the sophistication of contemporary tactics had altered the military needs of nations, they believed a well-organized militia most compatible with the ideological foundations of American republicanism. As David Humphreys noted, "With us, all should be soldiers as well as citizens." Repeatedly, writers warned of the dangers inherent in a military system that separated the responsibility for national defense from the functions of citizenship. Nevertheless, the citizen militia recommended in the Republican press and elsewhere had little in common with the decentralized system extant in America.

As had the Federalist proponents of militia reform in the previous decade, most commentators chose to merge a sensitivity for the growing complexity of modern warfare and society and a recognition of the national government's need to have access to a dependable emergency force with an appreciation for the republic's long-standing suspicion of standing

164   Creating a Peace Establishment

armies. The result was an assortment of recommendations for militia reform which, like the plan proposed by Henry Knox in 1790, urged the classification of the nation's militia by age as the best means to ensure national security. In its simplest manifestation, classification entailed little more than the imposition of more frequent training sessions for the nation's young men, its aim being only to develop a force capable of withstanding the initial thrusts of a foreign invader while giving valuable time for raising a regular army. Other proposals were more ambitious; one even envisioned a comprehensive militia system capable of replacing the regular army on the frontier during peacetime. These plans often included, as had the Knox plan, proposals for the establishment of military training camps and academies designed to instill both military discipline and republican virtues. In their most extreme form they urged that service in the national militia become a prerequisite for public office. Whatever the details prescribed, these proponents of militia reform stood together in agreeing that the structure of modern society and the sophistication of contemporary warfare required a reassessment of the assumptions supporting the existing militia structure.[21]

William Duane, the editor of the Philadelphia *Aurora* and one of the most persistent critics of American military preparedness, articulated as well as anyone the assumptions behind the continuing American unwillingness to abandon the militia for the military expertise offered by a professional army. Duane conceded that militia service had "become a matter of institution and positive law, rather than a habit or opinion." In part that was the result of the growing complexity of war. But it was also the consequence of the infusion of luxury and wealth into western European society that had followed the invention of the printing press, the discovery of America, and the rise of commerce. That understanding of the development of western society, borrowed of course from the political tracts of the radical Whigs, led Duane to link the rise of "new occupations, necessities, riches, and speculations" with the decline of "the practice of military exercises." In short, as money became the basis of exchange, the union of citizenship and military service that had ensured constitutional balance and political stability among free societies during the classical and feudal periods had been destroyed, making way for the rise of professional armies and the proliferation of political tyranny. For Duane, the lessons of history were inescapable. The nation that failed to provide itself with an armed and disciplined citizenry as it grew in wealth and economic complexity—by institutionalizing the citizen's obligation to perform militia service—faced the inevitable loss of its political freedom.[22]

The American republic was particularly vulnerable. Its growing wealth had made it an increasingly attractive target for external attack. At the same time, the republic had failed to develop a system of national defense capable of performing well in a modern war. The navy was too small, fortifications were too widely scattered, and the militia was too poorly disciplined and too inexperienced to provide an effective deterrent against surprise attack. Indeed, wrote Duane, Americans seemed bent on discouraging the cultivation of military skills. State governments had allowed their militias to deteriorate, and Congress had proven reluctant to legislate an effective national militia law. In his judgment the "current militia law seemed calculated to frustrate military discipline, to discourage patriotism, and to discredit [military] talents." With the renewal of hostilities between Britain and France and the growing likelihood that the United States would become involved in the conflict, the republic's very survival, he argued, depended upon the enactment of "some general law for enforcing an effective system of defence."[23]

Duane rejected out of hand any suggestion that the republic's interests might be best served by basing its military establishment around a core of professional troops. In a series of essays specifically refuting Godefroy's call for just such a force, he reminded Americans that the standing armies that supported the tyrannical governments of Europe had been created "when the holders of the soil ceased to be the armed defenders of the country." The small size of the free corps was immaterial. The introduction of fifty hired soldiers had provided the foundation for the huge army that supported the current oppressive government of Great Britain. The free corps could provide the same precedent and the same dangerous results. Representative government required a citizenry prepared by "skill and will" to defend it. "Any other system but militia, would be as fatal to the liberties of this country as any invading enemy could possibly be." Modern military maneuvers depended upon rigid discipline and tactical expertise; "the tactics of our revolution would not answer at the present times." But the former could be cultivated among the militia as easily as among the free corps, and the latter, Duane argued, was ultimately reducible to common sense. He was persuaded "that in the art of war, as in all other human affairs, there is a great deal more quackery among the professors than obscurity in the thing—and more common sense than the engrossers and retailers of worldly wisdom are willing to allow—or perhaps always comprehend."

Rejecting Godefroy's interpretation of the military history of the ancient republics, Duane claimed that the citizenries of Greece and Rome, "inspired by the love of liberty and their country, . . . were competent to repel and to resist for years the most profound and best disciplined armies and commanders of their times." The American militia could be expected to perform in a similar fashion. He warned Americans to be wary of plans to lift the burden of military service from the citizenry—Duane himself believed all men eighteen to forty-five should be enrolled in the active militia—and to be suspicious of claims that "vast scientific acquirements were indispensable to be competent to study tactics." Intrigue and deception had robbed free people of their liberties in the past. Only as long as "the citizens were the only soldiers" could the republic be secure from both external attack and internal intrigue. "It is for these solid reasons," concluded Duane, "that the whole wisdom and energy of the American nation should be directed to the perfection of that only system of safe and effective defence—a well organized, and well disciplined militia."[24]

The revival of militia plans reminiscent of Henry Knox's 1790 proposal embodied what was an attempt during the years before the War of 1812 to come to terms with the political ideology that had provided the basis for the Jeffersonian rise to political power and the realities of modern society and warfare. In a sense they represented a compromise between the divergent perceptions of the republic's military needs espoused by Priestley and Taylor. A professional military establishment was politically improbable, economically infeasible, and, some argued, militarily unnecessary. At the same time, the decentralized militia system implicit in Taylor's political theory was incompatible with the military needs of the national government and America's social and economic structure.

It was important, men like Duane believed, for America to prove wrong McHenry's claim that the militia could not satisfy the republic's military requirements. The ideological connotations of military professionalism demanded it. A classed militia system, as Knox had argued at the inception of the new national government, offered a means to institutionalize the citizen's obligation to serve the nation in arms. Regularly drilled in the complexities of war, such a militia promised to satisfy both the ideological demand for a citizen army and the political need for a militarily proficient force. Duane and others also agreed that only a national militia system could guarantee the level of military expertise understood to be essential for national security. The problem, of course, was that a national militia had been and would continue to be a political impossibility in America.

The Second Administration

The ideological considerations and institutional concerns outlined by Duane and the other proponents of an "organized militia" provided the context within which the Jefferson administration approached the increasingly urgent issue of military preparedness after 1805. With the renewal of hostilities in Europe threatening to draw the United States into the continuing conflict between Great Britain and France, Jefferson, along with Secretary of War Henry Dearborn and Secretary of the Navy Robert Smith, formulated during the autumn of 1805 a plan to class the militia by age. The president suggested the broad outlines of the plan in his annual message to Congress in December, along with an assortment of defense recommendations including funds for the improvement of coastal fortifications, the construction of gunboats, and the expansion of the seagoing navy.

The militia proposal, which was introduced on the Senate floor in January 1806, envisioned a milita composed of "every free, able-bodied white male citizen of the United States" between eighteen and forty-five years old. Each militia member would be assigned to one of four classes depending upon age. The junior class, men aged twenty-one to twenty-five, would bear the brunt of military service, being "liable to perform all active services within the United States, or the countries next adjacent, by tours of duty, not to exceed one year in any two." Members of the second class, twenty-six to thirty-five years old, would serve only in their own or adjoining states for tours not exceeding three months in a year. Men under twenty-one and over thirty-five (the minor and the senior classes) would be eligible for duty for the same period but only within their own state. Each class would be officered by men from its own ranks and exemptions from militia duty would be limited only to "religious scruples," though substitutes could be hired during times of actual mobilization.

The classification bill was structurally similar to the militia plan recommended by Henry Knox in 1790 and, like the latter, was designed to enable the national government "on any sudden emergency to call for the services of the younger portions [of the population], unencumbered with the old and those having families." It was, however, devoid of the detailed organizational and training apparatus that had helped defeat the Knox plan fifteen years earlier. Neither was it intended, as had been Knox's goal, as a means to centralize the military power of the citizenry in the hands of the national government. The Revolution of 1800 had promised an end to the centralization of power in the national government, and Jefferson remained reluctant to use militia reform as a means to expand federal prerogatives. The classed militia's function would be to provide "a competent number for offense or defence in any point where they may be wanted, and [to] give time for raising regular forces after the necessity of them shall become certain." The administration asked only that Congress impose on the state militia systems a selectivity and order that would add to the effectiveness and dependability of the militia when it was called into emergency service.[25]

The Senate passed the measure, but the bill never reached the House floor. A special committee chaired by Joseph Varnum recommended, and the House concurred, that it was "inexpedient to adopt measures for the classification or new organization of the militia." The reasons were numerous but ultimately reducible to two considerations, one constitutional and the other tactical—both of which ran contrary to the perception of national security implicit in the call for a classed militia. In the first place, Congress remained reluctant to alter the states' time-honored and ideologically significant control over the nation's militia. In the words of the congressional committee, "Congress did in the year 1792, pass an act [which] seems to embrace all the [constitutional] principles in the case delegated to Congress."

In a separate report assessing the nation's military capabilities, the Varnum committee also rejected the premise that the growing complexity of modern warfare necessitated a reconsideration of the institutional organization of the militia. It argued that American militia forces, often ill trained and usually supported by civilian governments in various states of disorganization, had fared well against Great Britain's trained regulars during the Revolutionary War, thanks to the patriotic sacrifices of the citizenry. The 1792 militia law, the establishment of stable constitutions at the state and national levels, and the presence of militia commanders, themselves veterans of the Revolutionary War, argued the committee, had rendered in recent years the nation's citizenry an even more formidable military force. Short of an actual invasion, which the committee agreed would require the enlistment of a regular army and not the reorganization of the militia, the existing militia structure could be expected to meet the nation's peacetime military requirements. Consequently, to satisfy the administration's concern about the nation's security, Congress passed legislation—in essence a renewal of the militia detachment act of 1803—providing the president access to one hundred thousand militia officers and men, organized through the structural apparatuses already existing in the states.[26]

Nevertheless, the administration remained committed to the classed militia idea. In messages to Congress and in private correspondence, Jefferson repeatedly urged that "nothing should be spared from this moment in putting our militia into the best condition possible." "Convinced that a militia of all ages promiscuously are entirely useless for distant service," he told James Madison in May 1807 that the "classification of our militia is now the essential thing the United States have to do." The nation needed to "transfer this service from the great Mass of our Militia to that portion of them to whose habits and enterprises active and distant service is most congenial." The volunteer corps legislation passed in 1807—to assuage concern that these units might become an extension of presidential power and influence, officers were to be appointed by the states and not the national government—was intended to accomplish that end. Nevertheless, Jefferson believed a classed militia would provide a force of greater size and dependability. The great armies of Europe could be deterred only by armies of equal strength and ability: "For these," he wrote in 1808, "we must depend on a classified militia . . . specially trained."[27]

Congress, however, remained uninterested in the plan. It debated and then rejected in January 1808 a modified militia classification scheme backed by the administration. Citing the reasons outlined in 1806, Congress once again preferred to grant the president access to one hundred thousand militiamen rather than alter the existing militia structure. Jefferson's parting request that Congress reform the militia with an eye to making it able to "repel a powerful enemy at every point of our territories exposed to invasion" also fell on deaf ears. A similar fate befell calls for militia reform issued by President James Madison during 1809 and 1810. Following the pattern set in 1806, congressional committees reported again and again, after having "carefully examined the subject, . . . that it would not be proper at this time, to make any alterations in the militia system of the United States."[28] Congress proved reluctant in 1810 even to authorize the continued use of the state-officered volunteer corps units, fearing an adverse effect on the existing militia structure.[29]

The only significant step taken during the prewar years toward making the militia the nation's principal defender during the "first moments of war" was legislation allocating two hundred thousand dollars annually for arming and equipping the "whole body of the Militia." But even that legislation was passed only after overcoming, on the one hand, concerns that the political independence of the citizenry and the constitutional prerogatives of the states might be undermined if the national government armed the militia and, on the other, the argument that the federal expenditures should be directed toward arming only the militia's most able soldiers.[30]

The deadlock between the executive and legislative branches over the militia reflected the ideological parameters within which the Jeffersonian leadership approached the nation's military requirements prior to the War of 1812. Cognizant of the ideological and constitutional implications of a militia force beyond the control of the states and committed to the belief that the existing militia structure was militarily sound, Congress refused to budge on militia reform. On the other hand, neither Jefferson nor his principal supporters in Congress successfully moved beyond the understanding of the nation's peacetime needs implicit in the classed militia. And, then, Republicans never perceived the classed militia as the vehicle for political and military centralization that was so important to Federalist militia planning. Whereas the Federalists, when confronted by a similar congressional reluctance to transform the militia into an effective national institution, began to look to the regular army and a nationally organized reserve force, the Republicans remained committed to transforming the militia into a reliable first line of national defense. The Jeffersonians never attempted to infuse into the ideological basis of American republicanism an understanding of the regular army as a principal part of the nation's peacetime military needs. A look at the debate sparked by legislation to triple the size of the regular army to over ten thousand men in 1808 makes that clear.

Confronted by an outspoken opposition committed to the axiom that the expansion of the regular army during peacetime was symptomatic of the social and political decay of a republican society, the administration's supporters in Congress explained the need for troops by pointing out that regular soldiers provided the only convenient means of garrisoning the nation's distant frontiers and extended coastlines. Repeatedly, advocates of the expanded peace establishment accepted their opponents' premise that it was "unwise in any nation . . . holding civil liberty in such high veneration . . . to relinquish their reliance on such a militia, and resort to regular military forces as their principal means of defence." But while the opposition used this premise to charge that the administration was embarking along a path of corruption and intrigue most recently followed by the Adams administration, proponents of administration policy contended that the expanded army was intended to supplement, not replace, the citizen militia.

The new troops were to be stationed in the most sparsely settled regions of the country, in areas where the population was "insufficiently numerous to defend themselves against the incursions of a foreign enemy, or the depredations of savage foe." Too small in number and too remotely located to pose a threat to civil liberties or to undermine the moral character of society, the expanded army would be an important addition to the nation's defenses while not challenging the primacy of the militia in the republic's peacetime establishment. It would protect "our frontiers, where there were no militia, and to which they could not be carried without great inconvenience to garrison fortifications, for which the militia are fitted neither by their discipline nor habits." The army then was a "necessary evil," a function of the demographic and geographic characteristics of a nation only recently doubled in size. "We only wish to reinforce the exposed points of attack," concluded one congressman, "mak[ing] these positions the rallying point; places of rendezvous for our militia."[31]

The point here is that the tone of the debate reflected the persistent influence of ideological tenets that looked to the citizen in arms to defend the nation against at least the initial thrusts of an invading force. Despite the theses posed by Joseph Priestley and Maximillian Godefroy, the expanded army was never explained as a reflection of the need to base the nation's peacetime military establishment around the capabilities of a professional military force. Indeed, the debate was remarkably devoid of any sense that the additional six thousand troops represented anything more than an addition to the nation's garrison force or at most a timely expansion of what some believed would most certainly become a wartime army. On the latter point, even the opposition conceded the unreliability and ineffectiveness of the militia during wartime and the necessity of regular soldiers to guarantee the order and discipline required during extended campaigns. They, however, demanded certain evidence of an impending invasion before supporting an expanded army. That the Jeffersonians failed to incorporate the logic of the moderate Whigs into their perception of the republic's military needs had important implications for the state of the nation's defenses on the eve of the War of 1812.

The Jeffersonians had come to power still burdened with the ideological baggage of their years in opposition. If they now sensed that a measure of military expertise was necessary for an effective peacetime establishment, they were intellectually incapable of supporting more than a militia classed by age. However, the ideology that drew the administration to the militia also prevented a majority in Congress from accepting even the minimal degree of military centralization implicit in the classed militia plans proposed by Jefferson. Thus, as Americans moved haltingly toward understanding that national security in a world dominated by armies trained in the increasingly complex science of military maneuvers and tactics demanded a peace establishment both well trained and responsive to national policy, they continued to rely on perceptions of constitutional balance and citizenship that had their origins in the works of men like Harrington, Sidney, Trenchard, and Burgh. Ironically, the ideological tenets that guided Republican perceptions of the nation's military needs in opposition and in power left the nation frighteningly vulnerable to external attack and dangerously ill prepared even for "the first moments of war."

10

Coda: A Call for Military Professionalism

War is an art, to attain perfection in which, much time and experience, particularly for officers, are necessary.
—John C. Calhoun, to the Speaker, House of Representatives, 12 December 1820, in *The Papers of John C. Calhoun*

The War of 1812 provided a poignant reminder of the new republic's failure to resolve the tension between ideology and policy that had plagued military considerations since its inception. Frantic efforts during the first six months of the Twelfth Congress to increase the nation's military capacity, including more than a dozen mobilization measures raising the army's authorized strength to just under thirty-six thousand men and the creation of a force of federal volunteers to number no more than thirty thousand men, reflected the impact of the ideological obstacles to military preparedness that had troubled Americans since the end of the Revolution. Simply put, the ideological and political divisions that had informed discussions of the military in American society since 1783 made an effective military response to mounting tensions with Great Britain impossible until war was at hand.

Congress and the Madison administration conceded that the militia's dispersed organizational structure and its inadequate level of training made it incapable of meeting the republic's wartime needs. The Republican leadership in Congress and the executive branch had little choice but to return to the long-standing American custom of relying on volunteers willing to serve lengthy enlistments to meet the exigencies of extended military campaigns. Unfortunately, few Americans were inspired to enlist in the army for the five-year term required or to enroll themselves for the eighteen-month tour with the volunteer units, this despite substantial land and monetary bounties provided for enlistment in either. Consequently, Congress was forced to authorize the president to call upwards of one hundred thousand militiamen for six months' service in the event future enlistments failed to materialize. By February 1813, nine months after war had been declared, enlistments had not markedly increased. The authorized strength of the regular army now numbered over fifty-eight thousand, but only a third of that number were under arms. More out of necessity than commitment, the republic turned to the militia to supplement its manpower needs, in the process leaving its fate in the hands of inexperienced regular officers, an assortment of untrained enlistees, and reluctant and undisciplined militia draftees.[1]

The performance of the republic's military hit its nadir in August 1814 when militia units fled before marauding British raiders near Bladensburg, Maryland, leaving the nation's capital unprotected and sending the Congress and the president scurrying into the Virginia countryside. If the war with Britain was a test of the republic's ability to survive, certainly the effectiveness of its military institutions continued to raise questions about the viability of a republican government in the modern world. Nevertheless, Congress refused to embrace a system of compulsory federal service which would have provided the nation with much-needed long-serving troops as well as the institutional centralization necessary for the effective coordination of manpower needs and strategic planning through the broad extent of the American republic. Such a plan, one developed by Secretary of War James Monroe in the fall of 1814, was rejected in favor of a continuation of the current ineffective recruiting system plus an increase in the land bounty offered new recruits. Few in Congress doubted the need for regulars during wartime, but fewer still would endorse Monroe's plan, which would have granted to the national government directly the power to organize and mobilize the nation's citizenry outside the existing militia structure. Congress was simply unwilling to accept Monroe's argument that the "commonwealth has the right to the service of all its citizens." The idea of a national government with the power to compel the citizenry to military service carried with it assumptions about political corruption unacceptable to congressmen still influenced by the ideological axioms that had sustained the American Revolution. Faced with the need to accept the expansion of the national government's powers in order to ensure military effectiveness, Congress declined. As a result, only the timely cessation of hostilities—coming within months after the decision to continue the system of bonuses and bounties to encourage enlistments—stopped the further degeneration of the army and the possible destruction of the American republic.[2]

Peace brought the immediate reduction of the regular army to ten thousand men. It also ushered in a general disinterest in the problems of military preparedness and effectiveness that had proven so chronic in the republic. There were those, however, among them John C. Calhoun—later secretary of war during the Monroe administration—who saw the cessation of hostilities as an opportunity to reassess the organizational and ideological foundations of the republic's military establishment. For Calhoun, the War of 1812 demonstrated once again the state-controlled militia's inability to provide effective officers and well-trained men able to meet the nation's wartime needs. Sensing that the militia would long remain the preserve of the states, he urged that the regular army become the source for the discipline and leadership needed to train and lead recruits quickly and effectively should the nation again be provoked to war. Calhoun believed that regular soldiers were necessary not only to meet the demands of extended campaigns but also as an essential part of the republic's peacetime military establishment.

In the aftermath of the War of 1812, Calhoun looked initially to the militia—better trained through an improved system of military academies and more systematically organized—to fulfill the nation's peacetime requirements.[3] But after watching Congress reject two postwar attempts by President Madison to secure a thorough reorganization of the militia, including the defeat of yet another plan to class the militia by age, Calhoun was prepared upon becoming Monroe's secretary of war to organize the nation's peace establishment around the principle of military professionalism. In December 1818 he justified the maintenance of a ten-thousand-man regular army, as Adam Smith might have, on the grounds that the nation's greater wealth, population, and size necessitated a larger regular force. Americans had long considered "a standing army . . . dangerous to the liberty of the country," conceded Calhoun, but he was quick to remind Congress that even the most zealous advocates of the militia had come to recognize that a "standing army, to a limmitted [sic] extent, is necessary" for national defense. A month later, he urged the House of Representatives to base the number of cadets at West Point on the nation's potential wartime needs instead of its peacetime requirements.

Calhoun understood that the nation would never support a peacetime army large enough to meet the expanded military burdens of war, and so he sought to create a body of regular and reserve officers capable of providing the leadership in an army placed on a wartime footing. Two years later, under congressional pressure to reduce the army from ten thousand to six thousand men, Calhoun clarified his thoughts on the nation's peacetime needs and integrated them into a peace establishment plan based on the assumption that "a standing Army in peace, in the present improved state of the military science, is an indispensable preparation . . . to resist with success its [war's] calamities and dangers."[4]

Calhoun contended that the nation's peace establishment should be organized with an eye to the army's wartime responsibilities. "The organization of the Army, ought to be such," he wrote, "as to enable the Government, at the commencement of hostilities to obtain a regular force, adequate to the emergencies of the country, properly organized and prepared for actual service." The militia having proven unable to meet the country's military needs while regulars were being trained and organized for long-term service, Calhoun hoped to organize the regular peace establishment so that the only difference between it and the wartime army would be size.

Calhoun proposed that the army's staff organization be kept intact during peacetime. Habits and procedures developed by staff officers during peace would ensure an effective and efficient wartime administration. Calhoun also wanted the army's battalion and regimental organizations, though only in skeletal form, retained during peacetime. Understaffed line units would require only additional manpower to be prepared for war. Had his plan been enacted, the army could have been doubled in size from just over six thousand men to just under 12,000 without adding a single officer; the addition of only 288 officers would have allowed for the tripling of the regular army's size without adding even an additional company to the army's administrative structure.

Of course, this organizational scheme would have required a far greater proportion of officers to men during peacetime than during war. That requirement, however, fit into Calhoun's overall perception of the function of the peace establishment. Besides providing the organizational foundation for an effective mobilization, "the military establishment in peace," in Calhoun's view, "ought to . . . create and perpetuate military skill and experience, so that, at all times, the country may have at its command a body of officers, sufficiently numerous, and well instructed in every branch of duty, both of the line and staff." Admittedly, such an arrangement would be costly, but it would eliminate the confusion and disorder that hindered mobilization during the War of 1812 when entirely new field units and organizational staffs had to be added to the army. Besides, as long as the country preferred not to keep a substantial number of enlisted men in the ranks of its peacetime army, a disproportionate number of officers would always be needed to train troops at the commencement of hostilities.[5]

The secretary of war's recommendation that the nation's peacetime security rest with an expandable professional army was far from original. Organizationally, the idea dated back to the peace establishment plans put forward by Washington's advisers in the aftermath of the Revolutionary War. Certainly his contention that "not [even] all the zeal, courage and patriotism of our militia" would protect the nation against invading regulars offered no new insights into the republic's wartime needs. Soldiers and statesmen had been making that claim since independence was declared in 1776. Neither did his proposal that the United States depend upon military professionalism as a means, "at the commencement of hostilities, to obtain a regular force, adequate to the emergencies of the country" represent an original contribution to the debate over the republic's military needs during war and peace. Some Federalists had had a similar goal in mind in the last months of the eighteenth century; they, of course, saw their plan blocked by a political and ideological environment that still associated military professionalism with moral decay, political corruption, and governmental instability.

What was new and very significant was that Calhoun's proposals for the nation's peace establishment brought the military theory of the Republican party's executive leadership into line with views of national security that had their origins in the writings of Daniel Defoe and Adam Smith and had been promoted by a small number of political and military thinkers in America since the 1780s. The party of Jefferson, long the defender of classical perceptions of the relationship between the citizen in arms and the freedom and security of a republican nation, allied itself for the first time with the proposition that the regular army could best fulfill the responsibilities vested in the military arm of the American constitution.

By repudiating the American militia tradition and by embracing the moderate Whig view that only professional military institutions could meet the demands of national security during war and peace in the modern world, Calhoun and the Monroe administration provided what should have been the necessary incentive to clear away the last major obstacle to the reconciliation of ideology and policy that had informed the evolution of the nation's military institutions. The ideological assumptions of revolutionary republicanism would no longer play an important role in the debate over the republic's military requirements. Still, not even in the nationalist-minded Era of Good Feelings was Congress willing to create the professional structure proposed by the secretary of war. The reasons, though, had less to do with the ideological considerations that had blocked earlier plans and much more to do with the changing world in which the republic found itself.[6]

In 1821, with memories of the second war for independence fading and as the United States entered the era of "free security" that characterized much of the nineteenth century, Congress reduced the regular army from ten thousand to six thousand men. It did not, however, implement the expandable army plan.[7] Instead, the army was relegated once again to the roles of frontier constabulary and guardian of the nation's arsenals and coastal fortifications—a role it had performed since 1796 and would continue to perform through most of the nineteenth century. Nevertheless, Calhoun's proposal, as Russell Weigley has pointed out, proved a permanent legacy. Nurtured by the army itself through the nineteenth century, it later became the centerpiece of Emory Upton's military reform program.[8]

That would not have been possible, of course, if it had not been for the basic change that had taken place in the American understanding of the military's place in a free society during the early-national period—a change, the result of which was embodied in Calhoun's expandable army plan. By 1826 the *North American Review* could editorialize that "the time has past [*sic*] in the United States, when any just fears are entertained by such a standing army, as may be required by the present system of general defence." Gone was the sense that military policy reflected the intrigue of "particular Administrations or parties." By the end of the first quarter of the nineteenth century, the army had come to be seen as a "settled system, founded on a true estimation of the permanent security and welfare of the country." No longer the agent of ambitious politicians anxious to undermine the rights secured during the war for independence, the American army had become "as much an institution of the country as the Constitution itself."[9]

Notes

Preface

1. The following is a composite definition drawn from David E. Apter, "Ideology and Discontent," 16–18; Clifford Geertz, "Ideology as a Cultural System," 47, 63–65, 71–72; J. G. A. Pocock, "Machiavelli, Harrington, and English Political Ideologies in the Eighteenth Century," 549; David W. Minar, "Ideology and Political Behavior," 327–30; Harry M. Johnson, "Ideology and the Social System," 7:77–83; Robert E. Shalhope, "Toward a Republican Synthesis," 78n; Bernard Bailyn, "The Central Themes of the American Revolution," 10–12.

Chapter 1

1. Russell F. Weigley, *History of the United States Army*, 4–9. Gary Huxford, "Origins of the American Military Tradition Reconsidered," 123. John Shy, *Toward Lexington*, 3–4, 44. Timothy H. Breen, "English Origins and New World Development," 76–81, 91–96. Douglas Edward Leach, *Arms for Empire*, 9–23. Darrett B. Rutman, "The Virginia Company and Its Military Regime," 1–20. *Backgrounds of Selective Service*, 1:32–39. Louis Morton, "The Origins of American Military Policy," 76–79. John Shy, "A New Look at the Colonial Militia," 176–77, 179. Herbert L. Osgood, *The American Colonies in the Seventeenth Century*, 1:496–526, 2:375–400. Timothy H. Breen, "Persistent Localism," 22–23. Morrison Sharp, "Leadership and Democracy in Early New England Defense," 250–60. Walter Millis, ed., *American Military Thought*, xvii–xix. Arthur A. Ekirch, Jr., *The Civilian and the Military*, 5–7. Jack P. Greene, *The Quest for Power*, 299.

2. Marvin A. Kreidberg and Merton G. Henry, *The History of Military Mobilization in the United States Army, 1775–1945*, 7–8. Morton, "American Military Policy," 80–82. Sharp, "Leadership and Democracy," 244–45. Leach, *Arms for Empire*, 21. Breen, "Persistent Localism," 22–23. Shy, *Toward Lexington*, 6–14. John Shy, "Colonial Militia," 177–81. John Shy, "The American Military Experience," 212–14. Frederick P. Todd, "Our National Guard," 74–82. Weigley, *United States Army*, 12.

3. *Statutes at Large*, 3:17–22, 82–83, 99–101, 119–21, 126–28. *Colonial Laws of New York from the Year 1664 to the Revolution*, 1:259, 272–74, 283–85, 315–16, 339, 369. *Charters and General Laws of the Colony and Province of Massachusetts Bay*, 229, 735, 737–40. Records of the States of the United States (hereafter cited as RSUS), Massachusetts, B [session laws], reel 1, unit 7, 229–30.

4. RSUS, Massachusetts, B, reel 1, unit 8, 351–54; unit 9, 402–4. *Backgrounds of*

Selective Service, vol. 2, part 6, Massachusetts, 172–73, 175–77, 178–80, 205–7, 214–18. *Colonial Laws of New York*, 3:595–98, 4:66–70, 167–73.

5. *Statutes at Large*, 4:33, 37, 5:94–96, 438–40, 6:115, 465–66, 525–28, 7:14–16, 31, 57–58, 70–72.

6. Shy, *Toward Lexington*, 40–44. Shy, "Colonial Militia," 179–81. Pauline Maier, *From Resistance to Revolution*, 16–18.

7. Slave patrol provisions were a regular part of militia legislation in the eighteenth-century South. On Maryland, see Osgood, *American Colonies*, 2:382–85. On South Carolina, see RSUS, South Carolina, B, reel 1a, unit 1, n.p.; reel 2a, unit 1, n.p.; reel 3, unit 1, n.p.; reel 2b, unit 2, n.p.; reel 3, unit 2, n.p. On Virginia, see *Statutes at Large*, 4:202. This act, passed in 1727, was continued regularly until 1748. It was revived in 1753 (ibid., 6:350).

8. Shy, *Toward Lexington*, 40. *Colonial Laws of New York*, 1:231–36, 611, 706, 3:3–14, 69–70, 148–50, 168–70. *General Laws of Massachusetts*, 262, 339–41, 432–44. RSUS, Massachusetts, B, reel 2, unit 1, 339–40. In Charleston, S.C., the night watch varied from a para-professional police force, e.g., in 1712, RSUS, South Carolina, B, reel 1a, unit 4, n.p., and in 1736, ibid., reel 2b, unit 3, n.p., to a more militia-based force, e.g. [1698], reel 1a, unit 3, n.p., which was updated periodically through 1707. Osgood, *American Colonies*, 1:509.

9. For a provocative account of the origins of the insular nature and tradition of the New England militia, see Breen, "English Origins," 74–96. Breen, "Persistent Localism," 22–23.

10. Exceptions to this general trend were in cases of total war, like the Louisburg campaign (1745), which had a very high percentage of Massachusetts men. Shy, "Colonial Militia," 181–85. Sharp, "Leadership and Democracy," 244–45. Kreidberg and Henry, *Mobilization*, 7–8. Stanley Pargellis, *Lord Loudoun in North America*, 83–100. Benjamin Quarles, "The Colonial Militia and Negro Manpower," 643–52. Richard B. Morris, *Government and Labor in Early America*, 282–93. Abbot E. Smith, *Colonists in Bondage*, 279–83. See also the military legislation cited above.

11. Leach, *Arms for Empire*, 271–79. Greene, *Quest for Power*, 297–309. Shy, "Colonial Militia," 181–85. Morton, "American Military Policy," 80–81. Maier, *From Resistance to Revolution*, 16–17. Richard Buel, Jr., "Democracy and the American Revolution," 175.

12. Leach, *Arms for Empire*, 82–91, 279–82. Alan Rogers, *Empire and Liberty*, 14, 21. Shy, "Military Experience," 212. Shy, *Toward Lexington*, 5–6, 14.

13. Pargellis, *Lord Loudoun*, 1–44, 79–80. Rogers, *Empire and Liberty*, 21, 51–58.

14. Pargellis, *Lord Loudoun*, 187–210. Bernard Bailyn, ed., *Pamphlets of the American Revolution, 1750–1776*, 1:702–3. Rogers, *Empire and Liberty*, 51–58, 75–89. Shy, *Toward Lexington*, 26–39. Jack P. Greene, "The South Carolina Quartering Dispute, 1757–1758," 193–204. Clarence E. Carter, "The Significance of Military Office in America, 1763–1775," 475–88.

15. Pargellis, *Lord Loudoun*, 103–24. Shy, *Toward Lexington*, 36, 99–100, 148–90, 250–58. Rogers, *Empire and Liberty*, 59–74 passim.

16. James Otis, *The Rights of the British Colonies Asserted and Proved*, in Bailyn, ed., *Pamphlets*, 1:451, 458–59, 468–70. See also Shy, *Toward Lexington*, 140–48; Eric

Robson, *The American Revolution*, 49–50. *Consideration upon the Rights of the Colonists to the Privileges of British Subjects, Introduced by a Brief Review of the Rise and Progress of British Liberty, and Concluded with Some Remarks upon the Present Alarming Situation.* . . . No doubt a few radical voices had already perceived the military presence as a threat to civil liberties. See Samuel Downer to New York Sons of Liberty, 21 July 1766, in Maier, *From Resistance to Revolution*, 147. See also ibid., 145–58. Samuel Adams to Christopher Gadsden, 11 December 1766, and S. Adams to Dennys de Berdt, 16 December 1766, *Writings of Samuel Adams*, 1:108–11, 112–13.

17. Shy, *Toward Lexington*, 140, 277–79, 348–59. *Four Dissertations, on the Reciprocal Advantages of a Perpetual Union between Great Britain and Her American Colonies*, essays 1 and 3.

18. Otis, *Rights*, in Bailyn, *Pamphlets*, 1:458–59, 468–70. Thomas Pownall, *The Exercise for the Militia of the Province of the Massachusetts-Bay*, 91–95.

19. For Pownall's intellectual ties with radical Whiggery, see John Shy, "The Spectrum of Imperial Possibilities," 46, 65–66.

Chapter 2

1. James Harrington, *James Harrington's Oceana*, 9–10, 16, 50–53. J. G. A. Pocock, "Machiavelli, Harrington, and English Political Ideologies in the Eighteenth Century," 553–55. J. G. A. Pocock, "James Harrington and the Good Old Cause," 46. Lance G. Banning, *The Jeffersonian Persuasion*, 25–33, 51–53. J. G. A. Pocock, "Civil Humanism and Its Role in Anglo-American Thought," 85–94. C. B. Macpherson, *The Political Theory of Possessive Individualism*, 160–93. Fera S. Fink, *The Classical Republicans*, 1–27, 52–68. J. G. A. Pocock, *Machiavellian Moment*, parts 1 and 2. Douglass G. Adair, "The Intellectual Origins of Jeffersonian Democracy," 65–80, 93–108.

2. Harrington, *Oceana*, 64–65, 78–85, 176–77. Fink, *Classical Republicans*, 73–80. See also Marchamont Nedham, *The Excellency of a Free State* (London, 1656), originally published in 1652, and Sir Henry Vane, *A Healing Question*, in Bernard Schwartz, ed., *The Bill of Rights*, 1:33–34, for similar reasoning about citizenship. Pocock, "James Harrington," 36–39.

3. Harrington, *Oceana*, 48–49. Fink, *Classical Republicans*, 69–70. Pocock, "English Political Ideologies," 559–62, 566–67, 569–71. Pocock, "James Harrington," 46. Pocock, *Machiavellian Moment*, 410–16.

4. Algernon Sidney, *Discourses Concerning Government*, 113–15 and passim. Caroline Robbins, "Algernon Sidney's *Discourses Concerning Government*," 285–87. Robert Molesworth, *An Account of Denmark, as It Was in the Year of 1692*, 42–46. Andrew Fletcher, *A Discourse of Government with Relation to Militias*, in *The Political Works of Andrew Fletcher*, 11–16. The same view of history was shared by the Earl of Shaftesbury, the author, probably John Locke, of *A Letter from a Person of Quality to His Friend in the Country* (1675), and Andrew Marvell, *An Account of the Growth of Popery and Arbitrary Government in England* (1677). Pocock, "Civic Humanism," 94–95. Pocock, "English Political Ideologies," 563–64. Banning, *Jeffersonian Per-*

suasion, 36–53. J. R. Western, *The English Militia in the Eighteenth Century*, 92–93. H. Trevor Colbourn, *The Lamp of Experience*, 21–56.

5. Sidney, *Discourses*, 113–15. Henry Neville, *Plato Redivivus or, A Dialogue Concerning Government* in *Two English Republican Tracts: Plato Redivivus or a Dialogue Concerning Government (c. 1681) by Henry Neville [and] An Essay Upon the Constitution of the Roman Government (c. 1699) by Walter Moyle*, 124–26. Fink, *Classical Republicans*, 129–37, 145–59. Pocock, "English Political Ideologies," 563–67. Robbins, "Sidney," 268–73. Fink, *Classical Republicans*, 149–69.

6. Fletcher, *Discourse of Government*, 39–42. Lois G. Schwoerer, "The Literature of the Standing Army Controversy, 1697–1699," 187–93, 197–201. Schwoerer, *"No Standing Armies!"* 178–79. Caroline Robbins, *The Eighteenth Century Commonwealthman*, 103–5. E. Arnold Miller, "Some Arguments Used by English Pamphleteers, 1697–1700, Concerning a Standing Army," 306–13. Western, *English Militia*, 77–94. Pocock, "English Political Ideologies," 572–73.

7. John Trenchard, *An Argument Shewing That a Standing Army Is Inconsistent with a Free Government and Absolutely Destructive to the Constitution of the English Monarchy*, 1:7–8, 10–13. Fletcher, *Discourse of Government*, 6–9, 39–42.

8. Trenchard, *An Argument*, 7, 13. Fletcher, *Discourse of Government*, 11–16, 31–35. Walter Moyle, *An Essay on Lacedaemonian Government*, in Moyle, *The Whole Works of Walter Moyle*, 49–77; and Moyle, *An Essay Upon the Constitution of the Roman Government*, in *Two English Republican Tracts*, especially 223, 228–29. Also Robbins's discussion of Moyle in *Two English Republican Tracts*, 21–33. Molesworth, *An Account of Denmark*, 42–46, 48–73, 75–98, 123–37, 224–25, 258–68. For Molesworth's impact in America, see Caroline Robbins, "'When It Is That Colonies May Turn Independent,'" 231–42.

9. John Trenchard, *A Short History of Standing Armies in England* (1698), 1:57–58. Fletcher, *Discourse of Government*, 31–37, 39–42, 68–69. Trenchard, *An Argument*, 15–17, 19–22, 27–29, 38–40. See also note 5.

10. Fletcher, *Discourse of Government*, 45–65. John Toland, *The Militia Reform'd, or an Easy Scheme of Furnishing England with a Constant Land-Force* (1698), 2:594–613.

11. Fletcher, *Discourse of Government*, 42–44. Toland, *Militia Reform'd*, 604. Western, *English Militia*, 93.

12. John Trenchard and Thomas Gordon, *Cato's Letters, or Essays on Liberty, Civil and Religious, and other Important Subjects*. For the relationship of free states and standing armies, see particularly letters 18, 25, 65, 94, 95. Banning, *Jeffersonian Persuasion*, 53–59. Bernard Bailyn, *The Ideological Origins of the American Revolution*, 35–36. For the views of Lord Bolingbroke, see Isaac Kramnick, *Bolingbroke and His Circle*. For similar developments in French Enlightenment thought relative to standing armies and citizen militias, see Montesquieu, *The Spirit of the Laws*, 1:98–99. Francis Hutcheson, *A System of Moral Philosophy*, in the *Collected Works of Francis Hutcheson* (1755) 2:323–25. *A System of Moral Philosophy* was originally published, posthumously, in 1755. See also Robbins, "Francis Hutcheson," 214–51 passim. William Blackstone, *Commentaries on the Laws of England*, 1:143–44, 408–15. Lawrence Delbert Cress, "Radical Whiggery on the Role of the Military," 52–53.

13. Oscar Handlin and Mary Handlin, "James Burgh and American Revolu-

tionary Theory," 43–47. Banning, *Jeffersonian Persuasion*, 60–62.

14. James Burgh, *Political Disquisitions*, 2:341, 359–60, 390–92, 398–400, 402, 424–25, 430–32, 441–42, 463–65. In analyzing the merits of the militia, Burgh quotes Blackstone, Molesworth, Trenchard, and Bolingbroke.

15. Ibid., 2:344–45, 374, 397–98, 406–7.

16. Ibid., 2:343–44, 348–53, 389, 432, 438–39, 443.

17. Ibid., 2:344–45, 374.

18. Schwoerer, "Standing Army Controversy," 194–95, 203–7.

19. Daniel Defoe, *A Brief Reply to the History of Standing Armies in England*, 7–14. *The Arguments against a Standing Army Rectified . . .* , 1–13. *The Case of Disbanding the Army at Present*, 1–5. *Some Queries Concerning the Disbanding of the Army*, 1–5. Defoe, *Some Reflections on a Pamphlet*, 17. John Somers, *A Letter, Ballancing the Necessity of Keeping a Land-force . . .* , 2–7. Defoe, *An Argument Shewing, That a Standing Army, with Consent of Parliament is Not Inconsistent with a Free Government* (1698), 39–41.

20. Defoe, *An Argument*, 36–39, 41–50. Defoe, *Brief Reply*, 5–6, 14–22. Somers, *Letter, Ballancing*, 14. *Some Queries*, 1–5. *An Argument Proving That a Small Number of Regulated Forces . . .* , 9–14.

21. Defoe, *Some Reflections*, 16. Defoe, *Brief Reply*, 14. Defoe, *Reflections on the Short History of Standing Armies in England*, 23–24. Somers, *Letter, Ballancing*, 7, 11. *Some Queries*, 5. *A Small Number of Regulated Forces*, 17.

22. Somers, *Letter, Ballancing*, 7–13. *A Small Number of Regulated Forces*, 15. *The Argument against a Standing Army Discussed*, 8–12.

23. Defoe, *Some Reflections*, 12–13, 16–22. Defoe, *Brief Reply*, 14. *Case of Disbanding the Army*, 5–7. *Some Queries*, 6–8. *A Small Number of Regulated Forces*, 15–16. Somers, *Letter, Ballancing*, 7–8.

24. *Parliamentary History of England*, 10:375–534 passim.

25. Adam Smith, *An Inquiry into the Nature and Causes of the Wealth of Nations*, 653–56, 658.

26. Ibid., 656–59.

27. Ibid., 659–60.

28. Ibid., 661–65.

29. Ibid., 665–66.

30. Ibid., 666–67.

31. Ibid., 667–68.

Chapter 3

1. Handlin and Handlin, "James Burgh," 38–47. Schwoerer, "Standing Army Controversy," 210. Robert E. Shalhope, "Toward a Republican Synthesis," 49–52. Robbins, "Francis Hutcheson," 231–42. Caroline Robbins, "The Strenuous Whig, Thomas Hollis of Lincoln's Inn," 268–73. David Lundberg and Henry F. May, "The Enlightened Reader in America," charts following p. 271. Colbourn, *Lamp of Experience*, 3–20, 199–232 passim. Bailyn, *Ideological Origins*, 35–36. Pocock, "English Political Ideologies," 573.

2. Lundberg and May, "Enlightened Reader," charts following p. 271.

3. Maier, *From Resistance to Revolution*, 42–46. Banning, *Jeffersonian Persuasion*, 70–83. Pocock, "Civic Humanism," 97–98. Bernard Bailyn, *The Origins of American Politics*, 54–56. Bailyn, *Ideological Origins*, 22–93. Bailyn, "The Central Themes of the American Revolution," 26–31. Buel, "Democracy and the Revolution," 165–90. Edmund S. Morgan, "The Puritan Ethic and the American Revolution," 6–7.

4. Shy, *Toward Lexington*, 204–23. Staughton Lynd, *Anti-Federalism in Dutchess County, New York*, 37–54. Gen. Gage to Sec. Conway, 15 July 1766, in *A Collection of Interesting, Authentic Papers, Relating to the Dispute between Great Britain and America*, 101–2. Maier, *From Resistance to Revolution*, 16–18.

5. Hiller B. Zobel, *The Boston Massacre*, 82–86. Shy, *Toward Lexington*, 294–303. Bailyn, *Ideological Origins*, 112–19. John R. Alden, *General Gage in America*, 156–64. Resolutions of a Convention of Towns and Districts of Massachusetts, 22 September 1768, printed in the *Boston Chronicle*, 26 September–5 October 1768. See also Josiah Quincy to John Eagleson, 15 September 1768, in *Memoir of the Life of Josiah Quincy, Junior, of Massachusetts*, 16–17.

6. Resolves of the Boston Town Meeting, 12 September 1768, printed in the *New York Journal*, 24 September 1768. Resolutions of the Convention of 22 September 1768, *Boston Chronicle*, 25 September–5 October 1768. Adams's comments appeared in the *Boston Gazette*, 19, 26 December 1768. [Samuel Adams], *An Appeal to the World*. Massachusetts House of Representatives Resolve of 1 July 1769, in the *New York Journal*, 13 July 1769. Massachusetts House to Governor Bernard, 17 July 1769, in *New York Journal*, 27 July 1769. The Boston Town Meeting Instructions to their Delegates to the Massachusetts House, 11 May 1769, *New York Journal*, 25 May 1769.

7. Speaker of the Massachusetts House of Representatives to Dennys de Berdt, agent for Massachusetts, 12 January 1768. These sentiments were echoed in petitions to the king and letters to Shelburne, Conway, Rockingham, Camden, and Chatham, written by the House during January and February 1768. These letters are in *True Sentiments of America*, 5–82. Among those composing the letters were Cushing, Otis, S. Adams, Colonel Otis, and Hancock (see William Tudor, *The Life of James Otis of Massachusetts*, 292). The Boston Town Meeting Instructions to their Representatives in the Assembly, June 1768, in the *New York Journal*, 30 June 1768. On the corruption of society through the proliferation of royal officials, see Morgan, "Puritan Ethic," 6–7. Oliver M. Dickerson, comp., *Boston under Military Rule [1768–1769] as Revealed in a Journal of the Times*, 4–5, 13, 43–57, 60–62, 64, 65, 74–75, 123. The "Journal of the Times" was written in Boston, but usually appeared in the *New York Journal* and *Philadelphia Pennsylvania Chronicle* before reaching the pages of the *Boston Evening Post*. Only Dickinson's *Pennsylvania Farmer* was more widely reprinted in the colonies and in England. The authors probably included Samuel Adams, Henry Knox, Benjamin Edes, publisher of the *Boston Evening Post*, William Greenleaf, an employee of Edes, Isaiah Thomas, later editor of the *Massachusetts Spy*, and William Cooper, the town clerk of Boston (ibid., viii–ix). [Adams], *Appeal*; and the public resolves and newspaper essays cited in note 6. De Berdt to Thomas Cushing, 1 June and 1 November 1769, in *Letters of Dennys de Berdt, 1757–1770*, 375, 382. Samuel Cooper to Thomas Pownall, 18

February, 11 May 1769, 2 July 1770, "Letters of Samuel Cooper to Thomas Pownall, 1769–1777," 304–5, 306, 319. Shy, *Toward Lexington*, 303–20. Zobel, *Boston Massacre*, 96–135. Bailyn, *Ideological Origins*, 144–59.

8. Massachusetts House to Governor Bernard, 15 June 1769, in *New York Journal*, 29 June 1769. *Boston Gazette*, 25 July 1768. Samuel Adams in ibid., 5, 26 December 1768, 19 February 1769. Massachusetts House Resolution, 1 July 1769, in *New York Journal*, 13 July 1769. Circular letter of the Boston Selectmen to the Selectmen of the Towns of Massachusetts, 14 September 1768, in ibid., 29 September 1768. Boston Town Meeting Petition to the Crown, summer 1769, in ibid., 3 August 1769. Declaration of the Town of Boston, 5 May 1769, in *Writings of Samuel Adams*, 1:349–52. Charles Thomson to Benjamin Franklin, 26 November 1769, *Papers of Charles Thomson*, 2:22–23. Dickerson, comp., *Journal of the Times*, 79. Shy, *Toward Lexington*, 378.

9. Dickerson, comp., *Journal of the Times*, 8, 9, 23, 39–40, 43, 47, and throughout. Adams's comments appeared in the *Boston Gazette*, 17 October and 12 December 1768. Samuel Cooper to Thomas Pownall, 18 February 1769, "Letters," 305. In the *Boston Gazette*, 8 February 1769, an anonymous commentator argued that the moral corruption of the British army was grossly exaggerated, the result of the misdeeds of a few "silly boys, fools, and madmen" carried out at the expense of the "honor, wisdom and benevolence" of the rest of the British army.

10. Shy, *Toward Lexington*, 277–90; Lawrence Delbert Cress, "The Standing Army, the Militia, and the New Republic," 96–108.

11. Massachusetts House of Representatives' response to Lieutenant Governor William Hutchinson's address to the opening of the 1770 legislative session, 7 April 1770, in Tudor, *Otis*, 371–74. Boston Town Committee to Diverse Gentlemen in London, 12 March 1770, *New York Journal*, 5 April 1770. A letter from Boston printed in the *New York Journal*, 12 April 1770. A letter from the *London Gazette*, 23 April 1770, printed in *New York Journal*, 26 July 1770. Cooper to Pownall, 26 March 1770, "Letters," 317–18. James Bowdoin, Joseph Warren, and Samuel Pemberton, *A Short Narrative of the Horrid Massacre in Boston*, 5–13. *An Account of a Late Military Massacre, or the Consequence of Quartering Troops in a Populous Town*, 1–2. Sermons delivered in commemoration of the Boston Massacre in 1771, 1772, and 1773 in Hezekiah Niles, ed., *Principles and Acts of the Revolution in America*, 17–37 passim.

12. Essays by Timothy Pickering in the Salem *Essex Gazette*, 31 January 1769, 21 February 1769, and in the *Boston Gazette*, 27 January 1772. Simeon Howard, *A Sermon Preached*, 40–41. Samuel Stillman, *A Sermon Preached*, 20–28. Nathaniel Robbins, *Jerusalem's Peace Wished*, 14–23. On the shift to radical Whig rhetoric in the Artillery Sermons, see Huxford, "Origins," 122–23. See Philip Davidson, *Propaganda and the American Revolution, 1763–1783*, 209, on the expanded influence of sermons when reprinted in pamphlets or the press.

13. Salem *Essex Gazette*, 31 January, 21 February 1769, and *Boston Gazette*, 21 September 1772. Ronald L. Boucher, "The Colonial Militia as a Social Institution," 125–28. Stillman, *A Sermon Preached*, 20–28. Robbins, *Jerusalem's Peace*, 14–23. Howard, *A Sermon Preached*, 22–30, 40–42. Jeremy Belknap, *A Sermon on Military Duty*, 7.

14. Howard, *A Sermon Preached*, 25–30.
15. Niles, ed., *Principles and Acts*, 17–37.
16. Ibid., 38–42. John Lathrop, *A Sermon Preached*, 1–27 and 30–39. See also Elisha Fish, *The Art of War Lawful and Necessary*, 2–17.
17. Josiah Quincy, *Observations on the Act of Parliament Commonly Called the Boston Port Bill*, 29, 41–43. Colbourn, *Lamp of Experience*, 78–80.
18. Quincy, *Observations*, 32–36, 39–41, 43–54, 58–63.
19. Ibid., 57.
20. Peter Force, ed., *American Archives*, vol. 1, is filled with local resolutions and commentaries taken from the press during the spring and summer of 1774. For resolutions typical in that they omit mention of the standing army while emphasizing no taxation and resistance to the tea tax, see Queen Anne, Md., Resolution, 30 March 1774, Baltimore County Resolution, 31 May 1774, Chestertown, Md., Resolution, 18 May 1774, Morris County, N.J., 27 June 1774, Lower Freehold, N.J., 6 June 1774, in Force, ed., *American Archives*, 1:366–67, 334–35, 452, 390, among many others in that volume. Also the resolutions of the county and corporate freeholders passed for the Virginia 1774 convention, convening 1 August 1774, in Robert L. Scribner, ed., *Revolutionary Virginia*, 1:111–68. Of the thirty county and municipal resolutions reprinted, only eight mention the standing army. These eight denounce the military for interfering in local police functions as proof of ministerial intrigue against colonial liberties. Resolutions of the colonial assemblies reveal the same trend. See the resolutions of Connecticut, New Jersey, Rhode Island, and South Carolina printed in the *New York Journal* on 16, 30 June, 7, 21 July 1774. Also the resolutions of the Philadelphia Town Meeting, in ibid., 23 June 1774. New York Town Meeting, 6 July 1774, in Force, ed., *American Archives*, 1:312–13. Resolves of the Virginia House of Burgesses meeting in Raleigh Tavern, 27 May 1774, and the Virginia Instructions to its delegates to the Continental Congress, Williamsburg, 8 August 1774, in *New York Journal*, 1 September 1774.
21. *The Papers of Thomas Jefferson*, ed. Boyd, 1:133–34. Pennsylvania instructions to its delegates to the Continental Congress, 16–21 July 1774, the "Argumentative Part," in Force, ed., *American Archives*, 1:564–92. Authorship is credited to Dickinson in Scribner, ed., *Revolutionary Virginia*, 2:155, n. 5. See also "An Essay," written during the fall of 1774, which repeated the same basic themes (John Dickinson, *The Political Writings of John Dickinson*, 1:353–60). Also letter 4, to the inhabitants of the British colonies in America, 15 June 1774, in ibid., 487–88.
22. For Jefferson's association with radical Whig thought, see H. Trevor Colbourn, "Jefferson's Use of the Past," 56–70. Also Merrill D. Peterson, *Thomas Jefferson and the New Nation*, 57–60. On Dickinson's intellectual heritage, see H. Trevor Colbourn, "John Dickinson, Historical Revolutionary," 273–86. Davidson, *Propaganda and the American Revolution*, 209.
23. Samuel Eliot Morison, ed., *Sources and Documents Illustrating the American Revolution, 1764–1788*, 119–22. *Journals of the Continental Congress*, 1:69, 96, 116. *No Standing Army in the British Colonies*, 4ff. Samuel Cooke, *The Violent Destroyed*, 23–26. John Lathrop, *A Discourse Preached*, 26–27. "Novanglus," no. 3 and no. 4, 5 February and 13 February 1774, in Bernard Mason, ed., *The American Colonial*

Crisis, 124, 126, 133–34, and 138–39. *New York Journal*, 1, 8 September 1774. Joseph Warren, Boston Massacre Oration, 5 March 1775, in Niles, ed., *Principles and Acts*, 24–30. An unsigned letter, 20 February 1775, Boston; "A Watchman," 24 December 1774, New Hampshire; unsigned letter, 17 February 1775, Portsmouth, N. H.; "Brecknock," 19 April 1775, London; all in Force, ed., *American Archives*, 1:1018 fn, 1063–65, 1246–47, 2:341–42. For resolutions leading to the Declaration of Taking Arms, 6 July 1775, see *Journals of the Continental Congress*, 2:128–29, 155–56. Also *Papers of Thomas Jefferson*, 1:213–18. See also the Provincial Congress of Massachusetts to the Continental Congress, 3 May 1775, and Twelve United Colonies . . . to the Inhabitants of Great Britain, 1 July 1775, *Journals of the Continental Congress*, 2:24–25, 165. Philadelphia Militia Association, ca. April 1775, and the Fairfield, Connecticut, Articles of Association, 15 August 1775, in Force, ed., *American Archives*, 2:399–400, and 3:141–43. John Carmichael, *A Self-Defensive War Lawful*, 4–16. David Jones, *Defensive War in a Just Cause Sinless*, 18–21.

24. *Journals of the Continental Congress*, 1:35. Richard Frothingham, *The Life and Times of Joseph Warren*, 362–66. Walter Millis, *Arms and Men*, 124–25. David Ammerman, *In the Common Cause*, 74–75.

25. Journal of the Massachusetts Provincial Congress, 26 October 1774, in Force, ed., *American Archives*, 1:843–45. Address of the Provincial Congress to the Inhabitants of Massachusetts-Bay, 4 December 1774, in Niles, ed., *Principles and Acts*, 108–10. On the militia organization in Massachusetts in early 1775, see Frothingham, *Joseph Warren*, 412–13. Ammerman, *In the Common Cause*, 140–42.

26. Maryland Convention Resolution, 8 December 1774, in Force, ed., *American Archives*, 1:1032. *Papers of George Mason*, 1:210–11, 212, 215–16. Ammerman, *In the Common Cause*, 142–44.

27. *Journals of the Continental Congress*, 3:506–7. Congress recommended that only company-level officers be elected.

28. Resolution of the Maryland Convention, 26 July 1775; Minutes of the New York Provincial Congress, 9 August 1775; Minutes of the New Jersey Provincial Congress, 16 August 1775; Pennsylvania Committee of Safety, 26 August 1775; Minutes of the Virginia Convention, 26 August 1775; New Hampshire Provincial Congress Minutes, 23 August 1775; North Carolina Provincial Congress, 31 August 1775; all in Force, ed., *American Archives*, 3:107–12; 525–26 and 542–46; 42–44; 506–10; 393–94 and 397–411; 595 and 622; 192–200 and 205. See also Patriotic Proceedings of the Convention of Deputies, Essex, New Hampshire, 25 January 1775, in Niles, ed., *Principles and Acts*, 13–14.

29. John Shy, "American Revolution," 121–56 passim.

30. Committee of Safety Resolution, New-Castle County, Delaware, 21 December 1774; Virginia Convention resolution on Military Preparedness, 23 March 1775, in Force, ed., *American Archives*, 1:1022 and 2:167–68. Petition of the Inhabitants of Kent County, Delaware, to Establish a Militia, 14 March 1775, in Niles, ed., *Principles and Acts*, 240. See also the Maryland and Fairfax County resolutions cited above. For post-Lexington comment reflecting the same sentiments, see "To the Inhabitants of Massachusetts," Sudbury, 5 September 1775, signed "Philo Patria," and Pennsylvania Committee of Safety to the Pennsylvania

House, 27 September 1775, in Force, ed., *American Archives*, 3:647–48 and 869–70. Samuel Adams to James Warren, 7 January 1776, *Writings of Samuel Adams*, 3:250–51. Carmichael, *A Self-Defensive War Lawful*, 16–19.

31. John Adams, "Novanglus," no. 3, 6 February 1775, in Mason, ed., *American Colonial Crisis*, 131.

Chapter 4

1. Charles Lee, *Strictures on a Pamphlet* (Philadelphia, 1774), in *The [Charles] Lee Papers*, 4:165–66. Lee to James Bowdoin, 30 November 1776, ibid., 5:323–24. John Shy, "Charles Lee," 22–32. Shy, "The American Revolution," 127–28. Colin Bonwick, *English Radicals and the American Revolution*, 31–32, 63–64.

2. Lee, *Strictures on a Pamphlet*, *Lee Papers*, 4:162–65. Lee to Bowdoin, 30 November 1776, and "Plan for an Army," ibid., 5:323–24, 382–89. Lee, "Plan for a Military Colony," ibid., 6:323–24.

3. Lee to George Washington, 13 April 1778, ibid., 5:382–83. Maurice de Saxe, *Reveries, or Memoirs upon the Art of War*. Alfred Vagts, *A History of Militarism*, 77–85. John F. C. Fuller, *The Conduct of War, 1789–1961*, 31–37. See Shy, "Charles Lee," 22–53, for an analysis which links Lee's views of the military with the *levée en masse*.

4. Lee, "Plan for a Military Colony," *Lee Papers*, 6:323–33.

5. George Washington to the President of Congress [John Hancock], 25 September 1776, in Millis, ed., *American Military Thought*, 9–11. Henry Knox shared Washington's views about the army (Knox to John Adams, 21 August 1776, and Knox to Adams, 25 September 1776, in Bernard Knollenberg, ed., "John Adams, Knox and Washington," 213–14, 216–17; Knox to William Knox, 23 September 1776, in Noah Brooks, *Henry Knox*, 70–71). See also Robert Morris to George Washington, 6 March 1777, *Correspondence of the American Revolution*, 1:348.

6. Washington to President of Congress [John Hancock], 25 September 1776, in Millis, ed., *American Military Thought*, 11–13. Washington to William Livingston, 24 January 1777, in Theodore Sedgwick, *A Memoir of the Life of William Livingston*, 224–25. Washington to Joseph Reed, 1 February 1776, and Reed to a member of Congress, n.d. [probably written in late 1776 or early 1777], in William B. Reed, *Life and Correspondence of Joseph Reed*, 1:149–50, 298–99. For other letters reflecting Washington's view of the army, see Elbridge Gerry to Horatio Gates, 24 June 1776, North Carolina Delegation to the North Carolina Council of Safety, 10 August 1776, *Letters of the Members of the Continental Congress*, 1:506, 2:44. William Hooper to the North Carolina Provincial Congress, 16 November 1776, *Colonial Records of North Carolina*, 10:907. Robert Morris to Commissioners for American Affairs in Europe, 28 March 1777, *The [Silas] Deane Papers*, 2:34–35. Richard Henry Lee to Thomas Jefferson, 29 April 1777, *The Letters of Richard Henry Lee*, 1:286. "To the American Soldiery," signed, A Soldier, Cambridge, 14 November 1775, and "To the Worthy Officers and Soldiers in the American Army," signed A Freeman, Cambridge, 24 November 1775, in Force, ed., *American Archives*, 4th ser., 3:1557–59, 1667–68.

7. Vagts, *History of Militarism*, 97–98. Weigley, *United States Army*, 33–34, 72–73. Shy, "American Revolution," 127–28. Russell F. Weigley, *Towards an American Army*, 4–70. Jonathan G. Rossie, *The Politics of Command in the American Revolution*, 17–44. Sidney Forman, "Why the U.S. Military Academy Was Established in 1802," 17–18. Walter Millis, *Arms and Men*, 26. John Adams to Henry Knox, 25 August 1776; William Ellery to Nicholas Cooke, 7 September 1776, *Letters of the Continental Congress*, 2:61, 79. See also John Adams, *Autobiography*, in *The Works of John Adams*, 3:48. Charles Royster, *A Revolutionary People at War*, 25–53.

8. On the terms of enlistment between June 1775 and September 1776, see Fred Anderson Berg, *Encyclopedia of Continental Army Units*, 139–40. The first effort to establish long-term enlistments appears to have been made in January 1776. See Richard Smith, diary, 19 January 1776, and James Duane, Notes on Debates, 22 February 1776, *Letters of the Continental Congress*, 1:319, 360–61. The first officially recorded effort to extend enlistments was on 21 June 1776 (*Journals of the Continental Congress*, 5:471). Simple duration enlistments, with no maximum service time, were established by Congress on 16 September 1776 (ibid., 762–63). Privates and noncommissioned officers were to receive twenty-dollar bounties upon enlistment and 100 acres at the end of the war. Officers serving for the duration would receive land grants ranging from 500 acres for colonels to 150 acres for ensigns. On these developments, see President of Congress [John Hancock], to the New Hampshire Assembly, 24 September 1776, in *Letters of the Continental Congress*, 2:99–100. On 12 November, faced with dwindling enlistments, Congress allowed soldiers to enlist for a maximum of three years or until Congress discharged them, on the grounds that duration enlistments prevented "men from inlisting who would otherwise readily manifest their attachment to the common cause." *Journals of the Continental Congress*, 6:944–45. The land bonus was retained only for those serving for the duration of the war. On the necessity of securing duration enlistments, see Richard Henry Lee to Patrick Henry, 15 September 1776, *Letters of Richard Henry Lee*, 1:215. Nicholas Cooke to John Hancock, 6 October 1776, and John Waterman to Cooke, 10 October 1776, in "Revolutionary Correspondence from 1775 to 1782," 6:127, 129. William Linn, *A Military Discourse*, 17–23. The initial articles of war adopted by Congress in June 1775 were not unlike the British articles. See *Journals of the Continental Congress*, 2:111–34, 3:352. The Articles of War, explicitly patterned after the British Articles, were adopted on 20 September 1776 (ibid., 5:788–807). The British Articles, of course, were only translations of the original Roman army codes. The only difference between the British and American articles was the severity of punishment in the British codes. Washington always believed that American punishments were not severe enough (Maurer Maurer, "Military Justice Under Washington," 9–16). Persons on the committee drawing up the revised Articles of War were Thomas Jefferson, John Adams, Edward Rutledge, and R. R. Livingston. See Edward Rutledge to R. R. Livingston, [19(?) August 1776], *Letters of the Continental Congress*, 2:54–56, and J. Adams, *Autobiography*, in *Works*, 3:68. The office of inspector general was created on 13 December 1777 (*Journals of the Continental Congress*, 9:1023–26).

9. Samuel Adams to James Warren, 7 January 1776, Warren to John Adams, 10 August 1777, *Warren-Adams Letters*, 197–98, 349. James Warren to Elbridge Gerry, 31 August 1777, 22 January 1778, in C. Harvey Gardiner, ed., *A Study in Dissent*, 79, 109. "On Standing Armies," 21 August 1772, signed Caractacus, in Force, ed., *American Archives*, 4th ser., 3:219–21. Benjamin Rush to John Adams, 1, 31 October 1777, Rush to Horatio Gates, 4 February 1778, on Rush's general suspicion of the military in society, see Rush to Catherine Macauly, 18 January 1769, all in *Letters of Benjamin Rush*, 1:155–57, 163–64, 198–99, 70–71. For an analysis of the popular perception of the Continental army, see Royster, *A Revolutionary People at War*, 54–189.

10. See notes 5, 6, and 9 above. The arrival of the French army with its career officers and professional soldiers in 1780 caused little public comment (William C. Stinchcombe, *The American Revolution and the French Alliance*, 135–36).

11. This summary is gleaned from the draft and enlistment laws passed in the states during the war years. A convenient compilation of the militia and draft laws in the states during the Revolution is *Backgrounds of Selective Service*, vol. 2, Connecticut, part 2, 173–250; Delaware, part 3, 26–35; Georgia, part 4, 117–49; Maryland, part 5, 119–43; Massachusetts, part 6, 220–60; New Hampshire, part 7, 79–117; New Jersey, part 8, 41–81; New York, part 9, 241–328; North Carolina, part 10, 48–128; Pennsylvania, part 11, 25–122; Rhode Island, part 12, 99–203; South Carolina, part 13, 57–102; Virginia, part 14, 255–421. See also Arthur J. Alexander, "Pennsylvania's Revolutionary Militia," 18–25; Arthur J. Alexander, "How Maryland Tried to Raise Her Continental Quotas," 184–93. Edward C. Papenfuse and Gregory A. Stiverson, "General Smallwood's Recruits," 117–32. For a different view of who served in the Continental army, and why, see Royster, *A Revolutionary People at War*, 190–254, 373–78. Not everyone in the South was enthusiastic about enlisting the poor and the landless. Edmund Pendleton once remarked, in typical radical Whig fashion, that "to point out any men and condemn t[hem] as Vagabonds or worthless without a Regular trial perhaps upon their being charged by a Spiteful neighbour, appears very exceptionable, not to take notice of the danger of trusting our defence to such people" (Pendleton to William Woodford, 29 November 1777, Pendleton to Washington, 22 December 1778, *The Letters and Papers of Edmund Pendleton, 1784–1803*, 1:238–39, 276–77).

12. Unless otherwise indicated, all citations to state constitutions are from *Federal and State Constitutions*. Citations refer to article or section number. Delaware (1776), Bill of Rights, 10, 19, 20, 21, in Schwartz, ed., *Bill of Rights*, 1:277–78. Maryland (1776) Declaration of Rights, 25, 26, 27, 28, 29. Massachusetts (1780) Declaration of Rights, 10, 17, 27, 28. New York (1777) Preamble. North Carolina (1776) Bill of Rights, 17. South Carolina (1778), 42. Pennsylvania, Declaration of Rights, 13. Virginia Bill of Rights, section 13, *George Mason Papers*, 1:282–89. See also the Jefferson drafts of the Virginia Constitution, *Thomas Jefferson Papers*, 1:338–45, 347–54, 356–64. New Hampshire adopted similar articles in its 1783 Bill of Rights, 24–27. For a general survey of state bills of rights, see Rutland, *The Birth of the Bill of Rights, 1776–1791*, 41–77. Connecticut

and Rhode Island only modified their colonial charters to reflect the break with England.

13. Massachusetts (1780), chapter 2, section 1, article 7. On the controversy over this grant of power see Robert J. Taylor, ed., *Massachusetts, Colony to Commonwealth*, 18–19, 56–57, 60–61, 63, 69–70, 71, 83–84, 120, and throughout. Also "Instructions of the Inhabitants of Malden, Mass., to their Representatives in Congress," 27 May 1776, in Niles, ed., *Principles and Acts*, 123. For other documents related to gubernatorial military power in Massachusetts between 1778 and 1780 see Records of the States of the United States (hereafter cited as RSUS), Massachusetts, C [constitutional records], reel 1, unit 2.

14. In most states the executive council was elected by the general assembly (Delaware [1776], 9, Maryland [1776], 33, North Carolina [1776], 18; Virginia [1776], in *Federal and State Constitutions*, 7:3817). The South Carolina constitutions did not mention militia embodiment, but the governor was not allowed to declare war or peace without consent of both houses ([1776], 26 [1778], 33). See also, John Adams, "Thoughts on Government," in *Works*, 4:194–98.

15. Article 33.

16. Section 20.

17. Delaware (1776), 18. Maryland (1776), 37 and 38. North Carolina (1776), 27. South Carolina (1776), 6 and 10; (1778), 9 and 20. Article 7 of the 1778 constitution also forbade the governor and lieutenant-governor from holding military commissions. Pennsylvania (1776), section 19, prohibited naval officers from holding various executive appointments. The following states also prohibited military suppliers from holding elected office: Delaware (1776), 18; North Carolina (1776), 27; Maryland (1776), 37 and 38.

18. Maryland (1776), 45. In Massachusetts militia officers were allowed to hold public office only after it was decided that they would be elected by the people. *Journal of 1780 Constitutional Convention*, 9, 15 February, 1, 2 March 1780, pp. 93, 113, 160, 166–67 in RSUS, Massachusetts, C, reel 1, unit 3.

19. New York (1777), 24. Virginia (1776), *Federal and State Constitutions*, 7:3817. *Thomas Jefferson Papers*, 1:367, 371, 377–83. Delaware (1776), 6, North Carolina (1776), 14, South Carolina (1776), 23, 25 (1778), 30–32, New Jersey (1776), 10. New Hampshire (1776), in *Federal and State Constitutions*, 4:2453. Pennsylvania (1776), section 5. Massachusetts (1780), chapter 2, section 1, article 10. See also note 13 above. Georgia did not designate the method of appointing militia officers in its constitution, but legislation was passed in 1777 making militia officers elective (*Backgrounds of Selective Service*, vol. 2, part 4, 117–40). The Maryland constitution was also silent on the issue, but the constitutional convention did reject a proposal to elect militia officers (*Journal of the Maryland Convention*, 5 November 1776, RSUS, Maryland, C, reel 1, unit 2).

20. Georgia (1777), 10. Delaware (1776), 28. Resolution of the Maryland Convention [Provincial Assembly], 3 July 1776, RSUS, Maryland, C, reel 1, unit 1.

21. The debates in Congress over the Articles recorded in the journals include no mention of the clauses concerning the army. *Journals of the Continental Congress*,

6:1076–85. Also Jefferson's Notes on Debates, ibid., 1098–1106. The official text of the Articles of Confederation is printed in ibid., 9:907–25.

22. Ibid., 5:548, Article 9.
23. Article 6.
24. Article 9. Don Higginbotham, *War of American Independence*, 206. Marcus Cunliffe, *Soldiers and Civilians*, 40–41.
25. To the General Assembly from Thomas Burke [December 1777], *Colonial Records of North Carolina*, 11:701–3. Burnett dates this letter 15 November 1777, *Letters of the Continental Congress*, 2:556n. "The Speech of the Hon. William Henry Drayton . . . Twentieth January 1778," in Niles, ed., *Principles and Acts*, 361–62, 371–72. Charles Lobingier, *The People's Law, or Popular Participation in Law Making*, 167–68.
26. *Journals of the Continental Congress*, 9:638, 640, 649–55.
27. Merrill Jensen, *The Articles of Confederation*, 185–97.
28. Washington, "Remarks on a Plan of Field Officers for Remodeling the Army," November 1777, *Writings of Washington*, 10:125–26. Committee of Congress to Washington, 10 December 1777, *Letters of the Continental Congress*, 1:585. *Journals of the Continental Congress*, 10:18–20, 285–86, 358–59; 11:502–3. William H. Glasson, *Federal Military Pensions in the United States*, 23–25, 27–30. H. James Henderson, *Party Politics in the Continental Congress*, 121–24.
29. On congressional action on half pay in 1779, see Washington to the Committee of Conference, 20 January 1779, *Writings of Washington*, 14:31–32; *Journals of the Continental Congress*, 14:638–39, 946–49, 973–97; 15:1335–37; James Lovell to Samuel Adams, 17 August 1779, and John Fell, Diary, 16, 17 August 1779, *Letters of the Continental Congress*, 4:381, 379. On congressional action and political developments leading up to lifetime pensions, see *Journals of the Continental Congress*, 17:773; Papers of the Continental Congress, item 21, 247–49, General Orders, 5 September 1780. Washington to the President of Congress [Henry Laurens], 11 October 1780, *Writings of Washington*, 19:504, 20:157–60. Henderson, *Party Politics*, 246–75. Half pay was passed on 21 October 1780 (*Journals of the Continental Congress*, 18:958–62). On the passage of half pay, see Abraham Clark to Josiah Hornblower, 31 October 1780, *Letters of the Continental Congress*, 5:435. Samuel Huntington to Jonathan Trumbull, 26 October 1780, *Trumbull Papers*, part 4, 7th ser., 3:152–53. James Warren to Elbridge Gerry, 3 December 1780, in Gardiner, ed., *Study in Dissent*, 149–50. See also Glasson, *Military Pensions*, 32–35.
30. On the organization of politics in Congress between 1780 and 1782, see Henderson, *Party Politics*, 281–349. Arthur Lee was a key southern parochialist with close ties to New England political leaders. Theodorick Bland, usually an ally of Lee, supported commutation. John Francis Mercer was another important southern parochialist in the half-pay debate. Parochialists sought to arrange for the states to settle the claims of their officers during the summer of 1782, but failed. See Charles Thomson, Notes of Debates, 31 July, 7 August 1782, *Letters of the Continental Congress*, 6:405–8, 432.
31. On the politics of commutation in the Continental Congress, see Henderson, *Party Politics*, 325–38. On the fiscal plight of the army and Robert Morris's role in commutation, see E. James Ferguson, *The Power of the Purse*, 133–34, 141,

155–64, 167–71. For the army's link with Hamilton and Morris and the pressure to pass commutation, see Richard H. Kohn, *Eagle and Sword*, 17–39. On the impost and its relationship with commutation, see Jackson Turner Main, *The Anti-Federalists*, 72–109 passim. Hamilton to Washington, 17 March 1783, *Letters of the Continental Congress*, 7:86–87. David Howell to Governor Greene, 30 July 1782, and Jonathan Arnold and Howell to Governor Greene, 15 October 1782, in William R. Staples, *Rhode Island in the Continental Congress, 1765–1790*, 381–82, 394–98. The suggestion that half pay be commuted to a single grant was included in the army's memorial to Congress, Papers of the Continental Congress, no. 42, vol. 6, 63. It was also recommended by General Alexander McDougall to Congress on 13 January 1783. See *Journals of the Continental Congress*, 25:852–53. On the urgency of resolving half pay see Henry Knox to General Lincoln, 20 December 1782, Knox to McDougall, 21 February 1783, Knox to Lincoln, 3 March 1783, in Francis Samuel Drake, *The Life and Correspondence of Henry Knox, Major-General in the American Revolutionary Army*, 76–80. On persistent reports of military unrest, see Henry Knox to Congress, December 1782, in *Journals of the Continental Congress*, 24:291–93; General McDougall and Colonel Ogden and Colonel Brooks, Report to Congress, 13 January 1783, in ibid., 25:852–53. Hamilton and Peters reported on the mood of the army to Congress on 20 February 1783, in ibid., 906–7. Concern over the military's conduct is discussed in Madison to Edmund Randolph, 25 February 1783, and Joseph Jones to Washington, 27 February 1783, *Letters of the Continental Congress*, 7:57–58, 61–62. On the resistance to half pay, see McDougall and Ogden to Knox, 8 February 1783, and Richard Peters to H. Gates, 5 March 1783, ibid., 7:35n–36n, 67. On the political pressure leading to the passage of commutation, see William Floyd to George Clinton, 12 March 1783, and McDougall to Knox, 15 March 1783, ibid., 7:72, 72n–73n; Madison to Nicholas P. Trist, 15 July 1827, *The Papers of James Madison*, 6:371n; and Madison, Notes on Debates, 20, 22 March 1783, ibid., 370, 375. On the crisis at Newburgh in mid-March 1783, see Maryland Delegation to William Paca, 18 March 1783, *Letters of the Continental Congress*, 7:88–89. Good general surveys of the passage of commutation include Merrill Jensen, *The New Nation*, 72–73; Louis C. Hatch, *The Administration of the American Revolutionary Army*, 151–78; Glasson, *Military Pensions*, 35–41, 49–50; Robert G. Bodenger, "Soldiers' Bonuses," 9–20.

32. James Lovell to Samuel Adams, 13 January 1778; Gerry to Washington, 13 January 1778; Henry Laurens to James Duane, 7 April 1778; Thomas Burke to Richard Caswell, 9 April 1778; Laurens to Governor Livingston, 19 April 1778; Laurens, "Notes on the Measure for Half Pay," [21 April 1778]; Laurens to Jacob Christopher Zahn, 28 April 1778; Laurens to Washington, 5 May 1778, all in *Letters of the Continental Congress*, 3:32, 33–34, 154, 162, 176–78, 183, 198–99, 221. Lovell to Samuel Adams, 18 April 1778, in Sedgwick, *Livingston*, 284. Gerry to James Warren, 26 May 1778, in Gardiner, ed., *Study in Dissent*, 120. Connecticut Delegation to Jonathan Trumbull, 18 May 1778, in *Trumbull Papers*, part 3, 7th ser., vol. 2, 231–33. Glasson, *Military Pensions*, 28–29.

33. [James Madison], Notes on Debates, 25, 28 January, 12, 19, 21, 25, 27 February 1783, *Madison Papers*, 6:130, 141–49, 225–26, 259–60, 270–74, 282–85,

297–99. Numerous proposals were put forward to commit half pay to the states or limit the proposed impost to cover only the military debt; see ibid., 130–378 passim. The delegates from Rhode Island and Connecticut had instructions to oppose any pension proposals; see ibid., 187, 189–90 (n. 10).

34. Massachusetts General Assembly to Congress, 11 July 1783, *Journals of the Continental Congress*, 25:607–9. "Cato," Boston *Continental Journal*, 30 January 1783. Glasson, *Military Pensions*, 43–48. Christopher Collier, *Roger Sherman's Connecticut*, 211–13, 216. Main, *Anti-Federalists*, 77–102, 106–9. Governor Greene to the Rhode Island Delegation, 10 May 1783, and Collins and Arnold to Governor Greene, 28 May 1783, in Staples, *Rhode Island in the Continental Congress*, 440, 440–41. Madison to Edmund Randolph, 8 September 1783, *Madison Papers*, 7:307–8. In the other states, opponents of nationalist policy linked commutation with the continuing efforts to secure a measure of fiscal independence for the national government, but most of their criticism centered on the new impost amendment sent the states within a month after the passage of commutation.

35. Extract from Farmington Revolutionary Records, 6 May 1783, quoted in Main, *Anti-Federalists*, 108–9. Resolutions of the town of Torrington, 15 July 1783, Hartford *Connecticut Courant*, 29 July 1783. Farmington Resolution, 4 August 1783, ibid., 12 August 1783. Killingworth Resolutions, 21 August 1783, ibid., 2 September 1783. Canaan Resolutions, 16 September 1783, ibid., 14 October 1783. "To the Editor," ibid., 13 May 1783. "Cives," ibid., 24 June 1783. "A Convention-Man," ibid., 3 February 1784. "To the Editor," ibid., 13 September 1783.

36. Ibid. Amenia Precinct, Dutchess County, New York, Resolutions, in *Connecticut Courant*, 12 August 1783. Simsbury Resolutions, 2 September 1783, ibid., 30 September 1783. Instructions of the town of Hartford to their delegates in the next General Assembly, 16 September 1783, ibid., 23 September 1783. "Desire," ibid., 30 September 1783.

37. The Society of the Cincinnati issue was introduced in the Killingworth Resolutions, 21 August 1783, in the *Connecticut Courant*, 2 September 1783. The Middletown convention of Connecticut towns met three times, 30 September, 16 December 1783, and 16 March 1784. The resolutions of these meetings are printed in ibid., 4 November, 23 December 1783, and 30 March 1784. Aedenus Burke, *Considerations of the Society or Order of Cincinnati*, 1–21. This pamphlet was written in South Carolina, but was republished in the mid-Atlantic and New England states during 1783 and 1784. It was recommended to the citizens of Connecticut during the December session and was the focus of debate in the March meeting of the Middletown convention. The best summary of reaction to the Cincinnati in New England is Wallace E. Davies, "The Society of Cincinnati in New England, 1783–1800," 4–13. Numerous private letters reflect the same concern for civil corruption if the Cincinnati were linked economically with the continental government. Samuel Osgood to John Adams, 14 January 1785, Osgood to Stephen Higginson, 2 February 1784, E. Gerry to S. Higginson, 13 May 1784, *Letters of the Continental Congress*, 7:416, 435, 522–23. Samuel Adams to E. Gerry, 19 April 1784, 23 April 1784, *Writings of Samuel Adams*, 298–300, 301–3. Chevalier de la

Luzerne to the Count de Vergennes, 15 February, ca. April, and 12 April 1784, *General Washington's Correspondence concerning the Society of the Cincinnati*, 77–80, 95–96, 135–39. See also Edgar E. Hume, "Early Opposition to the Society of the Cincinnati," 597–638.

38. Washington to the Committee of Congress with the Army, 29 January 1778, in *Writings of Washington*, 10:363–64. See also Washington to John Banister, 21 April 1778, ibid., 11:285–86. For a convenient collection of documents related to Washington's position on half pay from 1778 to 1783, see *A Collection of Papers Relative to Half-Pay and Commutation of Half-Pay Granted by Congress*.

39. Elbridge Gerry to Washington, 13 January 1778, *Letters of the Continental Congress*, 3:33–34. See also the summaries of the pro–half pay position in Connecticut Delegation to Jonathan Trumbull, 18 May 1778, *Trumbull Papers*, part 3, 7th ser., 2:231–33. Thomas Burke to Richard Caswell, 9 April 1778, *Letters of the Continental Congress*, 3:162. Henry Laurens to Governor Livingston, 19 April 1778, in Sedgwick, *Livingston*, 273.

40. See note 31, and *Connecticut Courant*, 12, 15, 22 August, 2, 9, 16, 23 September, 3 June, 7, 21 October 1783, 24 February, 2, 9, 16 March, 6 April 1784.

41. Webster, writing under the pseudonym Honorius, contributed regularly to the *Connecticut Courant* from late August through October 1783.

42. This summary of Webster's view of the military needs of a republic and the motives of an eighteenth-century soldier is gleaned from letters appearing in the *Connecticut Courant*, 9, 16, 30 September, 14, 21 October 1783. See also *Notes on the Life of Noah Webster*, 1:66–67, 74–75.

Chapter 5

1. For the ideological framework of the Revolution see Gordon S. Wood, *The Creation of the American Republic, 1776–1787*, 46–118 passim. Pocock, *The Machiavellian Moment*, 361–526 passim. Bailyn, *Ideological Origins*, 55–93. Morgan, "Puritan Ethic," 3–18. Banning, *The Jeffersonian Persuasion*, 22–69. Schwoerer, "No Standing Armies!" 188–200.

2. Kenneth A. Lockridge, "Social Change and the Meaning of the American Revolution," 403–39. Rowland Berthoff and John M. Murrin, "Feudalism, Communalism, and the Yeoman Freeholder," 256–88 passim. Gary B. Nash, "Social Change and the Growth of Prerevolutionary Urban Radicalism," 7–10. Main, *The Social Structure of Revolutionary America*.

3. Ramsay published his *History of the American Revolution* in Philadelphia in 1789. Warren's *History of the Rise, Progress and Termination of the American Revolution* . . . was not published until 1805 when three volumes were released in Boston, but a substantial part of the writing was completed in the 1780s (William R. Smith, *History as Argument*, 34–39).

4. Warren, *History*, 1:40–41, 43–45, 59–62, 66–67, 71–75, 91–97, 123, 157–60, 163, 311. See also Smith, *History as Argument*, 83–84, 88–91.

5. Warren, *History*, 1:177–78, 330–31, 362–63, 366–67, 2:187, 228, 236–39,

3:7, 268–80. Smith, *History as Argument*, 102–3. For an analysis of Warren's pervasive concern about public virtue and moral decay see Lester H. Cohen, "Explaining the Revolution," 200–18.

6. Ramsay, *History of American Revolution*, 1:191, 200, 206, 233–34, 294, 304, 305, 330–31; Smith, *History as Argument*, 59, 61–63.

7. Quotation from Ramsay, *History of the United States, from Their First Settlement as English Colonies, in 1607, to the Year 1808 . . .* , 2:357. Similar ideas are in his *History of American Revolution*, 1:191–96, 2:98–99, 115–16, 124–25.

8. The congressional committee was formed on 4 April 1783. Alexander Hamilton chaired the committee, which included James Madison, Samuel Osgood, Oliver Ellsworth, and James Wilson. See Madison, "Notes on Debates," 4 April 1783, *Papers of James Madison*, 6:432–43. See Hamilton to Washington, 9 April 1783, *Papers of Alexander Hamilton*, 3:322, for the committee's request for a report from Washington. See also Kohn, *Eagle and Sword*, 41–42.

9. Don Higginbotham, *War of American Independence*, 445–47; Kohn, *Eagle and Sword*, 41–42.

10. The quotations and the following discussion are from a series of letters sent in April 1783 to Washington: from Jean Gouvion, 16 April; from William Heath, 17 April; from Henry Knox, 17 April; from Timothy Pickering, 22 April; from Rufus Putnam, 25 April, with enclosures, "Thoughts on the Peace Establishment" and "For the Establishment of a Continental Militia"; and from Edward Hand [April 1783], "On the Peace Establishment"; all in George Washington Papers; from Jedediah Huntington, 16 April and from George Clinton, 17 April, *Correspondence of the American Revolution*, 4:27–28, 28–29; and from Friedrich von Steuben, 15 and 21 April, George Washington Papers. Friedrich von Steuben, *A Letter on the Subject of an Established Militia*.

11. Historians have analyzed the military plans of 1783. John McAuley Palmer, *Washington, Lincoln, Wilson*, 15–27, 55–69, 79–82, discusses the plans in the context of the post–World War I debate over the need for compulsory military training in twentieth-century America. Walter Millis, *Arms and Men*, 42–46, comments on the plans in much the same context. Both Palmer and Millis note that Washington's militia plan went well beyond the decentralized militia system that existed in the states at the war's end. Russell F. Weigley recognizes that Washington's plan did not envision a *levée en masse*, but he, too, associates Washington's thinking with mass conscription, "which historically has tied democratic political revolution to military revolution culminating in total war" (*Toward an American Army*, 11–15). Don Higginbotham surveys the plans largely within the interpretive framework provided by Palmer and Weigley (*War of American Independence*, 441–45). C. Joseph Bernardo and Eugene H. Bacon summarize the military plans of Washington, Hamilton, and Steuben as well as Knox's 1786 plan, pointing to the low level of military preparedness during the mid-1780s (*American Military Policy*, 47–66). Richard Kohn describes the plans submitted to Washington and traces the fate of his proposal in Congress ultimately linking the ideas expressed in the plans with what he believes to be the Federalists' rejection of a militia defense in 1792 (*Eagle and Sword*, 40–53). Nevertheless, none of these historians has noted the differences among the plans presented to Washington, nor

have they analyzed how these plans reflected efforts to blend revolutionary republicanism with the military realities of the postwar period.

12. Clinton to Washington, 17 April 1783, *Correspondence of the Revolution*, 4:28–29. Knox to Washington, 17 April 1783, George Washington Papers.

13. Steuben, *Letter on Established Militia*, 7–8. Pickering to Washington, 22 April 1783, George Washington Papers.

14. Pickering to Washington, 22 April 1783; enclosure "For the Establishment of a Continental Militia," in Putnam to Washington, 25 April 1783; Knox to Washington, 17 April 1783; in George Washington Papers. Steuben, *Letter on Established Militia*, 7–8, 11–15.

15. Pickering to Washington, 22 April 1783, and enclosure "For the Establishment of a Continental Militia," in Putnam to Washington, 25 April 1783, in George Washington Papers.

16. Steuben, *Letter on Established Militia*, 11–15.

17. Pickering to Washington, 22 April 1783, George Washington Papers.

18. Steuben to Washington, 15 April 1783, and "Peace Establishment," enclosure in Steuben to Washington, 21 April 1783, ibid. The letter of 21 April suggested a peacetime force of just under five thousand. Steuben refined that number to four thousand and expanded upon the general plans in these letters in *Letter on Established Militia*, 2–7. For a similar view of the peacetime regular establishment see Gouvion to Washington, 16 April 1783, George Washington Papers.

19. Putnam to Washington, 25 April 1783, enclosure "Thoughts on the Peace Establishment," in George Washington Papers. Clinton to Washington, 17 April 1783, *Correspondence of the Revolution*, 4:29–31. Hand to Washington, "On the Peace Establishment," [April 1783], George Washington Papers. None of these men offered estimates of the size of the force needed to accomplish these ends. See also Huntington to Washington, 16 April 1783, *Correspondence of the Revolution*, 4:27–28; John Patterson to Washington, 16 April 1783, George Washington Papers.

20. Pickering to Washington, 22 April 1783, George Washington Papers.

21. Clinton to Washington, 17 April 1783, *Correspondence of the Revolution*, 4:25–31.

22. Steuben to Washington, 21 April 1783. Edward Hand explicitly endorsed the Steuben proposal in a letter to Washington [April 1783]. Knox also suggested an academy plan similar to Steuben's, though it included provisions for separate naval and military academies (Knox to Washington, 17 April 1783, *Correspondence of the Revolution*, 4:27–28). Secretary of War Benjamin Lincoln also endorsed Steuben's plan (Lincoln to Hamilton, May 1783, Papers of the Continental Congress, item 38, 317–30). See also Palmer, *Washington, Lincoln, Wilson*, 62–65.

23. Washington to Steuben, 15 March 1784, in *Writings of Washington*, 27:360. See also Weigley, *Towards an American Army*, 10–13; Kohn, *Eagle and Sword*, 45.

24. "Sentiments on a Peace Establishment," in Washington to Hamilton, 2 May 1783, *Writings of Washington*, 26:388–89.

25. Ibid., 389–94. Washington was willing to institute a draft to compel service in the select militia if that should become necessary.

26. Ibid., 374–85. On enlistments in the British peacetime army see J. W.

Fortescue, *A History of the British Army*, 2:581–83.

27. "Sentiments on a Peace Establishment," in Washington to Hamilton, 2 May 1783, *Writings of Washington*, 26:396–97.

28. Washington to Steuben, 15 March 1783, ibid., 27:360.

29. "Sentiments on a Peace Establishment," ibid., 26:375, 392.

30. Steuben's plan was delivered to Hamilton's committee by Richad Peters of Pennsylvania (Peters to Steuben, 23 April, 6 May 1783, *Letters of the Continental Congress*, 7:150, 156). Secretary of War Benjamin Lincoln, working independently of Washington, also prepared recommendations for the peace establishment that were very similar to the commander in chief's (Lincoln to Hamilton, May 1783, and Lincoln's "Peace Establishment Plan" enclosed in Lincoln to the president of Congress, 3 May 1783, both in Papers of the Continental Congress, item 38, 317–30, 285–98).

31. The complete text of Hamilton's report is in *Journals of the Continental Congress*, 25:722–43. The comments concerning the militia are on pages 742–43. For summaries of Hamilton's report see Kohn, *Eagle and Sword*, 47–48, and Weigley, *Towards an American Army*, 14–15.

32. *Journals of the Continental Congress*, 25:722–38. Hamilton did not recommend a formal military academy, believing that "Military Knowledge is best acquired in service." Instead, he proposed that professors of mathematics, chemistry, natural philosophy, and civil architecture, and one drawing master be attached to the corps of engineers to provide advanced training in military arts (ibid., 732, 738).

33. Burnett dates the report as submitted on 17 June, as does Kohn. See *Letters of the Continental Congress*, 7:xxvii, and Kohn, *Eagle and Sword*, 321, n. 26. Syrett dates the report as 18 June 1783 in *Hamilton Papers*, 3:378n. Kohn and Burnett are probably correct.

34. The best discussion of the debate over the peace establishment during the summer of 1783 is Kohn, *Eagle and Sword*, 48–53. On the political significance of Congress's move to Princeton see Cress, "Whither Columbia?" 582–88. See also Kenneth R. Bowling, "New Light on the Philadelphia Mutiny of 1783: Federal-State Confrontation at the Close of the War for Independence," *Pennsylvania Magazine of History and Biography*, CI (1977), 419–50. On Washington's reaction to Hamilton's plan see Washington, "Observations on an Intended Report of a Committee of Congress on a Peace Establishment," 8 September 1783, in *Writings of Washington*, 27:140–44. The congressional resolution on frontier defense is in *Journals of the Continental Congress*, 24:806–7. On the parochialist opposition to the peace establishment see the letters written by members of Congress during July and August 1783, collected in *Letters of the Continental Congress*, 7:156, 167, 245, 263, 266, 8:842; and R. H. Lee to James Monroe, 5 January 1784, *Letters of Richard Henry Lee*, 2:287–89.

35. On the mood in Congress against the peace establishment see accounts in *Letters of the Continental Congress*, 7:415, 434, 492–93, 546–47, 576, 603, 8:116, 197; Knox to Washington, 28 May 1784, *Correspondence of the Revolution*, 4:68–69; and Massachusetts Delegation to the Massachusetts General Court, 4 June 1784, and Gerry to the Massachusetts General Court, 25 October 1784, in James T. Austin, *The Life of Elbridge Gerry*, 1:432–33, 460–63. Gerry's speech is in *Journals of the*

Continental Congress, 27:433-34. For the decision to reduce the army to eighty privates plus officers see ibid., 524. On the 1785 resolution see ibid., 28:28-29, 88-89, 223-24, 240-41, 247-48, 352-53, 390-91. The most complete discussion of Continental Congress politics in 1784 and 1785 is in H. James Henderson, *Party Politics in the Continental Congress,* 350-82. For an analysis centering on the political development of the army issue in the period see Kohn, *Eagle and Sword,* 54-62. See also Millis, *Arms and Men,* 38-46; Bernardo and Bacon, *American Military Policy,* 61-63; and Higginbotham, *War of American Independence,* 443-45.

36. Historians who have taken note of the Knox plan have considered it only as a restatement of Washington's view of the postwar military establishment. See Palmer, *Washington, Lincoln, Wilson,* 86-94, and Millis, *Arms and Men,* 50-51. Neither Kohn, *Eagle and Sword,* nor Higginbotham, *War of American Independence,* discusses the Knox plan.

37. Henry Knox, *A Plan for the General Arrangement of the Militia of the United States,* 1-6.

38. Ibid., 8, 11-14, 21-23, 25.

39. Ibid., 18-19, 22-24. Knox borrowed extensively from Andrew Fletcher, *A Discourse of Government with Relation to Militias,* in *The Political Works of Andrew Fletcher.*

40. Knox, *Plan for the Militia,* 10-15, 20, 24-25, 30-34.

41. Congressional committee endorsement is in *Journals of the Continental Congress,* 31:642. Ramsay to Knox, 12 March 1786, *David Ramsay, 1749-1815,* 98-99.

Chapter 6

1. Instructions to the Sheriff of Worcester from the Council Chamber, 2 September 1786, and Jonathan Warner to James Bowdoin, 3 September 1786, Massachusetts Archives, vol. 189, 7-8, vol. 190, 230, Massachusetts State Library. George R. Minot, *History of the Insurrection in 1786,* 40-41, 74-75, 92-94. Council Chamber Minutes, 7 and 9 September; Narrative of a riot in the County of Worcester, by Artemas Ward, 5 September 1786; Joseph Henshaw to James Bowdoin, 7 September 1786; Sheriff Greenleaf, Worcester County, to Bowdoin, 16 September 1786; Caleb Hyde, Sheriff of Berkshire County, to Bowdoin, 13 September 1786; William Shepard to Bowdoin, 25 and 29 September 1786; An Account [of events in Springfield] by Nathan P. Sargent and David Sewall, 2 October 1786; Shepard to Bowdoin, 4 December 1786; Jonathan Warner to Bowdoin, 5 January 1787; General Brooks to Bowdoin, 28 January 1787; all in Massachusetts Archives, vol. 189, 9-14, vol. 190, 131-33, 237-37a, 235-35a, 263-64, 266, 291-92, 294a-d, vol. 318, 202-3, 223, 299. Levi Lincoln to George Washington, 4 December 1786, George Washington Papers, ser. 4. [Commentary on the reluctance of the Third Division to support the government], undated and unsigned, Misc. Doc. Folder, Shays' Rebellion Collection. *Writ* vs. *Aaron Board,* 4 February 1787; Testimony and Trial of Dr. Isaac Chenery, 20 February 1787; *Writ* vs. *Major Francis Willson,* 28 February 1787; *Writ* vs. *Samuel Richardson*; General Court Martial, 2 June 1787; all in Shays' Rebellion Collection.

2. Proclamation, 2 September 1786; House and Senate Resolution, 4 February 1787; Bowdoin's Speech to the Massachusetts House and Senate, 28 September 1786; Bowdoin to Massachusetts House and Senate, 3 February 1787; all in Massachusetts Archives, vol. 189, 1–2, 108–9, vol. 190, 267–76, 330. Theophilus Parsons to Nathaniel Tracy, n.d. (probably soon after Shays' Rebellion), in Parsons, *Memoir of Theophilus Parsons, Chief Justice of the Supreme Judicial Court of Massachusetts*, 128–31.

3. Henry Lee to Washington, 3 September, 1 October, and 17 October 1786; Henry Knox to Washington, 28 October 1786; D. Humphreys to Washington, 1 November 1786; all in George Washington Papers. Washington to Henry Lee, 31 October 1786; Washington to James Madison, 5 November 1786; Washington to Levi Lincoln, 24 February 1787; all in *Writings of Washington*, 29:34–35, 51–52, 168. Knox to Washington, 14 January 1787, and Madison to Washington, 16 March 1787, in *Correspondence of the Revolution*, 4:161, 166–67. *Journals of the Continental Congress*, 31:891–93, 895–96. Edward Carrington to the Governor of Virginia [Edmund Randolph], 8 December 1786, *Letters of the Continental Congress*, 8:516–18. Bernardo and Bacon, *American Military Policy*, 66–69. Joseph P. Warren, "The Confederation and the Shays Rebellion," 42–67. Kohn, *Eagle and Sword*, 74–75. William Wiecek, *The Guarantee Clause of the U.S. Constitution*, 27–42. Van Beck Hall, *Politics without Parties*, 190–226. Robert J. Taylor, *Western Massachusetts in the Revolution*, 128–67. Also Robert A. East, "The Massachusetts Conservatives in the Critical Period," 380–91. On contemporary association of Shays' Rebellion with domestic turmoil in the ancient Greek republics, see Adair, "The Intellectual Origins of Jeffersonian Democracy," 105–21.

4. The relevant constitutional provisions are Article 1, sections 8 and 9, and Article 2, section 2. Bernardo Donahoe and Marshall Smelser, "The Congressional Power to Raise Armies," 202–12. Ernest R. May, "'The President Shall be Commander in Chief' (1787–1789),"4–21. Charles A. Lofgren, "War-Making under the Constitution," 674–702. Higginbotham, *War of American Independence*, 453–56. Samuel P. Huntington, *The Soldier and the State*, 163–70. Millis, *Arms and Men*, 47–50. Frederick B. Wiener, "The Militia Clause of the Constitution," 181–85. Howard White, *Executive Influence in Determining Military Policy in the United States*, 18–21. Ekirch, *Civilian and the Military*, 24–31.

5. Of the state constitutions, only those of North Carolina and Pennsylvania explicitly forbade raising armies in peacetime. Few Anti-Federalists attacked the value of military professionalism to the republic. Among those who did were "Brutus," no. 8, *New York Journal*, 10 January 1788; "A Democratic Federalist," *Pennsylvania Packet*, 23 October 1787; "Columbian Patriot [Elbridge Gerry]," "Observations on the New Constitution," in Paul Leicester Ford, ed., *Pamphlets on the Constitution of the United States*, 10; John Dawes, Virginia Convention, 23 June 1788, in *The Debates in the Several State Conventions on the Adoption of the Federal Constitution*, 3:611. Samuel Nason, Massachusetts Convention, 1 February 1788, ibid., 2:136–37; General Thompson, Massachusetts Convention, 23 January 1788, in *Debates and Proceedings in the Convention of Massachusetts*, 313; [Unsigned], *New York Journal*, 28 January 1788.

6. For the Anti-Federalist view of representation, see Cecelia M. Kenyon, "Men of Little Faith," 3–46. For a discussion of shifting views of representation during the 1780s, see Wood, *Creation of the American Republic*, part 5. On the unrepresentative nature of the national government and the potential for the abuse of its military powers, see "The Address and Reasons of Dissent of the Minority of the Convention of Pennsylvania to Their Constituents," in Cecelia M. Kenyon, ed., *The Antifederalists*, 55–57. George Mason, Virginia Convention, 16 June 1788, *George Mason Papers*, 3:1080–81. "Letters from a Federal Farmer," nos. 2 and 3, 9 October and 10 October 1787, in Kenyon, ed., *Antifederalists*, 213–14, 227–29. Kenyon and others have credited Richard Henry Lee with the authorship of these essays, but Gordon Wood casts doubt on that attribution in "The Authorship of the *Letters from the Federal Farmer*," 299–308. See also "Brutus," nos. 1 and 9, *New York Journal*, 18 October 1787 and 17 January 1788. "Brutus," no. 4, *Debates and Proceedings of Massachusetts*, 396.

7. Typically, Anti-Federalists compared the balance between the states and the federal government as outlined in the Articles of Confederation with the balance between the king and Parliament in England. General S. Thompson, Massachusetts Convention, 23 January 1788, *Debates in the Several State Conventions*, 2:79–81. William Lancaster, North Carolina Convention, 30 July 1788, ibid., 4:214. Patrick Henry, Virginia Convention, 16 June 1788, and John Dawes, Virginia Convention, 23 June 1788, ibid., 3:410, 611. "Brutus," no. 9, *New York Journal*, 17 January 1788. "Centinental," no. 2, ibid., 1 November 1787. "A Manifesto of a Number of Gentlemen from Albany Co.," ibid., 26 April 1789. George Mason, Virginia Convention, 14 June 1788, *George Mason Papers*, 3:1075–76.

8. John Lansing and Melanton Smith, New York Convention, 28 June, 1 July 1788, in *Debates in the Several State Conventions*, 2:375–76, 377. Patrick Henry, Virginia Convention, 5 June 1788, ibid., 2:73–74. "Cincinnati," no. 5, *New York Journal*, 29 November 1787.

9. "Brutus" [Robert Yates], nos. 1 and 4, *New York Journal*, 18 October 1787, and *Debates and Proceedings of Massachusetts*, 396. "Pennsylvania Minority Address," in Kenyon, *Antifederalists*, 57. John Dawes, Virginia Convention, 23 June 1788, *Debates in the Several State Conventions*, 3:611. "Federalist Farmer," nos. 2 and 3, in Kenyon, ed., *Antifederalists*, 214, 227. "The Federalist's Political Creed," in John B. McMaster and Frederick D. Stone, eds., *Pennsylvania and the Federal Convention, 1787–1788*, 2:548. Patrick Henry, Virginia Convention, 14 June, 16 June 1788, *Debates in the Several State Conventions*, 3:384–7 and 410–12.

10. Oliver Ellsworth, 18 August, and Elbridge Gerry and Luther Martin, 23 August 1787, in Madison's Notes of the Federal Convention, *The Records of the Federal Convention of 1787*, 2:330, 384–88. Unless otherwise noted, all references to convention speeches are to Madison's notes. Patrick Henry, Virginia Convention, 5 June 1788; William Grayson, Virginia Convention, 18 June 1788, *Debates in the Several State Conventions*, 3:47–48, 51–52, and 417–19. "Columbian Patriot" and "Observations," in Ford, ed., *Pamphlets*, 10–11. Luther Martin, "Defense of Gerry," 18 January 1788, *Records of the Federal Convention*, 3:259–60. Martin,

"Letter on the Federal Convention, 27 January 1788," *Debates in the Several State Conventions*, 1:372. See also Martin, *Genuine Information* . . . , delivered to the Maryland legislature, 29 November 1787, *Records of the Federal Convention*, 3:268–69. [Unsigned], *New York Journal*, 28 January 1788.

11. Luther Martin, no. 1, *Maryland Journal*, 18 March 1788, in Paul Leicester Ford, ed., *Essays on the Constitution of the United States*, 358–59. "Centinental," no. 3, *New York Journal*, 20 November 1787. "A Son of Liberty," ibid., 8 November 1787. Patrick Henry, Virginia Convention, 9 June 1788, *Debates in the Several State Conventions*, 3:169. The possibility that the militia might be neglected presented a particular problem for Martin because, as he argued in his "Letter on the Federal Convention," ibid., 1:372, "the citizens, so far from complaining of this neglect, might even esteem it a favor in the general government, as thereby they would be freed from the burden of militia duties, and left to their own private occupations and pleasures." See also Martin, *Genuine Information* . . . , ibid., 3:208–9; "Pennsylvania Minority Address," in Kenyon, ed., *Antifederalists*, 57; "A Manifesto," *New York Journal*, 22 April 1788; George Mason, Virginia Convention, 14 June 1788, *George Mason Papers*, 3:1075–76.

12. "Federal Farmer," no. 3, 10 October 1787, in Kenyon, ed., *Antifederalists*, 228. "Pennsylvania Minority Address," ibid., 57–58. George Mason, Virginia Convention, 18 June 1788, *Debates in the Several State Conventions*, 2:125–26. "A Countryman," no. 5, *New York Journal*, 22 January 1788. "Centinental," no. 9, in McMaster and Stone, eds., *Federal Constitution*, 2:630.

13. Martin, *Genuine Information* . . . , in *Records of the Federal Convention*, 3:218. Martin, "Letter on the Federal Convention," *Debates in the Several State Conventions*, 1:278–79. "An Officer of the Late Continental Army," *Independent Gazetteer*, 6 November 1787, in McMaster and Stone, eds., *Federal Constitution*, 1:180–82. "Cincinnatus," no. 3, *New York Journal*, 15 November 1787. "Brutus," no. 9, ibid., 17 January 1788. "Centinental," no. 2, ibid., 1 November 1787. "Federal Farmer," no. 3, in Kenyon, ed., *Antifederalists*, 227–29. Robert Miller, North Carolina Convention, 28 July 1788, *Debates in the Several State Conventions*, 4:114–15. George Mason, Virginia Convention, 5 June 1788, *George Mason Papers*, 3:1097–98. Patrick Henry, Virginia Convention, 5 June 1788, *Debates in the Several State Conventions*, 3:59–60. "Letters of Philadelphiensis," no. 9, *Independent Gazetteer*, 7 February 1788, and "Pennsylvania Minority Address," both in Kenyon, ed., *Antifederalists*, 72, 55–57. "Brutus," no. 1, *New York Journal*, 18 October 1787. "Tamony," ibid., 8 February 1788. "An Old Whig," ibid., 11 December 1787. "Cato [George Clinton]," no. 4, ibid., 8 November 1787. "Republican Federalist," no. 8, *Massachusetts Centinal*, 6 February 1788. Gerry, Federal Convention, 7 September 1787, *Records of the Federal Convention*, 2:508–9.

14. This point is explicit in the amendments to the Constitution offered in the state conventions and in the press. Repeatedly, attempts were made to keep the militia and the power to raise regular troops more in the hands of the states by calling for two-thirds or three-fourths votes in Congress to raise troops and by placing restrictions on the national government's power to call the militia out of the states. The right to bear arms was often claimed, but it was part of the concern that the militia system in the states not be purposely neglected by the national

government. See New Hampshire Convention, *Debates in the Several State Conventions*, 1:326; Rhode Island Convention, ibid., 1:334–36; North Carolina Convention, ibid., 4:244–47; Maryland Convention, ibid., 2:550–54; Virginia Convention, ibid., 3:659–60; Pennsylvania Convention, ibid., 2:545–46; New York Convention, ibid., 1:328, 330, and 2:406–8. Also George Mason, "An Amendment to the Constitution Is Needed to Prevent the Danger of a Standing Army," 14 June 1788, *George Mason Papers*, 3:1073–76. For amendments offered in the press, see "Federal Farmer," no. 3, "Pennsylvania Minority Address," and "Agrippa" to the Massachusetts Convention, *Massachusetts Gazette*, 5 February 1788, all in Kenyon, ed., *Antifederalists*, 228–29, 36–37, 156. Also "Brutus," nos. 2 and 10, *New York Journal*, 1 November 1787, 24 January 1788.

15. Wood, *Creation of the American Republic*, part 5. Pocock, *Machiavellian Moment*, chap. 15, especially 513–26. Douglass G. Adair, "'That Politics May Be Reduced to a Science,'" 343–60.

16. Madison, Federal Convention, 19, 29 June 1787, *Records of the Federal Convention*, 1:316, 318, 464–65. Edmund Randolph, Federal Convention, 16 June 1788, Yates Notes, ibid., 1:263. [Jay], *Federalist V*, in Jacob E. Cooke, ed., *The Federalist*, 23–27. All subsequent references to the *Federalist Papers* are to this edition. [Hamilton], *Federalist VI, VIII, XVI, XXI, XXV, LXXV*, 28–36, 44–47, 99–102, 130–32, 158–60, 588. [Madison], *Federalist XLI*, 270–73.

17. Madison, Federal Convention, 29 June and 23 August 1787, *Records of the Federal Convention*, 1:465, 2:388. Charles Pinckney, *Observations on the Plan of Government, Submitted to the Federal Convention* . . . , in ibid., 3:118–19. George Mason's comments in favor of national control over the militia, Federal Convention, 18 August 1787, ibid., 2:325. Also Mason and Madison, Federal Convention, 14 September 1787, ibid., 2:616–17. James Wilson, Pennsylvania Convention, *Debates in the Several State Conventions*, 2:521–22. Madison, Virginia Convention, 6 June 1788, ibid., 3:90. Madison, Wilson Nicholas, and Edmund Randolph, Virginia Convention, 14 June 1788, ibid., 3:381–83, 389–92, 400–401, and Madison, 16 June 1788, ibid., 412–13. "The Republican," *Connecticut Courant*, 7 January 1788. [Hamilton], *Federalist XXIX*, 181–85 and [Madison], *Federalist XLVI*, 308–10. Tench Coxe, *An Examination of the Constitution of the United States* . . . , in Ford, ed., *Pamphlets*, 151. Noah Webster, *An Examination of the Leading Principles of the Federal Convention*, ibid., 56–57. James Iredell, *Answer to Mr. Mason's Objections to the New Constitution*, ibid., 365. [Oliver Ellsworth], "The Landholder," no. 5, *Connecticut Courant*, 3 December 1787.

18. [Hamilton], *Federalist XXVI*, 164–71, and *XXIV*, 152–57. Iredell, *Answers to Mr. Mason's Objections*, Ford, ed., *Pamphlets*, 363–66. Iredell, North Carolina Convention, 26 July 1788, *Debates in the Several State Conventions*, 4:96–97. Madison, Virginia Convention, 16 June 1788, ibid., 3:413. Wilson, Pennsylvania Convention, 11 December 1787, ibid., 2:520. Thomas Dawes, Massachusetts Convention, 24 January 1788, ibid., 2:98. Alexander Contee Hanson, *Remarks on the Proposed Plan of a Federal Government*, in Ford, ed., *Pamphlets*, 234–35. Coxe, *An Examination* . . . , ibid., 15–51. Wilson Nicholas, Virginia Convention, 14 June 1788, *Debates in the Several State Conventions*, 3:391–93. N. Webster, *An Examination* . . . , in Ford, ed., *Pamphlets*, 51–52, 56–57. "A Citizen of New Haven,"

204 Notes to Pages 106–16

Connecticut Courant, 7 January 1788. "Plain Truth," *Independent Gazetteer*, 10 November 1787, in McMaster and Stone, eds., *Federal Constitution*, 1:191–95. "Candidus," *Providence Gazette*, 22 December 1787. Hugh Williamson, *Remarks on the New Plan of Government*, in Ford, ed., *Essays*, 401. "A North Carolina Citizen on the Federal Constitution, 1788," 50.

19. Hanson, *Remarks* . . . , in Ford, ed., *Pamphlets*, 234. N. Webster, *An Examination* . . . , ibid., 56–57. Edmund Randolph, Virginia Convention, 14 June 1788, *Debates in the Several State Conventions*, 3:400–401; Madison, 6, 14 June 1788, ibid., 90, 381–83; Wilson Nicholas, ibid., 389–93. [Madison], *Federalist XLVI*, 320–23. [Hamilton], *Federalist XXIV, XXV, XXIX*, 153–54, 160–63, 183–87. "Candidus," *Providence Gazette*, 22 December 1787.

20. [Hamilton], *Federalist XXV, XXVIII, VIII*, 158–63, 176–80, 47–48.

21. [Jay], *Federalist IV*, 18–23. [Madison], *Federalist LVI*, 380–81. [Hamilton], *Federalist XXIII*, 146–51. Madison, Virginia Convention, 6 June 1788, *Debates in the Several State Conventions*, 3:91. Pelatiah Webster, "Remarks on the Address of Sixteen Members of the Assembly of Pennsylvania to Their Constituents, Debated September 29, 1787," in McMaster and Stone, ed., *Federal Constitution*, 1:101. "James Wilson's Speech Delivered in the Statehouse," reported in the *Pennsylvania Packet*, 10 October 1787, in ibid., 1:145–46.

22. [Hamilton], *Federalist VIII*, 47, and *Federalist XXIV*, 156–57. Francis Corbin, Virginia Convention, 7 June 1788, Elliot, *Debates in the Several State Conventions*, 3:112–13. Edmund Randolph, 6 June, and Wilson Nicholas, 14 June 1788, ibid., 3:76–77, 388–89. Hanson, *Remarks*, in Ford, ed., *Pamphlets*, 235. Also "A Letter of His Excellency Edmund Randolph, Esq., on the Federal Convention, 10 October 1787," in *American Museum*, January 1788, vol. 3, 63; and "Pompilius" and "Further Remarks on Militia Laws, to Pompilius," in *American Museum*, September 1788, vol. 4, 224–26. These letters deal with the moral and economic shortcomings of militia service. See also Edward Mead Earle, "Adam Smith, Alexander Hamilton, Friedrich List," 117–18, 135–36.

Chapter 7

1. Weigley, *Towards an American Army*, 19–20. Palmer, *Washington, Lincoln, Wilson*, 96–101. Kohn, *Eagle and Sword*, 129–31. Kohn argues that the Knox plan did not represent a serious effort to make the militia an effective institution. At best, it was "most likely the first step in their plot to eliminate the militia altogether." Their real aim, Kohn believes, was to propose a militia system so burdensome that Congress would create what Hamilton and his followers wanted most, a large regular army (ibid., 279, 281, 283). This argument assumes that the administration expected a Congress supicious of the military power vested in the new government to accept a regular military establishment responsive to the national government as a viable alternative to a centralized militia system. It is equally plausible that the leaders of the Washington administration—cognizant of the popular suspicion of regular armies—proposed a comprehensive militia system because they recognized that it alone could meet the military needs of the national

government without arousing fears long associated with military professionalism. Indeed, the Federalist administration would have to have been guilty of considerable political naiveté to have approached the matter in any other way. Kohn's interpretation also overlooks the fact that the basic outline of Knox's plan had been favorably received in the Continental Congress in 1786. Certainly Washington had reason to believe that a similar reception awaited his recommendations for a national militia system.

2. Knox to Speaker, House of Representatives, 18 January 1790, *Debates and Proceedings in the Congress of the United States* (hereafter cited as *Annals of Congress*), vol. 2, appendix, 2087–2107.

3. Ibid., vol. 2, 1st Cong., 3rd sess., 1804–7, 1813–14, 1820–23. See also Philadelphia *Aurora*, 20, 24 January, 4 February, 6 June 1791. Elizabethtown *New Jersey Journal*, 14 April 1790.

4. *Annals of Congress*, vol. 2, 1st Cong., 3rd sess., 1804–26, vol. 3, 2nd Cong., 1st sess., 418–23, 552–55, 574–79.

5. The text of the Militia Act is in *Annals of Congress*, vol. 3, appendix, 1392–95. Concerning the passage of the act and its implications see Kohn, *Eagle and Sword*, 128–35. Kreidberg and Henry, *Mobilization*, 30–31. Palmer, *Washington, Lincoln, Wilson*, 110–23. Weigley, *Towards an American Army*, 20–21. John K. Mahon, *The American Militia*, 16–17, 27–28. Cunliffe, *Soldiers and Civilians*, 182–86. Wiener, "The Militia Clause," 187–88. Donald H. Stewart, *The Opposition Press of the Federal Period*, 374–75. Howard White, *Executive Influence*, 91–93.

6. Washington County, Hamilton District Resolutions, 11, 28 February 1794, Rawle Family Papers, 1:15, 18. Circular of the Western Insurgents to the Militia Officers, 28 July 1794; Resolves of Ohio County, Virginia, 9 September 1794; in *Pennsylvania Archives*, 2nd ser. (Harrisburg, 1887–96), 4:78–79, 269–71. Deposition of Francis Mentges, 1 August 1794, and Alexander Hamilton to George Washington, 5 August 1794, *Hamilton Papers*, 17:2–6, 54. James Wilson to Washington, 4 August 1794, and William Bradford to Washington, 17 August 1794, Pennsylvania Whiskey Rebellion Collection. Bradford to Washington, n.d. August 1794, George Washington Papers, 4th ser. Bradford to Elias Boudinot, 1 August 1794, Wallace Collection, vol. 2, Historical Society of Pennsylvania. Leland D. Baldwin, *Whiskey Rebels*, 116–28, 139–71. Eugene P. Link, *Democratic-Republican Societies, 1790–1800*, 51–52, 178–82. Robert W. Coakley, "Federal Use of Militia and the National Guard in Civil Disturbances," 18–19. David H. Pollitt, "Presidential Use of Troops to Execute the Laws," 122–29. The best account of the Washington administration's approach to the Whiskey Rebellion is Richard H. Kohn, "The Washington Administration's Decision to Crush the Whiskey Rebellion," 567–84. For an analysis of the factors contributing to the outbreak of the rebellion, see Jacob E. Cooke, "The Whiskey Insurrection," 316–48.

7. Hamilton to Washington, 2 August 1794, Henry Knox to Washington, 4 August 1794, Bradford to Washington, n.d. August 1794, George Washington Papers, 4th ser. Hamilton to Washington, 5 August 1794, *Pennsylvania Archives*, 2nd ser., 4:100–104. Bradford to Elias Boudinot, 7 August 1794, Wallace Collection, vol. 2.

8. Randolph to Washington, 5 August 1794, George Washington Papers, 4th

ser. See also Hugh Brackenridge to Tench Coxe, 8 August 1794, Virginia Executive Papers, box 86.

9. Mifflin to Washington, 5 August 1794, Randolph to Mifflin, 7 August and 30 August 1794, *Pennsylvania Archives*, 2nd ser., 4:104–9, 112–22, 220–31. Washington to Hamilton, 16 September 1792, *Writings of Washington*, 32:152–53. The federal commissioners were James Ross, James Yeates, and William Bradford. See the Commissioners to Secretary of State Randolph, 15, 17, 19, 22 August 1794, 5 September 1794, Pennsylvania Whiskey Rebellion Collection. See also Baldwin, *Whiskey Rebels*, 116–28, 139–82, 206–17.

10. Edward Smith to Edward Carrington, 17 August 1794, Virginia Executive Papers, box 86; James A. Bradley to Henry Lee, 12 September 1794, and "An Old Soldier," an enclosure; Benjamin Wilson to Lee, 2 September 1794; David Morgan to Lee, 7 September 1794; Arthur Campbell to Lee, 21 August 1794, ibid., box 87; Thomas Matthews to Lt. Gov. Wood, 12 October 1794, ibid., box 88. Henry Lee to Secretary of War Knox, 17 September 1794, and Lee Circular to the Delegates, Militia Commandants . . . in the District of Monogalia, 20 August 1794, in [Virginia] Governor's Letter Book. Proclamation of the Governor of New Jersey, 16 September 1794, in *Pennsylvania Archives*, 2nd ser., 4:306–7. Coakley, "Federal Use of Militia," 19–22.

11. Governor Thomas Lee to Henry Knox, 11 August 1794, Lee to Knox, 15 August 1794, Lee to Joseph Wilkinson, 4 September 1794, Lee to John Carlile, 4 September 1794, Lee to Alexander Hamilton, Lee to Henry Hollington, 5 September 1794, in [Maryland] Council Letter Book, 1793–96, 39, 40, 49, 51–52, 52–53. Lt. Col. William Oldham to Thomas Lee, 4 September 1794, and Brig. Gen. Uriah Forrest to Lee, 22 August 1794, in Maryland State Papers, ser. A, box 76, 5, 7. On the difficulty of raising troops see, ibid., box 76, 8, 14, 15, 16, 17A, 17B. On the problems faced in the western counties see Col. Henry Hollingsworth to Lee, 28 September 1794, and Brig. Gen. Montjoy Bayley to Lee, 23 August 1794, in [Maryland] Adjutant General's Papers, box 21, box 28. Also Thomas Lee to Hamilton, 13 September 1794, *Hamilton Papers*, 17:231–32.

12. Lee to Montjoy Bayley, 6 September 1794, Lee to James Lloyd, 8 September 1794, Lee to Philip Reed, 8 September 1794, Lee to Hamilton, 12 September 1794, Lee to Bayley, 13 September 1794, Lee to Samuel Smith, 13 September 1794, Lee to Hamilton, 13 September 1794, William Pinckney to Hamilton, 18 September 1794, Circular from Thomas Lee to Lt. C. Thomas Sprigg, Bezin Davis, Jr., and William Vanleer, 21 September 1794, Lee to Samuel Smith, 30 September 1794, in [Maryland] Council Letter Book, 53–54, 55–56, 57, 59–60, 60–61, 64–66, 71–73, 74–75, 78–79, 80–82. Sprigg to Lee, 22 September 1794, [Maryland] Adjutant General's Papers, box 57. [Maryland] Council Proceedings, 1793–99, 15 September 1794. John Lynn to Lee, 11 September 1794 and 25 September 1794, Maryland State Papers, ser. A, box 76, 35, 49.

13. Mifflin to General Harmar, 8 August 1794, Harmar to Brigade Inspectors, 27 August 1794, General Wilkins to Clement Biddle, 5 September 1794, Colonel Alexander Russell to Harmar, 6 September 1794, Mifflin to Harmar, 8 September 1794, Governor Mifflin's Address to the Militia of Philadelphia, 10 September 1794, Secretary of State Alexander Dallas's Report to the Pennsylvania Senate, 10

September 1794, Mifflin to the Militia of Lancaster, 26 September 1794, in *Pennsylvania Archives*, 2nd ser., 4:129–31, 209–10, 262, 263–64, 264–65, 273–74, 280–82, 373–75. David Morgan to Washington, 24 September 1794, George Washington Papers, 4th ser. Coakley, "Federal Use of Militia," 19–22.

14. Washington, Proclamation, 25 September 1794, Washington to Henry Lee, 20 October 1794, *Writings of Washington*, 33:207–9; 24:6. Thomas Matthews to Lt. Gov. Wood, 12 October 1794, Virginia Executive Papers, box 88. Governor Howell, General Orders, 1 September 1794, Josiah Harmar, General Orders, 20 September 1794, *Pennsylvania Archives*, 2nd ser., 4:232, 230.

15. Washington to Randolph, 16 October 1794, Washington to Lee, 20 October 1794, Washington's Sixth Annual Message to Congress, 19 November 1794, *Writings of Washington*, 34:3–4, 6, 34–35. General Samuel Smith's Address to the Maryland Troops, 15 November 1794, Secretary of War Knox to Governor Mifflin, 5 December 1794, *Pennsylvania Archives*, 2nd ser., 4:253–54, 486–87. The Act of Congress to Place Troops in the Western Counties, 14 November 1794, is in ibid., 478.

16. See the debate over select militia proposals in Congress during January and February 1795 and December 1796 in *Annals of Congress*, vol. 4, 3rd Cong., 2nd sess., 1067–71, 1214–20, 1233–37, vol. 6, 4th Cong., 2nd sess., 1675–91, 2099, 2223–24. See also Washington's Eighth Address to Congress, 7 December 1796, *Writings of Washington*, 35:319.

17. Stewart, *Opposition Press*, 85–89, 441–44. Adrienne Koch, *Jefferson and Madison*, 152. Mifflin to Washington, 5 August 1794, George Washington Papers. "Nestor," Philadelphia *Aurora*, 12 August 1794. Hugh Brackenridge to Tench Coxe, 8 August 1794, Virginia Executive Papers, box 86. Declaration of the Fayette County Committee, 10 September 1794, Albert Gallatin Papers. [Pennsylvania] Western Commissioners, Thomas McKean and William Irvine, to Governor Mifflin, 5 September 1794, Gallatin to Mifflin, 17 September 1794, *Pennsylvania Archives*, 2nd ser., 4:259–60, 316–19. On the link between regulars and the excise tax, see unsigned essay, Philadelphia *Aurora*, 18 June 1794; "Franklin," ibid., 22 August 1794. William Findley, *History of the Insurrection in the Four Western Counties of Pennsylvania*, 224; Findley, *A Review of the Revenue System*, 63–71. Positive assessments of the militia's performance include New Haven *Connecticut Journal*, 6 November 1794, and Philadelphia *Aurora*, 5 January 1795. Though the Democratic-Republican societies were accused by the Washington administration of perpetrating the Whiskey Rebellion, most societies actually supported the government's efforts to end the rebellion; see William Miller, "The Democratic Societies and the Whiskey Insurrection," 327, 331, 345. The Federalist press was strangely silent on the militia-related issues raised by the Whiskey Rebellion. Democratic societies were blamed for provoking the trouble and accused of undermining the representative structure of government. There was no discussion, however, of the difficulties experienced in getting the militia to turn out. See Philadelphia *Gazette of the United States*, July–December 1794 passim.

18. John Badollet to Albert Gallatin, 14 December 1794, Albert Gallatin Papers. Philadelphia *Aurora*, 4, 25, 26, 27 September, 2, 20 October, 24 November 1794.

19. Findley, *History of the Insurrection*, 153–68.

20. William Maclay's opposition to the creation of the original army establishment during the first session of Congress provides the only hint that a peacetime army was considered by some as incompatible with the tenets of American republicanism. He argued that no peace establishment was contemplated by the Constitution. The militia could serve the nation adequately in emergencies, giving time for the mobilization of an army for sustained fighting. By February 1791 he was convinced that the army and federal taxes were part of an administration scheme to destroy American liberties (William Maclay, *The Journals of William Maclay, United States Senator from Pennsylvania, 1789–1791*, 221, 226–27, 233, 235, 236–39, 369–78, 384). The best account of the legislative history of the army under Washington is Kohn, *Eagle and Sword*, 91–127, 174–86. See also Bernardo and Bacon, *American Military Policy*, 73–84.

21. *Annals of Congress*, vol. 3, 2nd Cong., 1st sess., 343–48.

22. Ibid., 337–42, 349–54. "Observer No. 1," Philadelphia *Aurora*, 20 February 1792. Philadelphia *National Gazette*, 18 February 1792. Philip Freneau, "Rules for Changing a Limited Republican Government into an Unlimited One," *National Gazette*, 4 July 1792.

23. Kohn, *Eagle and Sword*, 120–23, 147–48.

24. *Annals of Congress*, vol. 3, 2nd Cong., 2nd sess., 750, 762–88, 773–802.

25. Ibid.

26. Ibid., vol. 4, 3rd Cong., 1st sess., 534–35, 735–38, 774–79, 2nd sess., 1163–72, 1220–23, vol. 5, 4th Cong., 1st sess., 905–13, 1418–23. Timothy Pickering, "Objects of the Military Establishment of the United States," 3 February 1796, and James McHenry, "Report of the Peace Establishment," 14 March 1795, *American State Papers, Military Affairs* [hereafter cited as *ASP, MA*], 1:112–13, 114. "A Calm Observer," New York *Argus*, 12 May 1795. For other Republican antiarmy comments see Philadelphia *Aurora*, 3 January, 12 February, 31 March, 21 May, 22 May 1794, 30 May, 11 September 1795. Philadelphia *General Advertiser*, 22 May 1794. Boston *Independent Chronicle*, 5 June 1794. Stewart, *The Opposition Press*, 89, 92–94, 441–44. See also Kohn, *Eagle and Sword*, 174–89. White, *Executive Influence*, 116–17. Bernardo and Bacon, *American Military Policy*, 83–84.

Chapter 8

1. For the text of the Provisional Army Act and the New Army Act see *Debates and Proceedings in the Congress of the United States* (hereafter cited as *Annals of Congress*), vol. 9, appendix, 3729–33, 3743–44, 3785–87. The best account of the political context surrounding the passage of the Provisional and New Army acts is Kohn, *Eagle and Sword*, 193–255. Kohn, however, argues that Hamilton and a few followers envisioned a constitutional coup d'état through the creation of a classical, European standing army. See also, Ekirch, *The Civilian and the Military*, 40–44; William H. Gaines, Jr., "The Forgotten Army," 267–79; Bernardo and Bacon, *American Military Policy*, 85–87; White, *Executive Influence*, 155–63.

2. The periodic reprinting of political tracts from the revolutionary era underscores the mentality of the Republican opposition. For example, Josiah Quincy's *Observations on . . . the Boston Port Bill* was serialized in the Philadelphia *Aurora* between 20 February and 4 March 1799. It also appeared in the Boston *Independent Chronicle*. The *Aurora* reprinted Andrew Fletcher's *A Discourse of Government with Relation to Militias* in serial form between 23 and 27 November 1798. The *Independent Chronicle* reprinted part of Thomas Davies's 1781 Boston Massacre Oration under the title "On Standing Armies" on 28 March 1799. Excerpts pertaining to standing armies and militia from *Cato's Letters* appeared in the *Aurora* on 9 August 1798. See also Lance Banning, "Republican Ideology and the Triumph of the Constitution, 1789 to 1793," 181–88. Stewart, *Opposition Press*, 441–44.

3. Louisa County, Virginia, Resolutions, 18 October 1798, in Boston *Independent Chronicle*, 5 November 1798. Unsigned essay, ibid., 21 March 1799. "A Plain Countryman's Opinion," ibid., 15 April 1799. Spotsylvania County, Virginia, Resolution, 15 November 1798, ibid., 29 November 1798. Caroline County, Virginia, Memorial to the Virginia Assembly, 13 November 1798, ibid., 13 December 1798. "From Philadelphia," ibid., 10 December 1798. Unsigned essay, Philadelphia *Aurora*, 26 July 1798. "To the Electors of Northumberland County," ibid., 11 September 1799. Resolutions of Philadelphia Citizens, 11 February 1799, ibid., 13 February 1799.

4. Excerpts from Quincy's *Observations*, Boston *Independent Chronicle*, 6 August 1798. "Letter from a Virginia Congressman to a Constituent," ibid., 16 July 1798. Unsigned essay, ibid., 8 April 1799. Resolutions of the Citizens of Lexington, Kentucky, 29 August 1798, ibid., 25 October 1798. Louisa County, Virginia, Resolutions, 18 October 1798, ibid., 5 November 1798. Orange County, Virginia, Resolutions, n.d., ibid., 10 December 1798. Unsigned essays, ibid., 10 December 1798 and 14 January 1799. Unsigned essay, Philadelphia *Aurora*, 20 February 1799. Unsigned poem, ibid., 9 November 1799. Excerpt from *Cato's Letters*, ibid., 9 August 1798. Speech to Washington County, Pennsylvania, Militia Association, 28 February 1799, ibid., 16 May 1799. "A Customer to Mr. Greenleaf," with excerpts from "Mr. Poultrey's speech on the Motion to Reduce the Army [Parliament, 1738]," ibid., 2 May 1798. "CIRCUMSPECTION," ibid., 21 July 1798. Philadelphia County Militia to Governor Mifflin, 16 June 1798, ibid., 20 June 1798.

5. Petition from Washington County, Pennsylvania, to Albert Gallatin, 22 September 1798, Gallatin Papers. Editorial by William Duane, Philadelphia *Aurora*, 27 February 1800. Unsigned essay, Boston *Independent Chronicle*, 31 October 1799. Dinwiddie County, Virginia, Resolutions, 10 November 1798, ibid., 17 December 1798. Petition from the Citizens of Rutland, Vermont, to the United States Congress, 20 February 1799, ibid., 4 March 1799. "HONESTUS," ibid., 4 February 1799. "From Poughkeepsie," ibid., 28 February 1799. "Standing Armies," ibid., 13 December 1798.

6. "PILLIP," Philadelphia *Aurora*, 3 July 1798. Mifflin County, Pennsylvania, Resolutions, 11 January 1799, ibid., 23 January 1799. Unsigned essay, ibid., 6 December 1798. Speech to the Washington County, Pennsylvania, Militia Association, 28 February 1799, ibid., 16 May 1799. "Touchstone, No. II," ibid., 13 August 1800. "Elector," Boston *Independent Chronicle*, 1 April 1799. Dinwiddie

County, Virginia, Resolutions, 10 November 1798, ibid., 17 December 1798. "Democritus, #I 'On Standing Armies,'" ibid., 14 January 1799. Greene County, Pennsylvania, Resolutions, September 1798, Gallatin Papers.

7. "Democritus, 'On Standing Armies,'" Boston *Independent Chronicle*, 11 February 1799. Louisa County, Virginia, Resolutions, 18 October 1798, ibid., 5 November 1798. John Taylor of Caroline to the Virginia Assembly, 18 January 1799, ibid., 7 February 1799. "Democritus #II, 'On Standing Armies,'" ibid., 28 January 1799. Dinwiddie County, Virginia, Resolutions, 10 November 1798, ibid., 17 December 1798. Unsigned essay, ibid., 21 March 1799. Resolutions of a Meeting of Citizens in Philadelphia, 8 February 1799, Philadelphia *Aurora*, 11 February 1799. "A Republican," ibid., 2 April 1798. "Old Man of the Mountain," ibid., 23 June 1800. John Fowler to his Constituents, 15 May 1800, ibid., 9 June 1800. "To the REPUBLICAN CITIZENS of the County of Bucks [Pennsylvania]," ibid., 3 September 1799. Unsigned essays, ibid., 13 January, 29 August 1798, 26 May, 10 June, and 26 July 1799. Clark County, Tennessee, Resolutions, 24 July 1798, ibid., 1 September 1798. "A CITIZEN OF THE United States, 'Political Reflections,'" ibid., 23 February 1799. "Countryman," ibid., 20 February 1798. John Fowler to his Constituents, 20 July 1798, ibid., 8 September 1798. "CIRCUMSPECTION," ibid., 21 July 1798. "AN OLD SOLDIER," ibid., 3 August 1798. "MENTOR," ibid., 21 May 1799. Edmund Pendleton, Address to Citizens in Caroline County, Virginia, November 1798; and An Address, 20 February 1799, *Pendleton Papers*, 2:652–64, 658–69. Petition from Washington County, Pennsylvania, to Gallatin, 22 September 1798, Gallatin Papers.

8. *Annals of Congress*, vol. 8, 5th Cong., 2nd sess., 1525–42, 1631–1703 passim.

9. Ibid., 1703–7, 1725–72, 1934–54 passim.

10. "Humanus," Philadelphia *Aurora*, 6 September 1800. Address to the Citizens of the County of Lancaster, Pennsylvania, ibid., 18 September 1800. "A VIRGINIAN," ibid., 19 February 1799. "A Young a Very Young Citizen," ibid., 11 May 1798. Petition of the Citizens of Northampton, Pennsylvania, ibid., 12 February 1799. Spotsylvania County, Virginia, Resolutions, 6 November 1798, ibid., 20 November 1798. Hanover County, Virginia, Resolutions, 25 October 1798, Boston *Independent Chronicle*, 12 November 1798. Resolutions of the Citizens of Lexington, Kentucky, ibid., 25 October 1798. John Taylor of Caroline to the Virginia Assembly, 18 January 1798, ibid., 7 February 1799. John Fowler to his Constituents, 4 March 1799, Philadelphia *Gazette of the United States*, 4 May 1799.

11. Address to the Dorchester Militia Company, Boston *Constitutional Telegraphe*, 13 November 1799. Resolutions of the Citizens of Lexington, Kentucky, 29 August 1798, Boston *Independent Chronicle*, 25 October 1798. "Democritus, 'On Standing Armies,'" ibid., 11 February 1799. "People," ibid., 8 April 1799. Unsigned essay, ibid., 31 October 1799. Louisa County, Virginia, Resolutions, 18 October 1798, ibid., 5 November 1798. Orange County, Virginia, Militia Resolutions, ibid., 10 December 1798. Petition from the Citizens of Rutland, Vermont, to the U.S. Congress, 20 February 1799, ibid., 4 March 1799. "From Poughkeepsie," ibid., 28 February 1799. "People," Newark *Centinel of Freedom*, 7 May 1799. John Fowler to his Constituents, 4 March 1799, Philadelphia *Gazette of the United States*, 4 May 1799. Resolutions of a Meeting of Citizens in Philadelphia, 8

February 1799, Philadelphia *Aurora*, 11 February 1799. Unsigned poem, ibid., 9 November 1799. Dinwiddie County, Virginia, Resolutions, 10 November 1798, ibid., 17 December 1798. Essex County, Virginia, Resolutions, ibid., 7 December 1798. Mifflin County, Pennsylvania, Resolutions, ibid., 11, 23 January 1799. "American Citizens," ibid., 19 June 1800. "Thomas McKean to the Officer of the Militia of Lancaster," 26 February 1800, ibid., 7 March 1800. Newark, New Jersey, Toasts Celebrating the Disbanding of the Army, ibid., 19 June 1800. Fourth of July resolutions printed in the Republican press consistently referred to the glory of the militia, see for example, ibid., 9 July 1798.

12. *Annals of Congress*, vol. 8, 5th Cong., 2nd sess., 1525–42, 1631–1703 passim. Leading Federalists had considered the provisional army an alternative to the state militias since early 1794 when national security became an issue amidst mounting tensions between the United States and Great Britain. See Theodore Sedgwick's speech in the House of Representatives, 12 March 1794, *Annals of Congress*, vol. 4, 3rd Cong., 1st sess., 500–504. A similiar suggestion circulated among Federalists in the aftermath of the Whiskey Rebellion; see "Measures in the War Department Which It May Be Expedient to Adopt," [December 1794], *Hamilton Papers*, 17:582–84. Again in 1797, Hamilton described the provisional army as a means to provide the national government with an effective reserve freed from local entanglements, when he again recommended the plan to Secretary of State Timothy Pickering. See Hamilton to Pickering, 11 May 1797, ibid., 21:83–84. Also Hamilton to William Loughton Smith, 10 April 1797, ibid., 39–40. See also Kohn, *Eagle and Sword*, 220–21.

13. *Annals of Congress*, vol. 8, 5th Cong., 2nd sess., 1525–42, 1630–1703 passim. Except to note that the current diplomatic crisis with France required an expanded military establishment, the Federalist press was silent on the implications of the provisional army legislation.

14. Ibid., 1703–7, 1725–72, 1934–54 passim. Robert Goodloe Harper to his Constituents, 23 July 1798 and 20 March 1799, *Bayard Papers*, 55–59, 83–84. James Ross to James McHenry, 15 June 1798, in Bernard C. Steiner, *The Life and Correspondence of James McHenry* (Cleveland, 1907), 437–38. Harper to Hamilton, 27 April 1797, *Hamilton Papers*, 21:449. Kohn, *Eagle and Sword*, 226.

15. *Annals of Congress*, vol. 8, 5th Cong., 2nd sess., 1729–31, 1734–39, 1747, 1758. Hamilton to James Gunn, 22 December 1798, Steiner, *James McHenry*, 361. Hamilton to Pickering, 11 May 1797, [Hamilton], "The Stand, No. VI," originally published in the New York *Commercial Advertiser*, 19 April 1798, Hamilton to Sedgwick, 2 February 1799, Hamilton to Jonathan Drayton, [ca. October–November 1799], *Hamilton Papers*, 21:83–84, 438–49, 22:394, 453, 23:599–602. Secretary of War McHenry to John Adams, 24 December 1798, printed in Philadelphia *Aurora*, 10 January 1799.

16. Hamilton to McHenry [January 27–February 11?] 1798, Hamilton to Sedgwick, 1–5 March 1798, Hamilton to Pickering, 17 March 1798, Hamilton to Oliver Wolcott, Jr., 5 June 1798, Pickering to Hamilton, 9 June 1798, *Hamilton Papers*, 21:343, 361–63, 365, 386–87, 504–5.

17. General Orders, 6 June 1799, *Hamilton Papers*, 23:169–70. Washington to McHenry, 30 August and 15 October 1798, Hamilton to McHenry, 19 January

1800, in Steiner, *James McHenry*, 240–41, 346, 413. Washington to John Adams, 25 September 1798, Washington to William R. Davie, 24 October 1796, *Writings of Washington*, 36:457–58, 516.

18. *Annals of Congress*, vol. 10, 6th Cong., 1st sess., 304–6, 365.

19. James McHenry to Speaker, House of Representatives, 5 January 1800, with an endorsement by President John Adams, McHenry to Speaker, House of Representatives, 31 January 1800, *American State Papers, Military Affairs*, 1:133–35, 142–44. McHenry was closely associated with Alexander Hamilton, who long before had come to agree with Adam Smith's contention that regular soldiers were compatible with a free government. See Earle, "Adam Smith, Alexander Hamilton, Friedrich List," 129–34. Newspaper commentary reflecting similar insights include: Unsigned essays, Philadelphia *Gazette of the United States*, 31 March, 3 July, and 26 July 1799. "ALPHA," ibid., 12 April 1799. Minority Statement of the Virginia Legislature, ibid., 5 February 1799; [Hamilton], "The Stand, No. I," originally published in the New York *Commercial Advertiser*, 30 March 1798, *Hamilton Papers*, 21:386–87. See also McHenry to Washington, 4 August 1798, in Steiner, *James McHenry*, 339.

20. Kohn, *Eagle and Sword*, 256–73.

Chapter 9

1. Albany *Register*, 20 May 1800. Philadelphia *Aurora*, January to December 1800 passim, particularly 3, 21 March, 1 July, 25 October, 5 November 1800. Newark, *Centinel of Freedom*, 17 June 1800. *A Letter from Manlius, to John Marshall*, 4–5, 7–18. Benjamin Austin, *Constitutional Republicanism*, 46–47. Joseph B. Varnum, *An Address . . . to the . . . Massachusetts Militia*, 15–23.

2. Jefferson, "First Inaugural Address," 4 March 1801, and "First Annual Message to Congress," 8 December 1801, *Messages and Papers of the Presidents*, 1:322–23, 329–30. Edmund Pendleton, "The Danger Not Over," [October 5, 1801], *Pendleton Papers*, 2:695–99. Varnum, *An Address*, 19. Abraham Bishop, *Connecticut Republicanism*, 22–24. Jefferson to George Rogers Clark, 19 February 1781, *Jefferson Papers*, 4:653. Peterson, *Thomas Jefferson*, 214–15, 688–89.

3. An Act fixing the Military Peace Establishment of the United States, 16 March 1802, *Debates and Proceedings in the Congress of the United States* (hereafter cited as *Annals of Congress*), vol. 11, appendix, 1306–12. Jefferson, "First Annual Message to Congress," 8 December 1801, and "Second Annual Message to Congress," 15 December 1802, *Messages and Papers of the Presidents*, 1:329, 345. The House committee's response to the president's address is in *Annals of Congress*, vol. 12, 7th Cong., 2nd sess., 521–22. For the terms of the 1803 militia reform legislation, see ibid., appendix, 1566–67.

4. *Annals of Congress*, vol. 12, appendix, 1608–9.

5. Ibid., vol. 11, appendix, 1313. Jefferson asked for militia reform in every annual address to Congress during both administrations except 1803. David Humphreys, *Considerations on the Means of Improving the Militia for the Public Defence*, 16. Weigley, *Towards an American Army*, 26–29.

Notes to Pages 155–63   213

6. Joseph Priestley, *The Theological and Miscellaneous Works*, vol. 24, entitled, *Lectures on History and General Policy* . . . , 381–88. The text of the 1803 American edition was used for this collection.

7. Ibid., 387–88.

8. Ibid., 389–90.

9. Priestley's work was widely read in America, being owned by 49 percent of the nation's public and private libraries by 1813 (Lundberg and May, "The Enlightened Reader," charts following p. 271).

10. John Taylor of Caroline, *Arator*, 18, 21–23, 27, 37, 54–55, 290–92. John Taylor of Caroline, *An Inquiry into the Principles and Policy of the Government of the United States*, 623–24. Eugene T. Mudge, *The Social Philosophy of John Taylor of Caroline*, 6–7, 12–13, 15, 21, 50–52, 76–78. C. William Hill, Jr., *The Political Theory of John Taylor of Caroline*, 164–71, 236–48.

11. Taylor, *Inquiry*, 41–43, 69–77, 450–51, 594–95. Mudge, *John Taylor*, 105–11.

12. Taylor, *Inquiry*, 178–81, 451–53, 488–89, 624–25. Mudge, *John Taylor*, 54–55, 85, 103–4, 108–9.

13. Joel Barlow, "Advise to the Privileged Orders," in *The Political Works of Joel Barlow*, 24, 54–57, 62–66.

14. Barlow, "Letter to the National Convention of France," 16 September 1792, in *Political Works*, 176–97.

15. William Henry Harrison, Governor of Indiana Territory, to Charles Scott, Governor of Kentucky, 10 March 1810, n.d. April 1810, printed in the Washington *National Intelligencer*, 21 September, 1 October 1810, under the title "Militia Discipline." See also Walter James to James Monroe, 8 December 1811, Papers of James Monroe.

16. Harrison, "Militia Discipline," Washington *National Intelligencer*, 21 September, 1 October 1810. Thomas Baldwin, *A Discourse Delivered before the Ancient and Honourable Artillery Company*, 11–12, 22. "On the Military Constitution of Nations," Washington *National Intelligencer*, 18 November 1808. In the years before the War of 1812 newspapers frequently reprinted calls for militia reform issued by state governors. See, for example, James B. Richardson to the South Carolina Legislature, 27 November 1804, Washington *National Intelligencer*, 21 December 1804. Governor Thomas McKean to the Pennsylvania Legislature and Senate, 5 December 1805, ibid., 11 December 1805. Jonathan Trumbull to the Connecticut Assembly, October Session 1807, ibid., 23 October 1807.

17. David Humphreys, *Considerations on . . . the Militia*, 4–7. James Kendall, *Preparations for War*, 5–11. Epaphras Hoyt, *Practical Instructions for Military Officers*, iii–iv. Edward Gillespy, *The Military Instructor*, iii–iv. See also notes 15 and 16 above.

18. Maxmillian Godefroy, *Military Reflections, on Four Modes of Defence, for the United States*, 5–15, 21–22.

19. Ibid., 11–20.

20. Ibid., 23–38. See also Irene A. Lacroix, *Military and Political Hints*, throughout. Unsigned essay, Washington *National Intelligencer*, 25 July 1811. Unsigned essays in the *American Review of History and Politics* 3 (1812): 124–25,

125–26. An unsigned review of Charles Ganilh, *An Inquiry into the Various Systems of Political Economy*, in ibid., vol. 4 (1812), 320–33.

21. Humphreys, *Considerations on . . . the Militia*, 7–8, 16. Harrison, "Militia Discipline," Washington *National Intelligencer*, 21 September, 1 October 1810. Unsigned essay, ibid., 4 November 1807. "On the Military Constitution of Nations," ibid., 18 November 1808. "JURISCOLA," ibid., 17 October 1810. "AURORA," ibid., 14 December 1811. Kendall, *Preparations for War*, 22–23. See also Benjamin Tallmadge to Eden. Huntington, 18 December 1809, Huntington to Tallmadge, 4 January 1810, in *Annals of Congress*, vol. 21, appendix, 2409–18.

22. William Duane, *The American Military Library*, 1:i, 5–8, 29–36.

23. Philadelphia *Aurora*, 30 and 31 October 1807.

24. Ibid., 2, 3, 4, 5, 10, 11, 12, 14 November 1807. Duane, *American Military Library*, 1:i–iv.

25. Jefferson, "Fifth Annual Message to Congress," *Messages and Papers of the Presidents*, 1:385–87. The bill was introduced by Samuel Smith, brother of the secretary of the navy, in the Senate on 22 January 1807; see *Annals of Congress*, vol. 15, 9th Cong., 1st sess., 69–70. Richard A. Erney, "The Public Life of Henry Dearborn," 155–59. Peterson, *Thomas Jefferson*, 832–35. Dumas Malone, *Jefferson the President*, 507–23.

26. The congressional committee reports are in *Annals of Congress*, vol. 15, 9th Cong., 1st sess., 327–29, 1069–75. The debate over the militia detachment legislation can be followed in ibid., 398–408. The text of the final bill is in ibid., 1265–66. See also Erney, "Henry Dearborn," 163–65, 183.

27. Jefferson to Samuel Dupont de Nemours, 2 May 1808, Jefferson to Charles Pinckney, 30 March 1808, Thomas Jefferson Papers. Jefferson to James Madison, 5 May 1807, Jefferson to Henry Dearborn, 28 August 1807, Jefferson to John Armstrong, 2 May 1808, *Writings of Thomas Jefferson*, 9:49–50, 132, 193–94. Jefferson to the Governors of Ohio, Kentucky, Tennessee, and the Territories of Michigan, Indiana, Louisiana, Mississippi, Orleans, 21 March 1807, in Miscellaneous Letters Sent by the Secretary of War, 1800–1809, M 370, roll 3, volume 3, National Archives. Dearborn to the Governors of the States, 3 August 1807, ibid. See also Albert Gallatin to Jefferson, 25 July 1807, *Writings of Albert Gallatin*, 1:340–52. Jefferson, "Sixth and Seventh Annual Messages to Congress," 2 December 1806, 27 October 1807, *Messages and Papers of the Presidents*, 1:406–7, 410, 428–29. The text of the volunteer corps legislation is in *Annals of Congress*, vol. 16, appendix, 1259–60. Weigley, *U.S. Army*, 104–5. Huntington, *The Soldier and the State*, 196–97. Palmer, *Washington, Lincoln, Wilson*, 126–27. Forman, "Thomas Jefferson on Universal Military Training," 177–78.

28. The debate over the militia plan can be followed in *Annals of Congress*, vol. 18, 10th Cong., 1st sess., 1472–81, 1484–86, 1509–11, 1676. The text of the 1808 militia detachment act is in ibid., 2846. Jefferson's messages to Congress are in *Messages and Papers of the Presidents*, 1:443, 454–55. The House committee report quoted here was issued 3 January 1809 and is recorded in *American State Papers, Military Affairs* (hereafter cited as *ASP, MA*), 1:236. For the 1810 House report, see *Annals of Congress*, vol. 21, appendix, 2409–11. For the Senate, see ibid., vol. 20, 11th Cong., 2nd sess., 595, and the Senate Committee Report on the Militia, 6

May 1810, in *ASP, MA*, 1:256. Jefferson later blamed the nation's military problems during the War of 1812 on Congress's failure to class the militia. See Peterson, *Thomas Jefferson*, 933. For Madison's calls for militia reform, see his first and particularly his second annual messages to Congress, 29 November 1809, 5 December 1810, in *Messages and Papers of the Presidents*, 1:476, 486–87. Palmer, *Washington, Lincoln, Wilson*, 129–33. On related military matters after 1807 see: Erney, "Henry Dearborn," 193, 216–34. Mary P. Adams, "Jefferson's Military Policy with Special Reference to the Frontier, 1805–1809," 128–85, 242–71, 289–91, 305.

29. "Estimate for 50,000 Volunteers," 14 December 1808, Jefferson Papers. *Annals of Congress*, vol. 19, 10th Cong., 2nd sess., 946–69, 1168–70, 1192–1229. Resolution of the Delaware House of Representatives, 1 February 1809, in the Washington *National Intelligencer*, 13 February 1809. Henry Dearborn to House Committee [John Dawson, Chairman], 4 December 1809, Reports to Congress from the Secretary of War, 1803–7, M 220, roll 1, National Archives. *Annals of Congress*, vol. 20, 11th Cong., 2nd sess., 557–69 [Senate]. Ibid., vol. 21, 11th Cong., 2nd sess., 1471–79, 1497–1531, 1566–79, 1586–1605. James Breckinridge (Virginia) to his Constituents, 11 August 1810, *Circular Letters of Congressmen to Their Constituents, 1789–1829*, 2:681–82, 739. Samuel Taggert to John Taylor, 8 March 1810. "Letters of Samuel Taggert, Representative in Congress, 1803–1814," 346. Joseph Bloomfield to Benjamin Tallmadge, 9 December 1809, *Annals of Congress*, vol. 21, appendix, 2419–24.

30. The text of the legislation arming the militia is in *Annals of Congress*, vol. 18, appendix, 2860. The debate can be followed in ibid., vol. 27, 10th Cong., 1st sess., 1002–5, 1019–45, 2066–67, 2175–87, 2189–97. Henry Dearborn to John Ward, 5 November 1807, Miscellaneous Letters Sent by the Secretary of War, M 370, roll 3, vol. 3, National Archives.

31. The administration requested the expansion of the regular army on 25 February 1808. See *ASP, MA*, 1:227–28. John Randolph led the opposition to the expanded army. The debate over the request is in *Annals of Congress*, vol. 18, 10th Cong., 1st sess., 1512–22, 1620–39, 1714–15, 1855–57, 1860–68, 1873–83, 1901–73, 1977–2018, 2021–64. The text of the act expanding the army to 10,000 men is in ibid., 2850–52. Legislation suspending recruitment for the expanded army passed Congress in June 1809 (ibid., vol. 21, 11th Cong., 1st sess., 2511). Except for appropriation bills, no preparedness legislation passed Congress during the 11th Congress. See also Edwin Gray (Virginia) to his Constituents, n.d. April 1808, James M. Garnett (Virginia) to Freeholders of Caroline, Essex, King and Queen, and King William, 12 April 1808, George W. Campbell (Tennessee) to his Constituents, 14 April 1808, William B. Burnwell (Virginia) to his Constituents, 23 April 1808, Matthew Lyon (Kentucky) to his Constituents, 26 April 1808, in *Circular Letters*, 2:545, 561–62, 569, 584, 596. Weigley, *U.S. Army*, 109.

Chapter 10

1. Kreidberg and Henry, *Military Mobilization*, 42–46. Joseph C. Duggan, *The Legislative and Statutory Development of the Federal Concept for Military Service*, 12. Weigley, *U.S. Army*, 111–24.

2. For James Monroe's military plan see his "Report to the Senate Committee on Military Affairs," 17 October 1814, in *American State Papers, Military Affairs* (hereafter cited as *ASP, MA*), 1:514–17. On the public and official response to his plan, see Duggan, *Federal Concept for Military Service*, 13–17; Jack F. Leach, *Conscription in the United States*, chaps. 3 and 4.

3. Calhoun's speeches to the House of Representatives, 27 February 1815 and 2 January 1816, *The Papers of John C. Calhoun*, 1:277–78, 287–90.

4. The classing plan mentioned was submitted by Acting Secretary of War George Graham, 13 December 1816; see *ASP, MA*, 1:642–44. For the development of Calhoun's thought, see Calhoun to Speaker of the House, Henry Clay, 11 December 1818, *Calhoun Papers*, 3:374–78; Calhoun to the House of Representatives, 15 January 1819, *ASP, MA*, 1:834; Calhoun to Speaker, House of Representatives, 12 December 1820, *Calhoun Papers*, 5:481.

5. Calhoun to Speaker, House of Representatives, 12 December 1820, *Calhoun Papers*, 5:480–90.

6. The militia no longer occupied a position of importance in national discussions of the republic's military needs. See House Committee report on Militia Reform, 17 January 1817, *ASP, MA*, 1:633–35. The same report was quoted in its entirety by a House committee charged with militia reform in January 1819; see ibid., 824–27. See also, Carlton B. Smith, "Congressional Attitudes toward Military Preparedness during the Monroe Administration," 22–25. The decline in interest in the militia is revealed by the fact that Monroe never sought militia reform after his first year in office; see *Messages and Papers of the Presidents*, 2:7–8, 15–16, 45–46, 61–62, 78.

7. John C. Calhoun, "Reduction of the Army," 12 December 1820, and "Conditions of the Military Establishment and Fortifications," 27 November 1822, *ASP, MA*, 2:189–94, 450–51; Kreidberg and Henry, *Mobilization*, 61–62.

8. Weigley, *U.S. Army*, 142–45.

9. "Army of the United States," *North American Review* 23 (1826):245–46, 273. Weigley, *U.S. Army*, 144–72. Carlton B. Smith, "The American Search for a 'Harmless' Army," 34–36.

Bibliography

Primary Sources

NEWSPAPERS

American Museum. Philadelphia.
Argus. New York.
Aurora. Philadelphia.
Boston Chronicle.
Boston Gazette.
Centinel of Freedom. Newark.
Connecticut Courant. Hartford.
Connecticut Journal. New Haven.
Continental Journal. Boston.
Essex Gazette. Salem.
Gazette of the United States. Philadelphia.
General Advertiser. Philadelphia.
Independent Chronicle. Boston.
Journal. New York.
Massachusetts Centinel. Boston.
National Gazette. Philadelphia.
National Intelligencer. Washington.
New Jersey Journal. Elizabethtown.
New York Journal.
Providence Gazette.

ARCHIVAL MATERIALS

American Antiquarian Society. Worcester, Mass.
   Shays' Rebellion Collection. 1786–87.
Historical Society of Pennsylvania. Philadelphia.
   Rawle Family Papers.
   John William Wallace Collection.
Library of Congress. Washington, D.C.
   Albert Gallatin Papers.
   Thomas Jefferson Papers.
   James Monroe Papers.
   Pennsylvania Whiskey Rebellion Collection.
   George Washington Papers. 4th series. Microfilm.
National Archives. Washington, D.C.
   Papers of the Continental Congress. Microfilm.
   Records of the States of the United States. Session Laws and Constitutional Records. Microfilm.
   [Secretary of War.] Miscellaneous Letters Sent by the Secretary of War, 1800–1809. Microfilm.
   _____. Reports to Congress from the Secretary of War, 1803–7. Microfilm.
Maryland Hall of Records. Annapolis.
   [Maryland] Adjutant General's Papers.
   [Maryland] Council Letter Book, 1793–96.
   [Maryland] Council Proceedings, 1793–99.
   Maryland State Papers. Series A.

Massachusetts State Library. Boston.
  Massachusetts Archives. Vols. 189, 190, 191, 192, 318, 319.
Virginia State Library. Richmond.
  Virginia Executive Papers. Henry Lee. Boxes 86–89.
  [Virginia] Governor's Letter Book, July–December 1794.

PUBLISHED STATE PAPERS AND RELATED DOCUMENTS

American State Papers, Military Affairs. 7 vols. Walter Lowrie and Matthew S. Clarke, eds. Washington, 1838–61.
Backgrounds of Selective Service. Vol. 1, *A Historical Review of the Principles of Citizen Compulsion in the Raising of Armies.* Vol. 2, *Military Obligations: The American Tradition. A Compilation of the Enactments of Compulsion from the Earliest Settlements of the Original Thirteen Colonies in 1607 through the Articles of Confederation 1787.* Washington, 1947.
Charters and General Laws of the Colony and Province of Massachusetts Bay. Boston, 1814.
Colonial Laws of New York from the Year 1664 to the Revolution. 5 vols. Albany, 1894.
Colonial Records of North Carolina. 10 vols. William Clark, ed. Goldsboro, 1886–1907.
Debates and Proceedings in the Congress of the United States. Washington, 1834–53.
Debates and Proceedings in the Convention of the Commonwealth of Massachusetts . . . 1788. Boston, 1856.
The Debates in the Several State Conventions on the Adoption of the Federal Constitution. 5 vols. Jonathan Elliot, ed. Philadelphia, 1896.
The Federal and State Constitutions. 7 vols. Francis Newton Thorpe, ed. Washington, 1909.
Journals of the Continental Congress. 34 vols. W. C. Ford, et al., eds. Washington, 1904–36.
The Messages and Papers of the Presidents, 1789–1897. 10 vols. James D. Richardson, comp. Washington, 1898.
Parliamentary History of England. Vol. 10. William Cobbett, ed. London, 1812.
Pennsylvania Archives. 2nd series. Vol. 4. Harrisburg, 1887–96.
The Records of the Federal Convention of 1787. 4 vols. Max Farrand, ed. New Haven, 1937.
The Statutes at Large: Being a Collection of All the Laws of Virginia from 1619 to 1808. 13 vols. William W. Hening, ed. Richmond, 1819.

PUBLISHED CORRESPONDENCE

(Letters are included in some of the biographical works listed under secondary sources.)

Adams, John. *The Works of John Adams.* 10 vols. Charles F. Adams, ed. Boston, 1850–56.
Adams, Samuel. *The Writings of Samuel Adams.* 4 vols. Harry A. Cushing, ed. New York, 1904–8.
Bayard, James A. *Papers of James A. Bayard.* Elizabeth Donnan, ed. New York, 1971.

Calhoun, John C. *The Papers of John C. Calhoun*. Vols. 1–5. Robert L. Meriwether and W. Edwin Hemphill, eds. Columbia, 1959–71.
Circular Letters of Congressmen to Their Constituents, 1789–1829. 3 vols. Noble E. Cunningham, ed. Chapel Hill, 1978.
Cooke, Nicholas. "Revolutionary Correspondence of Governor Nicholas Cooke, 1775–1781." Matthew B. Jones, ed. American Antiquarian Society *Proceedings* 36 (1926): 231–53.
Cooper, Samuel. "Letters of Samuel Cooper to Thomas Pownall, 1769–1777." Frederick Tuckerman, ed. *American Historical Review* 8 (1903):301–30.
Correspondence of the American Revolution: Being Letters of Eminent Men to George Washington. 4 vols. Jared Sparks, ed. Boston, 1853.
Deane, Silas. *The Deane Papers*. 5 vols. New York Historical Society *Collections*, vols. 19–23. 1886–90.
de Berdt, Dennys. *Letters of Dennys de Berdt, 1757–1770*. Albert Matthews, ed. Cambridge, 1911.
Gallatin, Albert. *The Writings of Albert Gallatin*. 3 vols. Henry Adams, ed. New York, 1960.
Gardiner, C. Harvey, ed. *A Study in Dissent: The Warren-Gerry Correspondence, 1776–1792*. Carbondale, 1968.
Hamilton, Alexander. *The Papers of Alexander Hamilton*. 25 vols. Harold C. Syrett, ed. New York, 1962.
Jefferson, Thomas. *The Papers of Thomas Jefferson*. 19 vols. Julian P. Boyd, ed. Princeton, 1950.
———. *Writings of Thomas Jefferson*. Paul Leicester Ford, ed. New York, 1898.
Lee, Charles. *The Lee Papers*. 4 vols. New York Historical Society *Collections*, vols. 4–7. 1871–74.
Lee, Richard Henry. *The Letters of Richard Henry Lee*. 2 vols. James Curtis Ballagh, ed. New York, 1911.
Letters of the Members of the Continental Congress. 8 vols. Edmund C. Burnett, ed. Washington, 1921–36.
Madison, James. *The Papers of James Madison*. Vols. 6–7. William T. Hutchinson and William M. E. Rachal, eds. Chicago, 1969–71.
Mason, George. *The Papers of George Mason, 1725–1792*. 2 vols. Robert A. Rutland, ed. Chapel Hill, 1970.
Pendleton, Edmund. *The Letters and Papers of Edmund Pendleton, 1784–1803*. 2 vols. David John Mays, ed. Charlottesville, 1967.
Ramsay, David. *David Ramsay, 1749–1815: Selections from His Writings*. American Philosophical Society *Transactions*, vol. 55. Robert L. Brunhouse, ed. 1965.
"Revolutionary Correspondence from 1775 to 1782." Rhode Island Historical Society *Collections*, vol. 6. 1867.
Rush, Benjamin. *Letters of Benjamin Rush*, 2 vols. L. H. Butterfield, ed. Princeton, 1951.
Taggert, Samuel. "Letters of Samuel Taggert, Representative in Congress, 1803–14." George Henry Hayes, ed., American Antiquarian Society *Proceedings* 33 (1923): 113–226, 297–438.
Thomson, Charles. *The Papers of Charles Thomson, Secretary of the Continental Con-*

gress. New York Historical Society *Collections* 11 (1878):1–286.
Trumbull, Jonathan. *Papers.* Parts 1–4. Massachusetts Historical Society *Collections*, 5th ser., vols. 9–10 and 7th ser., vols. 2–3. 1885–1902.
Warren, James. *Warren-Adams Letters: Being Chiefly a Correspondence among John Adams, Samuel Adams, and James Warren, 1743–1777.* Massachusetts Historical Society Collections, vols. 72–73. 1917.
Washington, George. *Correspondence concerning the Society of the Cincinnati.* Edgar Erskine Hume, ed. Baltimore, 1941.
———. *The Writings of George Washington, from the Original Manuscript Sources, 1747–1799.* 39 vols. John C. Fitzpatrick, ed. Washington, 1931–44.

CONTEMPORARY BOOKS, TRACTS, AND PAMPHLETS

An Account of a Late Military Massacre, or the Consequences of Quartering Troops in a Populous Town. New York, 1770.
[Adams, Samuel]. *An Appeal to the World: Or a Vindication of the Town of Boston.* Boston, 1769.
Adams, Zabdiel. *The Evil Designs of Men.* Boston, 1783.
The American Review of History and Politics. Vols. 3–4 (1812).
The Argument against a Standing Army Discussed. London, 1698.
The Argument against a Standing Army Rectified, and the Reflections and Remarks upon It in Several Pamphlets Considered. London, 1697.
An Argument Proving That a Small Number of Regulated Forces . . . Cannot Damage Our Present Happy Establishment. London, 1698.
"Army of the United States." *North American Review* 23 (1826): 245–74.
Austin, Benjamin. *Constitutional Republicanism.* Boston, 1803.
Baldwin, Thomas. *A Discourse Delivered before the Ancient and Honourable Artillery Company.* Boston, 1807.
Barlow, Joel. *The Political Works of Joel Barlow.* New York, 1796.
Barnard, Thomas. *A Sermon Preached at the Request of the Antient and Honourable Artillery Company.* Boston, 1789.
Belknap, Jeremy. *A Sermon on Military Duty.* Salem, 1773.
Bishop, Abraham. *Connecticut Republicanism.* Albany, 1801.
Blackstone, William. *Commentaries on the Laws of England.* 4 vols. London, 1809.
Bowdoin, James, Joseph Warren, and Samuel Pemberton. *A Short Narrative of the Horrid Massacre in Boston.* Boston, 1770.
Burgh, James. *Political Disquisitions.* 2 vols. London, 1775.
Burke, Aedanus. *Considerations of the Society or Order of Cincinnati.* Hartford, 1784.
Carmichael, John. *A Self-Defensive War Lawful.* Lancaster, 1775.
The Case of Disbanding the Army at Present, Briefly and Impartially Considered. London, 1698.
A Collection of Interesting, Authentic Papers, Relative to the Dispute between Great Britain and America: Shewing the Course and Progress of That Misunderstanding, from 1764–1775. John Almond, comp. London, 1777.
A Collection of Papers Related to Half-Pay and the Commutation of Half-Pay Granted by Congress. George Washington, comp. Fishkill, 1783.

Bibliography   221

Considerations upon the Rights of the Colonists to the Privileges of British Subjects. New York, 1766.
Cooke, Samuel. *The Violent Destroyed.* Boston, 1777.
Cooper, Thomas. *Political Essays.* Philadelphia, 1800.
Croswell, Andrew. *Part of an Exposition of Paul's Journey . . . with an Appendix on Military Cruelties by Another Hand.* Boston, 1768.
Defoe, Daniel. *An Argument Shewing, That a Standing Army, with Consent of Parliament, Is Not Inconsistent with a Free Government.* 1698. Printed in *Daniel Defoe.* Edited by James T. Boulton. New York, 1965.
―――. *A Brief Reply to the History of Standing Armies in England.* London, 1698.
―――. *Reflections on the Short History of Standing Armies in England.* London, 1698.
―――. *Some Reflections on a Pamphlet Lately Published, Entitled, an Argument Shewing That a Standing Army Is Inconsistent. . . .* London, 1697.
Dickinson, John. *Political Writings of John Dickinson.* 2 vols. Wilmington, 1801.
Duane, William. *The American Military Library: Or, Compendium of Modern Tactics.* Philadelphia, 1809.
Findley, William. *History of the Insurrection in the Four Western Counties of Pennsylvania.* Philadelphia, 1796.
―――. *A Review of the Revenue System.* Philadelphia, 1794.
Fish, Elisha. *The Art of War Lawful and Necessary.* Boston, 1774.
Fletcher, Andrew. *The Political Works of Andrew Fletcher.* London, 1737.
Four Dissertations, on the Reciprocal Advantages of a Perpetual Union between Great Britain and Her American Colonies. Philadelphia, 1766.
Gillespy, Edward. *The Military Instructor: Or, New System of European Exercise and Drill.* Boston, 1809.
Godefroy, Maximillian. *Military Reflections, on Four Modes of Defence, for the United States.* Baltimore, 1807.
Harrington, James. *James Harrington's Oceana.* Edited by Sten Boduar Liljegren. Heidelberg, 1924.
Howard, Simeon. *A Sermon Preached to the Ancient and Honourable Artillery-Company.* Boston, 1773.
Hoyt, Epaphras. *Practical Instructions for Military Officers.* Greenfield, Mass., 1811.
Humphreys, David. *Considerations on the Means of Improving the Militia for the Public Defence.* Hartford, 1803.
Hutcheson, Francis. *Collected Works.* Edited by Bernhard Fabian. Vol. 6. Hildeshiem, 1969.
Jones, David. *Defensive War in a Just Cause Sinless.* Philadelphia, 1775.
Kendall, James. *Preparations for War: The Best Security for Peace.* Boston, 1806.
Knox, Henry. *A Plan for the General Arrangement of the Militia of the United States.* Philadelphia, 1786.
Lacroix, Irene A. *Military and Political Hints.* Boston, 1808.
Lathrop, John. *A Discourse Preached.* Boston, 1774.
―――. *A Sermon Preached to the Ancient and Honourable Artillery-Company.* Boston, 1774.
A Letter from Manlius, to John Marshall. Richmond, 1800.

Linn, William. *A Military Discourse.* Philadelphia, 1776.
Maclay, William. *The Journal of William Maclay, United States Senator from Pennsylvania, 1789–1791.* New York, 1927.
Minot, George R. *History of the Insurrection in 1786.* Worcester, 1788.
Molesworth, Robert. *An Account of Denmark, as It Was in the Year of 1692.* London, 1694.
Montesquieu. *The Spirit of the Laws.* Translated by Thomas Nugent. 2 vols. London, 1773.
Moyle, Walter. *Whole Works.* London, 1727.
"A North Carolina Citizen on the Federal Constitution, 1788." Edited by Julian P. Boyd. *North Carolina Historical Review* 16 (1939): 36–53.
No Standing Army in the British Colonies: Or an Address to the Inhabitants of the Colony of New York, against Unlawful Standing Armies. New York, 1776.
Notes on the Life of Noah Webster. Compiled by Emily E. F. Ford. 2 vols. New York, 1912.
Pickering, Timothy. *An Easy Plan of Discipline for a Militia.* Salem, 1775.
Pownall, Thomas. *The Exercise for the Militia of the Province of the Massachusetts Bay.* (1758) Printed in *The Remembrancer, or Impartial Repository of Public Events . . . , 1775–1784,* vol. 8. London, 1775–84.
Priestley, Joseph. *The Theological and Miscellaneous Works,* vol. 24. London, 1826.
Quincy, Josiah. *Observations on the Act of Parliament Commonly Called the Boston Port Bill: With Thoughts on Civil Society and Standing Armies.* Boston, 1774.
Ramsay, David. *History of the American Revolution.* 2 vols. Philadelphia, 1789.
———. *History of the United States, from Their First Settlement as English Colonies, in 1607, to the Year 1808.* 3 vols. Philadelphia, 1816.
Robbins, Nathaniel. *Jerusalem's Peace Wished.* Boston, 1772.
Saxe, Maurice de. *Reveries, or Memoirs upon the Art of War.* London, 1757.
Sidney, Algernon. *Discourses Concerning Government.* London, 1751 ed.
Smith, Adam. *An Inquiry into the Nature and Causes of the Wealth of Nations.* New York, 1937.
Somers, John. *A Letter, Ballancing the Necessity of Keeping a Land-force. . . .* n.p., 1697.
Some Queries Concerning the Disbanding of the Army. n.p., 1698.
Steuben, Friedrich von. *A Letter on the Subject of an Established Militia.* New York, 1784.
Stillman, Samuel. *A Sermon Preached to the Ancient and Honorable Artillery Company.* Boston, 1770.
Taylor, John, of Caroline. *Arator: Being a Series of Agricultural Essays, Practical and Political.* Washington, 1813.
———. *An Inquiry into the Principles and Policy of the Government of the United States.* Fredericksburg, 1814.
Toland, John. *The Militia Reform'd, or an Easy Scheme of Furnishing England with a Constant Land-Force.* London, 1698. Printed in *A Collection of State Tracts Published on Occasion of the Late Revolution in 1688 and during the Reign of King William III.* Vol. 2. London, 1706.
Trenchard, John. *A Short History of Standing Armies in England (1698).* Printed in *A*

Bibliography 223

Collection of Tracts, vol. 1. Edited by John Trenchard and Thomas Gordon. London, 1751.
Trenchard, John, and Thomas Gordon. *Cato's Letters, or Essays on Liberty, Civil and Religious, and other Important Subjects*, 4 vols. London, 1755 ed.
[Trenchard, John, and Walter Moyle(?)]. *An Argument Shewing a Standing Army Is Inconsistent with a Free Government and Absolutely Destructive to the Constitution of the English Monarchy*. London, 1697. Printed in *A Collection of Tracts*. Vol. 1. Edited by John Trenchard and Thomas Gordon. London, 1751.
True Sentiments of America: Contained in a Collection of Letters Sent from the House of Representatives of the Province of Massachusetts Bay to Several Persons of High Rank in This Kingdom. Compiled by Thomas Hollis. London, 1768.
Two English Republican Tracts: Plato Redivivus or, a Dialogue Concerning Government (c. 1681) by Henry Neville [and] an Essay upon the Constitution of the Roman Government (c. 1699) by Walter Moyle. Edited by Caroline Robbins. Cambridge, 1969.
Varnum, Joseph B. *An Address . . . to the . . . Massachusetts Militia*. Cambridge, 1800.
Warren, Mercy Otis. *History of the Rise, Progress and Termination of the American Revolution*. 3 vols. Boston, 1805.

MISCELLANEOUS COLLECTIONS

Bailyn, Bernard, ed. *Pamphlets of the American Revolution, 1750–1776*. Vol. 1. Cambridge, 1965– .
Cooke, Jacob E., ed. *The Federalist*. Middletown, Conn., 1961.
Dickerson, Oliver M., comp. *Boston under Military Rule [1768–1769] as Revealed in Journal of the Times*. Boston, 1939.
Force, Peter, ed. *American Archives*. 4th series, vols. 1–3. Washington, 1837–53.
Ford, Paul Leicester, ed. *Essays on the Constitution of the United States, . . . 1787–1788*. Brooklyn, 1892.
_____. *Pamphlets on the Constitution of the United States, . . . 1787–1788*. Brooklyn, 1888.
Kenyon, Cecelia M., ed. *The Antifederalists*. Indianapolis, 1966.
McMaster, John Bach, and Frederick D. Stone, eds. *Pennsylvania and the Federal Constitution, 1787–1788*. 2 vols. Philadelphia, 1970 ed.
Mason, Bernard, ed. *The American Colonial Crisis: The Daniel Leonard-John Adams Letters to the Press, 1774–1775*. New York, 1972.
Millis, Walter, ed. *American Military Thought*. Indianapolis, 1966.
Morison, Samuel Eliot, ed. *Sources and Documents Illustrating the American Revolution, 1764–1788*. New York, 1965.
Niles, Hezekiah, ed. *Principles and Acts of the Revolution in America*. Baltimore, 1876 ed.
Schwartz, Bernard, ed. *The Bill of Rights: A Documentary History*. 2 vols. New York, 1971.
Scribner, Robert L., ed. *Revolutionary Virginia: The Road to Independence*. 2 vols. Charlottesville, 1973– .
Taylor, Robert J., ed. *Massachusetts, Colony to Commonwealth: Documents on the Formation of Its Constitution, 1776–1780*. Chapel Hill, 1961.

Secondary Sources

BOOKS

Alden, John R. *General Gage in America: Being Principally a History of His Role in the American Revolution*. Baton Rouge, 1948.

Ammerman, David. *In the Common Cause: American Response to the Coercive Acts of 1774*. New York, 1976.

Austin, James T. *The Life of Elbridge Gerry, with Contemporary Letters*. 2 vols. Boston, 1829.

Bailyn, Bernard. *The Ideological Origins of the American Revolution*. Cambridge, 1967.

──────. *The Origins of American Politics*. New York, 1967.

Baldwin, Leland D. *Whiskey Rebels: The Story of a Frontier Uprising*. Pittsburgh, 1939.

Banning, Lance G. *The Jeffersonian Persuasion: Evolution of a Party Ideology*. Ithaca, 1978.

Berg, Fred Anderson. *Encyclopedia of Continental Army Units: Battalions, Regiments, and Independent Corps*. Harrisburg, 1972.

Bernardo, C. Joseph, and Eugene H. Bacon. *American Military Policy: Its Development since 1775*. Harrisburg, 1955.

Bonwick, Colin. *English Radicals and the American Revolution*. Chapel Hill, 1977.

Brooks, Noah. *Henry Knox, A Soldier of the Revolution*. New York, 1900.

Colbourn, H. Trevor. *The Lamp of Experience: Whig History and the Intellectual Origins of the American Revolution*. Chapel Hill, 1965.

Collier, Christopher. *Roger Sherman's Connecticut: Yankee Politics and the American Revolution*. Middletown, 1971.

Cunliffe, Marcus. *Soldiers and Civilians: The Martial Spirit in America, 1775–1865*. Boston, 1968.

Davidson, Philip. *Propaganda and the American Revolution, 1763–1783*. Chapel Hill, 1941.

Drake, Francis Samuel. *The Life and Correspondence of Henry Knox, Major-General in the American Revolutionary Army*. Boston, 1873.

Duggan, Joseph C. *The Legislative and Statutory Development of the Federal Concept for Military Service*. Washington, 1946.

Ekirch, Arthur A., Jr. *The Civilian and the Military*. New York, 1956.

Ferguson, E. James. *The Power of the Purse: A History of American Public Finance, 1776–1790*. Chapel Hill, 1961.

Fink, Fera S. *The Classical Republicans: An Essay in the Recovery of a Pattern of Thought in Seventeenth-Century England*. Evanston, 1945.

Fortescue, J. W. *A History of the British Army*. Vol. 2. London, 1910.

Frothingham, Richard. *The Life and Times of Joseph Warren*. Boston, 1865.

Fuller, John F. C. *The Conduct of War, 1789–1961: A Study of the Impact of the French, Industrial, and Russian Revolutions on War and Its Conduct*. New Brunswick, 1961.

Glasson, William H. *Federal Military Pensions in the United States*. New York, 1918.

Greene, Jack P. *The Quest for Power: The Lower Houses of Assembly in the Southern Royal*

Colonies, 1689–1776. Chapel Hill, 1963.
Hall, Van Beck. *Politics without Parties: Massachusetts, 1780–1791.* Pittsburgh, 1972.
Hatch, Louis C. *The Administration of the American Revolutionary Army.* New York, 1904.
Henderson, H. James. *Party Politics in the Continental Congress.* New York, 1974.
Higginbotham, Don. *The War of American Independence: Military Attitudes, Policies, and Practices, 1763–1789.* New York, 1973.
Hill, C. William, Jr. *The Political Theory of John Taylor of Caroline.* Cranbury, N.Y., 1977.
Huntington, Samuel P. *The Soldier and the State: The Theory and Politics of Civil-Military Relations.* Cambridge, 1957.
Jensen, Merrill. *The Articles of Confederation: An Interpretation of the Social-Constitutional History of the American Revolution, 1774–1781.* Rev. ed. Madison, 1970.
―――. *The New Nation: A History of the United States during the Confederation, 1781–1789.* New York, 1950.
Koch, Adrienne. *Jefferson and Madison: The Great Collaboration.* New York, 1950.
Kohn, Richard H. *Eagle and Sword: The Beginnings of the Military Establishment in America.* New York, 1975.
Kramnick, Isaac. *Bolingbroke and His Circle: The Politics of Nostalgia in the Age of Walpole.* Cambridge, 1968.
Kreidberg, Marvin A., and Merton G. Henry. *The History of Military Mobilization in the United States Army, 1775–1945.* Washington, 1955.
Leach, Douglas Edward. *Arms for Empire: A Military History of the British Colonies in North America, 1607–1763.* New York, 1973.
Leach, Jack F. *Conscription in the United States: Historic Background.* Rutland, Vt., 1952.
Link, Eugene P. *Democratic-Republican Societies, 1790–1800.* New York, 1942.
Lobingier, Charles S. *The People's Law, or Popular Participation in Law Making.* New York, 1909.
Lynd, Staughton. *Anti-Federalism in Dutchess County, New York: A Study of Democracy and Class Conflict in the Revolutionary Era.* Chicago, 1962.
Macpherson, C. B. *The Political Theory of Possessive Individualism: Hobbes to Locke.* Oxford, 1962.
Mahon, John K. *The American Militia: Decade of Decision, 1789–1800.* Gainesville, 1960.
Maier, Pauline. *From Resistance to Revolution: Colonial Radicals and the Development of American Opposition to Britain, 1765–1776.* New York, 1972.
Main, Jackson Turner. *The Anti-Federalists: Critics of the Constitution, 1781–1788.* Chapel Hill, 1961.
―――. *The Social Structure of Revolutionary America.* Princeton, 1965.
Malone, Dumas. *Jefferson the President: Second Term, 1805–1809.* Boston, 1974.
Millis, Walter. *Arms and Men: A Study of American Military History.* New York, 1958.
Morris, Richard B. *Government and Labor in Early America.* New York, 1946.

Mudge, Eugene T. *The Social Philosophy of John Taylor of Caroline*. New York, 1939.
Osgood, Herbert L. *The American Colonies in the Seventeenth Century*. 2 vols. New York, 1904.
Palmer, John McAuley. *Washington, Lincoln, Wilson: Three War Statesmen*. Garden City, 1930.
Pargellis, Stanley. *Lord Loudoun in North America*. New Haven, 1933.
Parsons, Theophilus. *Memoir of Theophilus Parsons, Chief Justice of the Supreme Judicial Court of Massachusetts*. Boston, 1859.
Peterson, Merrill D. *Thomas Jefferson and the New Nation*. New York, 1970.
Pocock, J. G. A. *The Machiavellian Moment: Florentine Political Thought and the Atlantic Republican Tradition*. Princeton, 1975.
Quincy, Josiah. *Memoir of the Life of Josiah Quincy, Junior, of Massachusetts*. Boston, 1825.
Reed, William B. *Life and Correspondence of Joseph Reed*. 2 vols. Philadelphia, 1847.
Robbins, Caroline. *The Eighteenth-Century Commonwealthman: Studies in the Transmission, Development, and Circumstances of English Liberal Thought from the Restoration of Charles II until the War with the Thirteen Colonies*. Cambridge, 1961.
Robson, Eric. *The American Revolution: In Its Political and Military Aspects, 1763–1783*. New York, 1966.
Rogers, Alan. *Empire and Liberty: American Resistance to British Authority, 1755–1763*. Berkeley, 1974.
Rossie, Jonathan G. *Politics of Command in the American Revolution*. Syracuse, 1975.
Royster, Charles. *A Revolutionary People at War: The Continental Army and American Character, 1775–1783*. Chapel Hill, 1979.
Rutland, Robert A. *The Birth of the Bill of Rights, 1776–1791*. Chapel Hill, 1955.
Schwoerer, Lois G. *"No Standing Armies!" The Anti-Army Ideology in Seventeenth Century England*. Baltimore, 1974.
Sedgwick, Theodore. *A Memoir of the Life of William Livingston*. New York, 1833.
Shy, John. *Toward Lexington: The Role of the British Army in the American Revolution*. Princeton, 1965.
Smith, Abbot E. *Colonists in Bondage: White Servitude and Convict Labor in America, 1607–1776*. Chapel Hill, 1947.
Smith, William Raymond. *History as Argument: Three Patriot Historians of the American Revolution*. The Hague, 1966.
Staples, William R. *Rhode Island in the Continental Congress, 1765–1790: With the Journal of the Convention That Adopted the Constitution*. Edited by Reuben A. Guild. New York, 1971.
Steiner, Bernard C. *The Life and Correspondence of James McHenry*. Cleveland, 1907.
Stewart, Donald M. *The Opposition Press of the Federal Period*. Albany, 1969.
Stinchcombe, William C. *The American Revolution and the French Alliance*. Syracuse, 1969.
Taylor, Robert J. *Western Massachusetts in the Revolution*. Providence, 1954.
Tudor, William. *The Life of James Otis of Massachusetts*. Boston, 1823.
Vagts, Alfred. *A History of Militarism: Romance and Realities of a Profession*. New York, 1937.

Weigley, Russell F. *History of the United States Army*. New York, 1967.
──── . *Towards an American Army: Military Thought from Washington to Marshall*. New York, 1962.
Western, John R. *The English Militia in the Eighteenth Century: The Story of a Political Issue, 1660–1802*. London, 1965.
White, Howard. *Executive Influence in Determining Military Policy in the United States*. Urbana, 1924.
Wiecek, William M. *The Guarantee Clause of the U.S. Constitution*. Ithaca, 1972.
Wood, Gordon S. *The Creation of the American Republic*. Chapel Hill, 1969.
Zobel, Hiller B. *The Boston Massacre*. New York, 1970.

ARTICLES

Adair, Douglass, G. "'That Politics May Be Reduced to a Science': David Hume, James Madison, and the Tenth Federalist." *Huntington Library Quarterly* 20 (1957): 343–60.
Alexander, Arthur J. "How Maryland Tried to Raise Her Continental Quotas." *Maryland Historical Magazine* 42 (1947): 184–96.
──── . "Pennsylvania's Revolutionary Militia." *Pennsylvania Magazine of History and Biography* 69 (1945): 15–25.
Apter, David E. "Ideology and Discontent." In *Ideology and Discontent*, edited by David E. Apter, pp. 15–46. New York, 1964.
Bailyn, Bernard. "The Central Themes of the American Revolution: An Interpretation." In *Essays on the American Revolution*, edited by Stephen G. Kurtz and James H. Hutson, pp. 3–31. Chapel Hill, 1973.
Banning, Lance. "Republican Ideology and the Triumph of the Constitution, 1789–1793." *William and Mary Quarterly*, 3d ser., vol. 31 (1974): 167–88.
Berthoff, Rowland, and John M. Murrin. "Feudalism, Communalism, and the Yeoman Freeholder: The American Revolution Considered as a Social Accident." In *Essays on the American Revolution*, edited by Stephen G. Kurtz and James H. Hutson, pp. 256–88. Chapel Hill, 1973.
Boucher, Ronald L. "The Colonial Militia as a Social Institution: Salem, Massachusetts, 1764–1775." *Military Affairs* 37 (1973): 125–30.
Bowling, Kenneth R. "New Light on the Philadelphia Mutiny of 1783." *Pennsylvania Magazine of History and Biography*, 101 (1977): 419–50.
Breen, Timothy H. "English Origins and New World Development: The Case of the Covenanted Militia in Seventeenth-Century Massachusetts." *Past and Present* 57 (1972): 74–96.
──── . "Persistent Localism: English Social Change and the Shaping of New England Institutions." *William and Mary Quarterly*, 3d ser., vol. 32 (1975): 3–28.
Buel, Richard, Jr., "Democracy and the American Revolution: A Frame of Reference." *William and Mary Quarterly*, 3d ser., vol. 21 (1964): 165–90.
Carter, Clarence E. "The Significance of Military Office in America, 1763–1775." *American Historical Review* 28 (1923): 475–88.
Coakley, Robert W. "Federal Use of Militia and the National Guard in Civil

Disturbances: The Whiskey Rebellion to Little Rock." In *Bayonets in the Streets: The Use of Troops in Civil Disturbances*, edited by Robin Higham, pp. 17–34. Lawrence, 1969.

Cohen, Lester H. "Explaining the Revolution: Ideology and Ethics in Mercy Otis Warren's Historical Theory." *William and Mary Quarterly*, 3d ser., vol. 37 (1980): 200–218.

Colbourn, H. Trevor. "Jefferson's Use of the Past." *William and Mary Quarterly*, 3d ser., vol. 15 (1958): 56–70.

———. "John Dickinson, Historical Revolutionary." *Pennsylvania Magazine of History and Biography* 83 (1959): 271–92.

Cooke, Jacob E. "The Whiskey Insurrection: A Re-Evaluation." *Pennsylvania History* 30 (1963): 316–46.

Cress, Lawrence Delbert. "Radical Whiggery on the Role of the Military: Ideological Roots of the American Revolutionary Militia." *Journal of the History of Ideas* 40 (1979): 43–60.

———. "Whither Columbia? Congressional Residence and the Politics of the New Nation, 1776 to 1787." *William and Mary Quarterly*, 3d ser., vol. 32 (1975): 581–600.

Davies, Wallace E. "The Society of Cincinnati in New England, 1783–1800." *William and Mary Quarterly*, 3d ser., vol. 5 (1948): 3–25.

Donahoe, Bernardo, and Marshall Smelser. "The Congressional Power to Raise Armies: The Constitutional and Ratifying Conventions, 1787–88." *Review of Politics* 33 (1971): 202–12.

Earle, Edward Mead. "Adam Smith, Alexander Hamilton, Friedrich List: Economic Foundations of Military Power." In *Makers of Modern Strategy*, edited by Edward Mead Earle, pp. 117–54. Princeton, 1952.

East, Robert A. "The Massachusetts Conservatives in the Critical Period." In *Era of the American Revolution*, edited by Richard B. Morris, pp. 349–91. New York, 1939.

Forman, Sidney. "Thomas Jefferson on Universal Military Training." *Military Affairs* 11 (1947): 177–78.

———. "Why the U.S. Military Academy Was Established in 1802." *Military Affairs* 29 (1965): 16–25.

French, Allen. "The Arms and Military Training of Our Colonizing Ancestors." Massachusetts Historical Society *Proceedings* 47 (1941–44): 3–21.

Gaines, William H., Jr. "The Forgotten Army: Recruiting for a National Emergency (1799–1800)." *Virginia Magazine of History and Biography* 46 (1948): 267–79.

Geertz, Clifford. "Ideology as a Cultural System." In *Ideology and Discontent*, edited by David E. Apter, pp. 47–76. New York, 1964.

Greene, Jack P. "The South Carolina Quartering Dispute, 1757–1758." *South Carolina Historical Magazine* 60 (1959): 193–204.

Handlin, Oscar, and Mary Handlin. "James Burgh and American Revolutionary Theory." Massachusetts Historical Society *Proceedings* 73 (1961): 38–57.

Hume, Edgar E. "Early Opposition to the Society of the Cincinnati." *Americana* 30 (1936): 597–638.

Huxford, Gary. "Origins of the American Military Tradition Reconsidered." *Rocky Mountain Social Science Journal* 8 (1971): 119-25.
Johnson, Harry M. "Ideology and the Social System." *International Encyclopedia of the Social Sciences*, 7:76-85. New York, 1968.
Kenyon, Cecelia M. "Men of Little Faith: The Anti-Federalists on the Nature of Representative Government." *William and Mary Quarterly*, 3d ser., vol. 12 (1955): 8-43.
Knollenberg, Bernard. "John Adams, Knox, and Washington." American Antiquarian Society *Proceedings* 56 (1946): 207-38.
Kohn, Richard H. "The Washington Administration's Decision to Crush the Whiskey Rebellion." *Journal of American History* 5 (1972): 567-84.
Lemisch, Jesse. "The American Revolution from the Bottom Up." In *Towards a New Past: Dissenting Essays in American History*, edited by Barton J. Bernstein, pp. 3-45. New York, 1968.
Lockridge, Kenneth A. "Social Change and the Meaning of the American Revolution." *Journal of Social History* 6 (1973): 403-49.
Lofgren, Charles A. "War-Making under the Constitution: The Original Understanding." *Yale Law Journal* 81 (1971-72): 672-702.
Lundberg, David, and Henry F. May. "The Enlightened Reader in America." *American Quarterly* 28 (1976): 262-71, and charts following.
Maurer, Maurer. "Military Justice under Washington." *Military Affairs* 28 (1964-65): 8-16.
May, Ernest R. "'The President Shall Be Commander in Chief' (1787-89)." In *The Ultimate Decision: The President as Commander in Chief*, edited by Ernest R. May, pp. 3-20. New York, 1960.
Miller, E. Arnold. "Some Arguments Used by English Pamphleteers, 1697-1700, Concerning a Standing Army." *Journal of Modern History* 18 (1946): 306-13.
Miller, William. "The Democratic Societies and the Whiskey Insurrection." *Pennsylvania Magazine of History and Biography* 58 (1938): 324-49.
Minar, David W. "Ideology and Political Behavior." *Midwest Journal of Political Science* 5 (1961): 317-31.
Morgan, Edmund S. "The Puritan Ethic and the American Revolution." *William and Mary Quarterly*, 3d ser., vol. 24 (1965): 3-43.
Morton, Louis. "The Origins of American Military Policy." *Military Affairs* 22 (1958): 75-82.
Nash, Gary B. "Social Change and the Growth of Prerevolutionary Urban Radicalism." In *The American Revolution: Explorations in the History of American Radicalism*, edited by Alfred F. Young, pp. 3-36. DeKalb, 1976.
Papenfuse, Edward C., and Gregory A. Stiverson. "General Smallwood's Recruits: The Peacetime Career of the Revolutionary War Private." *William and Mary Quarterly*, 3d ser., vol. 30 (1973): 117-32.
Pocock, J. G. A. "Civic Humanism and Its Role in Anglo-American Thought." In *Politics, Language, and Time: Essays on Political Thought and History*, pp. 80-103. New York, 1971.
――――. "James Harrington and the Good Old Cause: A Study of the Ideological Context of His Writings." *Journal of British Studies* 10 (1970): 30-48.

———. "Machiavelli, Harrington, and English Political Ideologies in the Eighteenth Century." *William and Mary Quarterly*, 3d ser., vol. 22 (1965): 549–83.

Pollitt, David H. "Presidential Use of Troops to Execute the Laws: A Brief History." *North Carolina Law Review* 36 (1957–58): 117–41.

Quarles, Benjamin. "The Colonial Militia and Negro Manpower." *Mississippi Valley Historical Review* 45 (1959): 643–52.

Robbins, Caroline. "Algernon Sidney's *Discourses Concerning Government*: Textbook of Revolution." *William and Mary Quarterly*, 3d ser., vol. 4 (1947): 267–96.

———. "The Strenuous Whig, Thomas Hollis of Lincoln's Inn." *William and Mary Quarterly*, 3d ser., vol. 7 (1950): 406–53.

———. "'When It Is That Colonies May Turn Independent': An Analysis of the Environment and Politics of Francis Hutcheson (1694–1746)." *William and Mary Quarterly*, 3d ser., vol. 11 (1954): 214–51.

Rutman, Darrett B. "The Virginia Company and Its Military Regime." In *The Old Dominion: Essays for Thomas Perkins Abernathy*, edited by Darrett B. Rutman, pp. 1–20. Charlottesville, 1964.

Schwoerer, Lois G. "The Literature of the Standing Army Controversy, 1697–1699." *Huntington Library Quarterly* 28 (1965): 187–212.

Shalhope, Robert E. "Toward a Republican Synthesis: The Emergence of an Understanding of Republicanism in American Historiography." *William and Mary Quarterly*, 3d ser., vol. 29 (1972): 49–80.

Sharp, Morrison. "Leadership and Democracy in Early New England Defense." *American Historical Review* 40 (1945): 244–60.

Shy, John. "The American Military Experience: History and Learning." *Journal of Interdisciplinary History* 1 (1971): 205–28.

———. "The American Revolution: The Military Conflict Considered as a Revolutionary War." In *Essays on the American Revolution*, edited by Stephen G. Kurtz and James H. Hutson, pp. 121–56. Chapel Hill, 1973.

———. "Charles Lee: The Soldier as Radical." In *George Washington's Generals*, edited by George A. Billias, pp. 22–53. New York, 1964.

———. "A New Look at the Colonial Militia." *William and Mary Quarterly*, 3d ser., vol. 20 (1963): 175–85.

———. "The Spectrum of Imperial Possibilities." In *A People Numerous and Armed*, pp. 35–72. New York, 1976.

Smith, Carlton B. "The American Search for a 'Harmless' Army." *Essays in History* 10 (1964–65): 29–43.

———. "Congressional Attitudes towards Military Preparedness during the Monroe Administration." *Military Affairs* 40 (1976): 22–25.

Todd, Frederick P. "Our National Guard: An Introduction to Its History." *Military Affairs* 5 (1941): 73–86.

Warren, Joseph P. "The Confederation and the Shays Rebellion." *American Historical Review* 11 (1905): 42–67.

Wiener, Frederick B. "The Militia Clause of the Constitution." *Harvard Law Review* 54 (1940): 181–220.

Wood, Gordon S. "The Authorship of the *Letters From the Federal Farmer*." *William and Mary Quarterly*, 3d ser., vol. 31 (1974): 299–308.

DISSERTATIONS

Adair, Douglass G. "The Intellectual Origins of Jeffersonian Democracy: Republicanism, the Class Struggle, and the Virtuous Farmer." Yale University, 1943.

Adams, Mary P. "Jefferson's Military Policy with Special Reference to the Frontier, 1805–9." University of Virginia, 1958.

Bodenger, Robert G. "Soldiers' Bonuses: A History of Veterans' Benefits in the United States, 1776–1967." Pennsylvania State University, 1971.

Cress, Lawrence Delbert. "The Standing Army, the Militia, and the New Republic: Changing Attitudes toward the Military in American Society, 1768–1820." University of Virginia, 1976.

Erney, Richard A. "The Public Life of Henry Dearborn." Columbia University, 1957.

Index

Adams, John, 35, 49, 58, 145, 148
Adams, Samuel, 35, 37, 39, 58
Anti-Federalist thought: on representation, 98–100, 101; on standing armies, 99–100; on the role of the militia, 100; on executive military power, 100–101; use of radical Whig thought by, 101–2
Army: threat of, 11, 18–19, 21, 23–25, 37–39, 45–46, 47, 48, 63–66, 77, 88–89, 98–100, 103–4, 105–7, 130–32, 137–43; American peacetime, 62–63, 64, 82–84, 85–86, 87–88, 93, 129–34, 137, 170–71, 173–77. *See also* Anti-Federalist thought; British army; Colonial military institutions; Continental army; Corruption, army as agent of; Military professionalism
Articles of Confederation, 74, 81, 87, 95, 98–99, 107; on military professionalism, 62–63; on the militia, 63; on centralization of military power, 63–65; amendments to proposed, 63–65, 69
Aurora (Philadelphia), 127, 128, 138, 140, 151, 164
Austin, Benjamin, 150

Bache, Benjamin Franklin, 128
Baldwin, Thomas, 161
Barlow, Joel, 159–60
Barnard, Thomas, 111–12
Bernard, Francis, 37, 38, 63
Blackstone, William, 22, 55
Bolingbroke, Henry St. John, Viscount, 22

Boston Massacre, 41, 42; orations commemorating, 41, 44, 47
Boston Tea Party, 44
Bowdoin, James, 95, 96
Bradford, William, 122
British army, 4, 5, 7, 9–11, 12, 35, 36–37, 47; colonial attitude toward, 11, 12, 13; in Boston, 36–41, 44, 46, 47, 135; moral impact of, 39–40. *See also* Colonial military institutions; Military professionalism
Burgh, James, 22–24, 28, 32, 35, 56, 140, 171. *See also* Radical Whig thought
Burke, Aedanus, 70–71
Burke, Thomas, 63

Calhoun, John C.: on military professionalism, 174–77
Cato's Letters, 21, 25, 77. *See also* Radical Whig thought
Cincinnati, Society of the, 70–71, 77
Citizenship, 22; responsibilities of, 16–17, 19. *See also* Citizen-soldier
Citizen-soldier, 1, 12–13, 15, 16, 23, 58, 59, 65, 76, 78, 79, 112, 113, 117–18, 126, 161, 162–63, 173; relationship to liberty, 42–46, 55–56. *See also* Anti-Federalist thought; Barlow, Joel; Duane, William; Federalist party; Knox, Henry; Militia, political significance of; Peace Establishment Plans of 1783; Priestley, Joseph; Republican party; Smith, Adam; Taylor, John, of Caroline; Washington, George
Civil disobedience, 39, 111, 121–25

234 Index

Clairborne, W. C., 141
Clinton, George, 79–84
Coercive Acts, 41, 42, 44, 45, 46, 77
Colonial assemblies: power over military affairs, 8, 9, 10–11, 47
Colonial military institutions, 3–10, 13–14, 35–36, 38, 39, 40, 41, 46, 47, 53
Commonwealth of Oceana, 16, 34, 159. See also Harrington, James
Constitutional balance, 15, 16–17, 24–25, 25, 32–33; in Oceana, 16–17; in the ancient constitutions, 17, 19, 21, 23; militia's role in, 20–21, 23–24, 24, 42–44, 45, 46, 48–50, 66, 96, 116–19, 120; moderate Whigs on, 25, 26, 27, 28; American understanding of, 36, 65–66, 73, 74. See also Anti-Federalist thought; Articles of Confederation; Barlow, Joel; Duane, William; Federalist thought; Half pay; Militia, reform of; Peace Establishment Plans of 1783; Republican party; Smith, Adam; State constitutions; Taylor, John, of Caroline
Continental army, 55, 76, 147; motivation for service in, 57, 59, 60, 67, 68, 71, 72–73; professional foundations of, 58–60, 67, 73–74, 77; composition, 59, 60; ideological implications of, 66
Continental Congress, 46, 48, 63, 67–69, 78, 92; response to Shays' Rebellion, 96–97, 103
Corbin, William, 108
Corruption, 11, 13, 17–18, 21, 22, 23–24, 27, 46, 77; of the Gothic constitution, 17–18; of citizens, 18, 24; impact of military professionalism on, 20, 22, 23–24; moderate Whigs on, 28; American understanding of, 26, 36, 37–40; ministerial conspiracy and, 13, 37–40, 42, 46, 48; army as agent of, 18, 19–20, 21, 22, 24, 26, 36, 37–40, 42, 44, 46, 47–48, 65, 67, 76. See also Anti-Federalist thought; Articles of Confederation; Duane, William; Federalist thought; Half pay; Militia, reform of; Peace Establishment Plans of 1783; Republican party; Smith, Adam; State constitutions; Taylor, John, of Caroline
Coxe, Tench, 104

Dawes, Thomas, 105
Dearborn, Henry, 167
Defoe, Daniel, 15, 25, 26, 28, 32, 89, 176
Dickinson, John, 35, 47, 62
Drayton, William Henry, 63
Duane, William, 138, 151, 153, 154; on the militia and standing armies, 164–66

English Bill of Rights, 10, 11, 26, 36, 37, 38, 105
Expeditionary forces: use of, 5–8, 12; composition, 5–7, 8, 12, 53; control of, 5, 8–9. See also Colonial military institutions

Federal Constitution: military provisions of, 97
Federalist Papers, 102, 103, 105, 106, 107
Federalist party: on military professionalism, 131–32, 146–49; on militia ineffectiveness, 143–44; on volunteer corps, 143–45; on the New Army, 145–46; on the provisional army, 145. See also Military professionalism; Nationalists
Federalist thought: on representation, 102–3; use of radical Whig thought, 103; on centralized military power, 103–5; on a national militia, 104–5; on abuse of military power, 105–7; on military professionalism, 107–8
Findley, William: on militia reform, 128–29
Fitzsimmons, Thomas, 119

Fletcher, Andrew, 18, 20, 21, 22, 35, 55
France, 1, 3, 4, 5, 26, 159, 160, 167
Franklin, Benjamin, 35
Freneau, Philip, 131

Gage, Thomas, 37, 44
Gallatin, Albert, 140, 141, 142
George II, 22
George III, 24
Gerry, Elbridge, 88, 89
Giles, William, 133
Glorious Revolution, 1, 13, 18, 25, 27, 32, 37, 40, 47
Godefroy, Maximillian, 165, 171; on military professionalism, 162–63
Gordon, Thomas, 21, 22, 35, 77
Gothic constitution, 17, 23, 25, 32
Great Britain: military requirements of, 25, 26, 28

Half pay, 64, 74; legislative history of, 67–68; as a threat to civil liberties, 68–70; defense of, 71–73
Hamilton, Alexander, 78, 89, 92, 95, 103, 105, 106, 107, 108, 122, 125, 145, 149; military establishment plan, 87–88; support for military professionalism, 87–88
Hancock, John, 35, 44
Hand, Edward, 79–84
Harper, Robert Goodloe, 144
Harrington, James, 19, 22, 24, 28, 34, 35, 53, 56, 89, 159, 171; concept of citizenship, 16–17; nature of corruption, 17; use of history, 17
Harrison, William Henry, 160; on military professionalism, 161
Henry, Patrick, 99, 100
Hillsborough, Wills Hill, 2d Viscount of, 37, 38
History: American use of, 11, 12, 43, 45, 84, 142, 162, 165; Harrington's use of, 16, 17; radical Whig use of, 17, 19, 27; Burgh's use of, 22–23; moderate Whig use of, 27, 28; Anti-Federalists' use of, 101–2; Federalists' use of, 103–4, 108; Priestley's use of, 155–56. *See also* Smith, Adam
Hollis, Thomas, 34–35
Howard, Simeon, 43–44
Howell, David, 88
Humphreys, David, 154, 162, 163
Hutcheson, Francis, 22, 28

Ideology: defined, xi-xii

Jackson, James, 119
James II, 19, 26
Jay, John, 103
Jefferson, Thomas, 35, 47, 58, 153, 167, 168, 169, 171; on wartime military requirements, 151–52; on classed militia, 167–69
Jefferson administration: on militia reform, 142–43, 153–54, 166–70; on regular army, 153, 170–71. *See also* Republican party
"Journal of the Times," 38, 39, 41

King George's War, 6
King William's War, 5, 6
Knox, Henry, 35, 75, 79, 122, 131, 142, 145, 148; military proposals of 1783, 80–84; military plan of 1786, 90–92; military plan of 1790, 116–19, 164, 166, 167; on military centralization, 118–19

Lansing, John, 99
Lathrop, John, 45
Laurens, Henry, 68
Lee, Arthur, 88
Lee, Charles, 54, 58; on citizen-soldiers, 55–56; on military professionalism, 55; plan for a military colony, 56
Lee, Henry, 124, 146
Lee, Thomas, 124, 125

236 Index

Lincoln, Benjamin, 198 (n. 30)
Livingston, Robert R., 58
Loudoun, John Campbell, 4th Earl of: powers and relations with colonial assemblies, 9–10
Lovell, James, 41, 68

McDowell, Joseph, 141
McHenry, James, 145, 166; on military professionalism, 146–48
Machiavelli, 23, 55
Madison, James, 69, 102, 103, 104, 106, 120, 128, 140, 168, 169
Mason, George, 35, 49
Mercer, John, 130–31
Mifflin, Thomas, 122, 125
Military academy, 83–84, 86, 146–48, 154, 164. *See also* Military professionalism
Military professionalism, 3, 7–8, 12–13, 15, 17–18, 20, 21–23, 25–32, 35, 39–41, 43–47, 48, 56–57, 66, 72–73, 74, 77–78, 83, 85–86, 101, 107–8, 131, 143–44, 146–49, 155–57, 162–63, 174–77
Militia: political significance of, 3, 9, 11, 12–14, 15, 16–17, 18, 20–21, 22–23, 27–28, 29–30, 41–46, 48–50, 55–56, 58, 65, 76, 77, 79–80, 84, 88–89, 90–91, 100, 106, 126, 128–29, 151–52, 157–60; control of, 4, 5, 7, 13, 81–82, 85, 87, 91, 100, 118, 119–20, 126–27, 153–54, 168; use of, 4–5, 7, 12–13, 30, 58, 77–78, 96–97, 121–22, 124–26, 130, 143, 168, 170, 173; reform of, 20–21, 55–56, 79–82, 84–85, 87, 90–92, 104–5, 116–21, 127–28, 145, 153–54, 160–62, 164–66, 167–70, 174; composition of, 43–44, 55, 126; mobilization, 48–49, 58, 59, 73, 77, 78, 95–96, 124–25. *See also* Citizen-soldier; Colonial military institutions
Moderate Whig thought, 15, 25–32, 35, 57, 60, 97, 108, 131, 157, 171; on military professionalism, 25–26, 27, 28; on threat of military dictatorship, 26; on the militia, 27–28; use of history, 27, 28; influence in America, 33, 35. *See also* Smith, Adam
Molesworth, Robert, 19, 35
Monroe, James, 173
Morgan, Daniel, 124
Morris, Robert, 72, 88. *See also* Nationalists
Moyle, Walter, 18

Nationalists, 67–68, 74, 88, 92, 95, 112. *See also* Federalist thought
New Army Act, 137
Newburgh, 68
North American Review, 177

Opposition thought, 13, 14, 15, 16, 32. *See also* Radical Whig thought
Otis, Harrison Grey, 146
Otis, James, 35, 38; threat to American liberties, 11; preference for militia soldiers, 11; significance of British army in America, 11, 12

Parliament, 1, 10, 13, 18, 35, 40, 41; constitutional prerogatives of, 26
Parochialists, 68–69, 88, 92, 112. *See also* Anti-Federalist thought
Parsons, Theophilus, 96
Peace Establishment Plans of 1783, 78–90, 103. *See also* Knox, Henry
Peace of Ryswick, 18, 25
Pendleton, Edmund, 140, 151
Pennsylvania Farmer, 47
Pickering, Timothy, 43, 90, 145; on military needs in 1783, 79–84
Political Disquisitions, 22, 32, 35
Pownall, Thomas, 3, 12, 13
Priestley, Joseph, 154, 162, 166, 171; on citizen-soldiers, 155–56; on military professionalism, 155, 156–57. *See also* Smith, Adam
Provisional Army Act, 137

"Publius." See *Federalist Papers*
Putnam, Rufus, 79–84

Quartering soldiers, 10–11
Quincy, Josiah, 45
Quincy, Josiah, Jr., 35, 45

Radical Whig thought, 17–21, 27, 29, 30, 31, 41, 42, 43, 45, 47, 48, 50, 53, 54, 55, 60, 65, 66, 67, 77, 82, 91, 92, 97, 101, 104, 120, 132, 137, 149, 159, 164; on nature of corruption, 17–18, 19–20, 21; on standing armies, 18–20, 25; writers of, 18–19, 22; on citizen-soldiers, 19, 20–21; on national defense needs, 20–21; read in America, 13, 18, 21, 22, 25, 34–35, 37, 47
Ramsay, David, 77–78, 79, 92
Randolph, Edmund, 108, 122–23
Representation, 42, 47; American perception of, 37–38. See also Anti-Federalist thought; Federalist thought
Republican party, 149; on the militia, 127–28, 142–43, 152; on the provisional army, 137–38, 140–41; on military centralization; 133; on military professionalism, 133; on the New Army, 138–40, 146; on the volunteer corps, 141–42; on Federalist military policy, 130–34, 136, 150–51; on wartime military needs, 152. See also Calhoun, John C.; Jefferson administration
Revolution of 1688. See Glorious Revolution
Rush, Benjamin, 35, 58

St. Clair, Arthur, 120, 130
Saxe, Maurice Comte de, 55–56
Seven Years' War, 6–7, 9–10, 35; quartering in, 10, 12
Shays' Rebellion, 95–97, 103; Republican party's view of, 128–29

Sidney, Algernon, 18, 35, 45, 89, 171
Smith, Adam, 28, 35, 53, 54, 56, 89, 108, 115, 155, 162, 174, 176; on military professionalism, 29–32; use of history, 29, 31. See also Priestley, Joseph
Smith, Robert, 167
Somers, John, 25, 26
South Sea Bubble, 21
State constitutions, 66, 100–101; appointment of military officers, 61–62; military powers of governors, 61–62; military powers of representative assemblies, 61; restrictions on military officers, 61, 62
Steuben, Friedrich von, 75, 90, 108, 120; on military needs in 1783, 79–84

Taylor, John, of Caroline, 139–40, 154, 160, 166; on nature of corruption, 157, 158–59; on significance of the militia, 158–59
Toland, John, 18, 20, 21
Townshend duties, 37, 39, 42
Trenchard, John, 18, 21, 22, 35, 43, 47, 55, 77, 171

Uniform Militia Act of 1792, 120–21, 122
United States: defense requirements in peacetime, 76–78, 79, 82, 89, 90, 93, 104, 107, 111, 112, 113, 115, 117, 130, 131, 132, 133–34, 136, 146–49, 152, 170–71, 173–77. See also Peace Establishment Plans of 1783
Upton, Emory, 177

Valley Forge, 67
Varnum, Joseph B., 151, 168

Wadsworth, Jeremiah, 131
Walpole, Robert, 24, 28
War of 1812: militia's performance during, 173; mobilization, 172–73
Warren, James, 58

Warren, Mercy Otis, 77, 78, 81, 88, 92
Washington, George, 49, 54, 56, 58, 78, 90, 95, 116, 121, 122, 146, 148; on military professionalism, 57; on the motivation of soldiers, 57; on militia ineffectiveness, 57; on half pay, 71–72; on Military Establishment Plans of 1783, 84–87; on Hamilton's military establishment plan of 1783, 88; on the Whiskey Rebellion, 126
Wayne, Anthony, 132
Wealth of Nations, 28, 32, 56. *See also* Smith, Adam

Webster, Noah, 106; on military professionalism, 72; on motivation of soldiers, 72–73
Whiskey Rebellion, 121, 126, 143, 144; difficulty raising troops to put down, 112–25; Washington's cabinet's response to, 122–23, implications for civil order, 126–27
Wilkes, John, 22
William III, 15, 18, 21, 25, 28, 34
Wilson, James, 35, 105, 121, 122

Yates, Robert, 99

www.ingramcontent.com/pod-product-compliance
Lightning Source LLC
Chambersburg PA
CBHW021400290426
44108CB00010B/321